INTERNATIONAL
RELATIONS THEORY

2ND EDITION

INTERNATIONAL
RELATIONS THEORY
THE ESSENTIALS
OLIVER DADDOW

Los Angeles | London | New Delhi
Singapore | Washington DC

Los Angeles | London | New Delhi
Singapore | Washington DC

SAGE Publications Ltd
1 Oliver's Yard
55 City Road
London EC1Y 1SP

SAGE Publications Inc.
2455 Teller Road
Thousand Oaks, California 91320

SAGE Publications India Pvt Ltd
B 1/I 1 Mohan Cooperative Industrial Area
Mathura Road
New Delhi 110 044

SAGE Publications Asia-Pacific Pte Ltd
3 Church Street
#10-04 Samsung Hub
Singapore 049483

Editor: Natalie Aguilera
Editorial assistant: James Piper
Production editor: Katie Forsythe
Copyeditor: Rosemary Campbell
Proofreader: Derek Markham
Marketing manager: Sally Ransom
Cover design: Wendy Scott
Typeset by: C&M Digitals (P) Ltd, Chennai, India
Printed and bound by CPI Group (UK) Ltd,
Croydon, CR0 4YY

© Oliver Daddow 2013

First edition published in 2009. Reprinted twice in
2010 and once in 2011.
This edition first published 2013.

Library of Congress Control Number: 2012947811

British Library Cataloguing in Publication data

A catalogue record for this book is available from the
British Library

ISBN 978-1-4462-5623-7
ISBN 978-1-4462-5624-4 (pbk)

MIX
Paper from
responsible sources
FSC® C013056
www.fsc.org

CONTENTS

ABOUT THE AUTHOR

Oliver Daddow is Reader in International Politics at the University of Leicester. His research interests are in interpretivist international relations, British foreign policy and discourse analysis: he is the author of *New Labour and the European Union: Blair and Brown's Logic of History* (Manchester University Press, 2011) and *Britain and Europe since 1945: Historiographical Perspectives on Integration* (Manchester University Press, 2004). He edited *Harold Wilson and European Integration: Britain's Second Application to Join the EEC* (Frank Cass, 2003). With Jamie Gaskarth he co-edited *British Foreign Policy: The New Labour Years* (Palgrave Macmillan, 2011), and with Mark Bevir and Ian Hall he co-edited *Interpreting Global Security* (Routledge, 2013). He has written book chapters and peer reviewed journal articles across his research interests, including in *International Affairs*, *Political Quarterly*, *British Journal of Politics and International Relations*, *Cambridge Review of International Affairs* and *Review of International Studies*.

ACKNOWLEDGEMENTS

This book began life at the British International Studies Association conference at St Andrews in December 2005. It was during a chat with David Mainwaring in the publisher's exhibition that we spotted a potential gap in the market for a pedagogically inclined book aimed at students new not just to the study of IR in general but to the increasingly diverse field of IR theory in particular. I can safely say that had that conversation not taken place this book would certainly not have been written – such are the fortuitous vagaries of academic life. This substantially revised and rejigged version is the product of a series of meetings and discussions at conferences around the globe with my current editor, Natalie Aguilera. Natalie has been an equally inspirational editor, bringing a real zest to this updated edition that has helped see it through from my rough early ideas for change to the finished product. My thanks to everyone at Sage who, as usual, has worked so hard on the manuscript on my behalf, and to the six anonymous reviewers who gave detailed and constructive feedback on how to improve on the first edition of the text.

Adrian Gallagher read through some of my first stabs at trying to summarize these theories in a couple of thousand words and his astute comments were most helpful, particularly on the detail of English School theorizing. Thanks, finally, to all my students of International Theory at the University of Leicester and elsewhere who have, to varying degrees probably, enjoyed and suffered my sometimes clunky attempts to distil the complexity of this subject matter into manageable sized chunks for academic consumption. Many elements of both formal and informal feedback on my teaching have helped me refine this text enormously. Magnus Evjebraten, Matthew Breeds and Chris Hills were particularly helpful.

INTRODUCTION: WHY YOU SHOULD BUY THIS BOOK

(Or: Why Have I Written it?)

I have written this book with one very clear aim in mind: to help students new to the study of International Relations Theory (IRT) find their way in to what can be a beguiling, complex, yet ultimately fascinating subject of study at university level. IRT is beguiling because there are so many different theoretical perspectives on offer, all claiming to offer important insights into what makes the world of international affairs 'tick'. How do we know which theory is 'best'? IRT is complex because it is often a brand new field of study for students, even those who come from a Politics or History background. Many school- and college-level courses deal with issues in international relations such as globalization, war and peace, but the 'theory' element is the vital addition that sets university-level programmes in International Relations apart. And no one *really* enjoys doing theory, do they? If nothing else, I hope this book helps you lose all fear of theory, theorizing and, yes, theorists!

And this is why IRT is fascinating. We might not realize it when we watch news reports about the Arab Spring, the War on Terror, or the crisis in the Eurozone, but underpinning all political and media coverage of global politics is a theoretical take on events. News media tell us which actors are important, frame how they are interacting on the global stage, speculate on their motivations for doing so and debate the possible outcomes of the decisions they make. Sometimes these are routine, day-to-day decisions, at other times they are hastily concocted in a crisis. The point is that in selecting to present the views of a few actors, in a certain way, and with an editorial slant that can cue you, the consumer of news, to view some actors or causes more sympathetically than others, theoretical choices have been made. After reading this book you will, I hope, be in a better position to 'see through' some of the dominant ways in which the world is simplified for understanding through these significant but often hidden theoretical choices. As a result, the book should help you discover how and where you can acquire the skills of critical engagement with the world around you on your course in IRT. And let's face it, if students of politics and international affairs can't take a critically informed perspective on those who govern us around the world, who can?

A note on terminology: 'International Relations', written with capitalized 'IR', denotes the formal study of international relations: there is a discipline of International Relations which studies international relations going on 'out there' in the world. In different universities, courses in IR go by the names 'international politics', 'global politics' or 'world politics', each containing varying amounts of theory. This book abbreviates International Relations Theory to IRT.

The book has been explicitly written for the newcomer to IRT with the goal of helping you manage your learning on your IRT course. It has been structured to make it easy to dip in and out of, and might also be used either as a refresher or adjunct to courses that deal with international affairs and which demand engagement with perhaps the odd popular theory such as Realism and Liberalism. The skills element (how to plan, research and write essays as well as revise for exams) is a hugely important feature of this book and, here, students from across politics and related disciplines should find something to help them through assessed and non-assessed work at university.

It can be a daunting prospect beginning the study of new subjects. There are long reading lists to plough through, unfamiliar concepts to learn and apply, difficult ideas to digest and many new ways of thinking to master in a relatively short space of time. The volume of reading and the depth of information required to succeed can be overwhelming for any student. This book should help you navigate your way through the complexity of IRT in three main ways. First, it summarizes the main components of the key theories you are likely to encounter on your course. Second, it shows how all these theories interrelate and influence each other in constructive dialogue over time. Third, it introduces the background to each theory and gives you a clear sense of how this apparent jumble all 'fit' together in the discipline. The book provides you with a clear overview of your IRT course that will allow you to fill in the detail as and when required. Furthermore, it offers practical advice and guidance on putting together assessed and non-assessed coursework (essays and presentations), and tips on how to do your best in exams.

HOW TO USE THE BOOK (OR: TAKING OWNERSHIP OF YOUR LEARNING ABOUT IRT)

This book is designed to help you succeed in your undergraduate or postgraduate level course in International Relations Theory. Theories of IR are likely to crop up in many and sometimes unexpected places during your degree programme; they are not only studied on courses specifically called 'International Relations Theory'. Theory regularly features in courses variously titled International Politics, International Relations since 1945, World Politics since 1945, the Contemporary World Arena, Foreign Policy Analysis and Methods in International Relations. Any module on International Security or Security Studies is likely to have a strong theoretical component based around debates between Realists and 'the rest', on, for example, the utility of nuclear weapons as security guarantors in the modern world. Theoretical concerns underpin the material on all these courses, and this book should therefore be useful whether your course is specifically on IRT or whether you need it as a handy introduction to the theories that crop up on related Politics and IR degree level modules.

The principal aim of the book is to help you succeed at coursework assignments, pass your exams, and overall to get the best out of your course in IRT. It has been designed and written to provide you with an accessible guide to the topics, themes and issues you will encounter on a typical IRT course, and the ways of thinking, writing and presenting evidence your tutors will be looking to see when they assess your written work and/or oral presentations (depending on the mode of assessment for the module you are on). I have not written the book to be another textbook on IRT – there are plenty of very good ones on the market already. Nor is this book meant to be read instead of textbooks, academic journal articles and other wider readings for your course. Given the succinct 'overview' nature of my coverage of the theories, this book should be read as a basic introduction *before*, and, if necessary, *alongside* the more advanced and in-depth scholarship which you will undoubtedly need to engage with to impress your tutors, who will be encouraging you to go beyond textbook treatments of all the subjects you take at university level. The introductory nature of my coverage together with the skills element of the book means that you should also find it useful to return to this book as you near the end of modules dealing with IRT and/or as you begin preparing for essays, exams and other assessed work. In sum, I hope this book is both primer and refresher, and that it is easy to navigate in and out of when you need to support your learning about IRT.

Students of International Relations and International Relations Theory are well served by a host of textbooks coming at the subject from a range of perspectives. These textbooks, in turn, are synthesizing often dense and complex writings from academic research monographs and articles in scholarly journals, where you will find the latest cutting-edge research on the subject. This book is intended for use in supporting the information and learning skills you develop by reading the main course texts and the 'original' theoretical and empirical work on IRT. It will help familiarize you with the basics of the discipline and give you an 'insider's' (tutor's) perspective on how to prepare effectively for putting together coursework essays and sitting exams. In terms of the key skills tested in such assessments, the book helps you organize your thoughts effectively, plan persuasive and logical arguments, and express those arguments clearly in speech and writing.

The aims of this book are:

- To introduce you to the subject matter of International Relations
- To survey the key theories of International Relations
- To provide help in developing the essential skills needed to meet the learning outcomes on courses in International Relations that have a theory component
- To act as a study aid alongside the textbook and more advanced reading you should be doing on your course.

There are many different theories of IR and it is rare to find a course that covers all of them. The time allowed at universities to deliver individual modules is very tight indeed and your tutor will have to make choices about which theories to teach you and which to leave out or cover only briefly. Tutors will not be expecting you to know everything about every theory, but they will be looking for a serious engagement with the theories that are covered. I would strongly advise you to consult the information about your particular course in IRT as soon as it is available, and to compare what you will cover on your course with the contents of this book. You will then only need to concern yourself with the chapters of the book that are directly relevant to your studies. In sum, it is unlikely that you will need to know each theory in detail, so concentrate your efforts only on the ones that are relevant to the course you are studying.

There are many more theories about international relations than there are weeks in the average semester to study them all. Make sure you know from the beginning of your course which theories you need to know in detail, and which are either not covered or less important to the overall make-up of your studies. Knowledge of other theories is useful but not a prerequisite for success, so plan your time and channel your energy and reading time wisely.

NAVIGATION AND MAIN FEATURES

This book is divided into four main parts. Part I gives you an orientation to the field of International Relations and International Relations Theory. Chapter 1.1 introduces the contested subject matter of IR, arguing that if you grasp the reasons for scholarly disputes over the object of study and how to study it, you will quickly understand why so many theories about IR have emerged and developed over the years. Chapter 1.2 begins by introducing why academics use theory and then focuses on why it is important to study International Relations theoretically. In Chapter 1.3 I sketch out what your course in IR theory might look like and what your tutor's expectations of you will be in terms of effort, participation and workload. Chapter 1.4 expands on the main themes from Chapter 1.2 in that it gives a more formal introduction to the development of the discipline of International Relations after its foundation in 1919. By the end of Part I you should be comfortable with what to expect on your course and to have begun thinking about the big questions that animate scholars working in this fascinatingly diverse discipline.

Part II is the real nitty-gritty of the book where I present an overview of the main IR theories you will come across on your course. You may cover some, you may cover them all, so feel free to pick and choose the relevant chapters as you see fit. Chapter 2.1 explores Liberalism, Chapter 2.2 considers Realism, while Chapter 2.3 introduces the updated variants of each, Neoliberalism and Neorealism. Chapter 2.4 delves into English School theory and Chapter 2.5 summarizes Social Constructivism. After that we move to theories that deal with issues in IR overlooked or ignored by these earlier 'mainstream' theories. Chapter 2.6 is on Marxism, Chapter 2.7 covers Critical Theory, Chapter 2.8 examines Feminism, Chapter 2.9 introduces Postmodernism, Chapter 2.10 examines Post-colonialism and, finally, Chapter 2.11 considers Environmentalism. By the end of Part II you should have a solid foundation of knowledge about each theory of IR and know where to look to find more detail about them.

Each chapter in Part II contains the following features:

- **New terms** appear in bold and their meaning is clearly explained in the Glossary at the end of the book.
- In order to highlight key points in each chapter I have inserted a series of 'Tips boxes' (example below) which will help you remember the most important issues raised in each chapter.

Remember, this book should not be seen as a substitute for the coverage of the theories you will get from lectures, seminars and course readings but as an accompaniment to them.

- I have also included hints in the form of 'Common pitfalls' boxes. These come from my experiences of teaching IRT and watching how students learn about it (or not, as the case may be!) Avoiding these pitfalls will help you enormously.
- Scattered throughout the book are 'Taking it further' boxes (see p. 11), where issues of particular significance within the discipline are developed in a little more detail than in the body text. I hope these will be useful in stimulating you to read more widely around the issues they raise.
- For each of the chapters on the substance of IR theories I have provided a list of key terms associated with those theories. You might wish to make a list of these key terms with all the different definitions and interpretations placed upon them by IR academics, for two reasons. First, it will help you understand the 'language' scholars use to debate issues in IR and

IRT. Second, you will generate a stock of critical reference material for use in your coursework and exam essays.

- I have provided a series of 'Questions to ponder' at the end of each of the chapters, together with a brief overview of how you might wish to set about tackling each one. Thinking about how you carve up essay and exam questions is a real skill to develop at university and my summary of what tutors look for should help you appreciate where you need to be in your written work, empirically and theoretically but crucially also in terms of logic and argument.
- At the end of each chapter there are 'References to more information' where you will find a list of sources you could read to deepen your understanding of the issues raised in the chapter. Your tutor will doubtless provide you with an extensive reading list for each theory so the two together should give you plenty to go on. I have tried to include less well known sources along with the canonical texts. It is usually obvious from the title what the book or article is about, but for several entries I have included a few pointers by way of explanation.

Part III is all about study skills. It offers advice and practical guidance in study, writing and revision skills so that you can present your knowledge in the most effective possible way in university level essays, exams and other coursework assignments, such as individual or group presentations. Chapters 3.1 and 3.2 explain how you can get the most out of university lectures and seminars by developing techniques and strategies for critically engaging with the relevant material before and during lectures, and for consolidating your knowledge in seminars (or tutorials, depending on what your university chooses to call them). Chapter 3.3 surveys the different types of feedback you will receive at university and how to get the maximum profit from it. Chapter 3.4 considers the difficult process of planning and writing academic essays. It encourages you to appreciate the importance of essay structure and modes of argumentation, and gives you practical steps to help deliver well balanced, well argued and clearly structured answers. Chapter 3.5 showcases examples of best practice in exam writing from real IRT essays I have marked in the past (and, yes, the students are still living to tell the tale).

> Developing good essay technique is vital for succeeding at courses in IRT. The ingredients of a good coursework essay are the same that go into cooking up a good exam answer.

Chapter 3.6 considers an increasing bane of the modern marking and assessment experience for tutors: plagiarism. It explains in simple terms what plagiarism is, and, crucially, how to avoid being accused of academic malpractice in the form of plagiarism. There is a very simple way, of course: do not plagiarize! Forearmed is forewarned. Chapters 3.7 and 3.8 consider the two things you need to do to succeed at exams: revise effectively and clearly communicate your thoughts in writing under not inconsiderable time pressure. By the end of Part III you should be in a position to prepare robustly argued, finely balanced, critically informed and academically sound coursework submissions. You should also be in a position to reflect on how to make the most of your revision time and how to do the very best you can in an exam on IRT.

In Part IV, you will find the Glossary and the References.

THINKING LIKE AN IR THEORIST

What do IR theorists *do*? When approaching a new programme of study it is important to grasp as early as you can what it is the scholars who have preceded you in the discipline are trying to achieve.

- IR theorists are interested in explaining the interactions between **states** in the international system.
- IR theorists have become increasingly interested in the behaviour of other actors in the international system which operate across, or transcend, state borders. They include supranational organizations such as the United Nations (UN) and the European Union (EU), **multinational corporations** such as Shell or Nike, loose transnational networks such as Al Qaeda, and transnational pressure groups such as Greenpeace, Human Rights Watch or Médecins Sans Frontières.
- Over time, IR academics have devised a variety of theories to explain the particular interaction or set of interactions that interest them the most, and which they feel best explain the 'international relations' they take to be important.
- IR theorists use evidence, logic and reasoned argument with other academics around the world to build their theories, test those theories and refine them over time.
- IR theorists use case studies from the 'real world' of politics, economics, history and law to ground their interpretations in the realm of 'facts'.
- Different IR theories can explain or interpret the same event or process in different ways. IR theorists might agree on some aspects of international affairs but not others and they can be quite 'tribal' as a result.

- IR theory is eclectic in that it draws upon evidence, ideas and arguments from across several disciplines in the humanities and social sciences: philosophy, law, politics, economics and history all feature in various theories to differing degrees.

> It is vital that you try and learn to think like an IR theorist. Courses in IRT are likely to test a lot more than simply your knowledge about the individual theories themselves. They will also look to see you engaging with debates about the role and value of 'theorizing' international relations. The experts whose works you read on this course have to grapple with these difficult questions every day and if you can show that you comprehend their predicament, you are likely to succeed at your course.

Appreciating what IR theorists do on a day-to-day basis helps us understand a bit more about the academic enterprise itself. Every academic discipline has its own terminology, shared language and concepts that sometimes unite and sometimes cause disagreements between scholars. Academic disciplines and sub-disciplines such as IRT have, over time, generated practices and shared expectations about what counts as knowledge and progress in the field. It is a bit like taking part in a sport you have not played before; what you do is useless unless you understand the following: first, the basic rules and laws of the game; second, the spirit in which these rules and laws are to be implemented during play (the unfolding **norms** of the sport); third, who is supposed to do what within your team, if it is a team sport – everything from tactical positioning to strategic aims for the team; and finally, the shared meanings behind the actions of the various players in the game, in particular the designation of 'winners' and 'losers' (or runners up).

In football (soccer), for example, it is only when you understand how the offside rule works that you can appreciate why the referee blows his or her whistle and the players stop the game when the linesperson raises his/her flag. Learning skills is one thing, but acquiring knowledge of the tactics and techniques for keeping onside is a key part of being a successful footballer. So it is in the academic world that the best students tend to be the ones who most quickly understand the 'rules of the game' and have the patience to spend time getting into the mindset of the experts they read and for whom they write essays and exam answers. Familiarity with conventions enhances comprehension and speeds adaptation to the expectations on you as a student. This book will give you advice on how to get to grips with the discipline of IRT and help you express your thoughts in the language or authorial 'voice' of the IR theorist. In short, it will help you better understand the rules of the game in IRT – what it is that IR theorists seek to do when they go to work every morning.

> On your course you are likely to be assessed on two main grounds: (1) your understanding of each of the theories you cover on the curriculum; and (2) your ability to critique each of those theories.

RUNNING THEMES

There is a wide assortment of IR theories, all of which claim to make sense of the subject or at least some significant aspect of it. Throughout your course you will be exposed to, and expected to engage with, aspects of all these debates about the role, nature and value of theorizing international relations. Here are five of the most common dimensions of the debate about theory you will probably encounter:

1 **The nature of theory** – while there are many elements of overlap, there is no single view common to all scholars of IR on what theory *is*. The word 'theory' is often used interchangeably with words like 'approaches', 'perspectives', 'traditions', or even 'images', indicating that there are real and ongoing disputes over what 'makes' a theory and when a particular body of writing is sufficiently well developed to constitute a distinct theory of IR.

2 **Ontology** – or the object of study. The problem, issue or set of events different writers or groups of writers are trying to explain will necessarily affect both how they study IR and the nature of the evidence they deploy to develop, test and refine their theory. The question of ontology is therefore vital: do you think different theorists are viewing the same world (do they share an ontology of IR), or are they 'seeing' different worlds (are their ontologies of IR at odds with each other)?

3 **Epistemology** – or the theory of knowledge. The stuff of international relations is not as tangible and easy to put under a microscope as, for example, atoms are for physicists, molecules are

for chemists, or as fingerprints are for Crime Scene Investigators. IR theorists often involve themselves in quite heated disputes about epistemology: what counts as reliable evidence about a particular problem area.

4 **Logic and argument** – IR theorists use narrative arguments to try and persuade readers of the strength of their case. This use of argumentation usually has two dimensions to it. The theorist has to construct a theory that flows logically from the evidence gathered and the ontological assumptions s/he has made about the object of study, meaning the theory must have *internal* logic. The theorist will often also question the assumptions, interpretations and evidential base of other theorists; this is the *external* dimension where rival theories look outward to try to critique and knock down rival theories.

5 **Positivist/normative divide** – returns us to disputes about the nature of theory. For positivists, the study of the social sciences can proceed using the same methods as in the natural sciences to produce generalizations, predictions and laws about IR. Normative theorists question the applicability of methods drawn from the natural sciences and tend to be more open about the agendas to which they write and the uses to which their theories might be put in the 'real world' of politics and public policy.

'Theory' is a disputed term. Think about how each writer you study either defines the word explicitly in their work or what they would implicitly understand 'theory' to mean. You should soon see how they might position themselves in unfolding disciplinary discussions about the uses, nature and foundations of theory.

TAKING IT FURTHER

IR is a multidimensional discipline, so naturally a course on the theories about International Relations will reflect the intrinsic diversity of the field. It is testament to the scale of the task at hand (theorizing the world, to put it simply!) that we have so many theories and so many claims to provide an objective, 'scientific' account of the broad sweep of international relations. Studying the subject at university level will provide you with a flavour of the main debates that have shaped the field as well as the latest cutting-edge research. The onus is on you to do as much wider reading as you see fit to expand your knowledge base and follow up on the aspects of IR and IRT that interest you the most.

To this end I have interspersed the book with 'Taking it further' sections which cover material that may well lie outside the scope of your course, but which add depth or a new dimension to the themes we cover in the main text. Taking things further in this way is useful for you for three main reasons.

First of all, *following up wider debates* and points of interest will help you understand more about how the individual theories you examine on your course fit together to make the discipline of IR.

Common Pitfall

Many students tend to 'play it safe' and concentrate only on the essential textbook reading for their course. It is advisable to go that extra mile and seek out the original academic readings that get quickly summarized in the textbooks as a way of helping you develop your critical capabilities and familiarity with the original core texts.

Second, you will *learn more effectively* about this subject – any subject for that matter – if you spend time thinking seriously about the underlying disputes about how to study a subject, what 'counts' as evidence, and how to present your findings appropriately in an academic context. Reflecting on what you have learnt and reading around a topic will help you understand the material you cover on your IRT course, as well as helping you think through the big philosophical and theoretical issues associated with research and debates in politics and the social sciences more generally. Reading what scholars have had to say about how to study IRT will help you come to a position within these debates and help you articulate and justify your opinion in essays and exams.

The third reason is perhaps the most important to you at this stage of your studies: showing your module tutor that you have *actively engaged with IR theory.* An active and informed dialogue with yourself and your peers about the nature, value and role of IRT will come across clearly to your tutor when they mark your work. The average student might know what some of the theories say about IR, whereas the better student will be able to dissect the assumptions of each theory and be able to critique the theories using information they have taken from wide reading around the subject. In exams you will not necessarily be expected to show the same level of depth and critical capability, but you will need to take a stance on a given issue or theory and justify your interpretation with logic and evidence from key writings. Trying to gain an overall impression of the recurring debates that animate the discipline will help develop your intellectual abilities no end.

> Although your course is an essentially theoretical one, it is important that you do not forget that the theorists whose work you study have been influenced by events in the world at their respective times of writing. Try and identify the influence of practice on theory when you read academic books and articles.

QUESTIONS TO PONDER

As you plough through the lecture and seminar reading for your course in IR theory it is beneficial to consider the kinds of IRT-related questions you might have to answer in exams or essays during and/or at the end of the module. Essay questions with deadlines will usually be available at the beginning of your module, but if they are not included in your course resources from the outset your course tutor may be willing to let you have copies of past essay titles before they are published. For exams the obvious resource is past exam papers, so check your course materials early on in your studies and scrutinize them carefully. These will show you the kinds of themes, issues, concepts and ideas your tutor will push through the lectures, and invite you to reflect upon in assessed work.

The nub of the matter is to take an *active* approach to your learning about IRT. Learning from books and articles is not just about concentrating on the fabric of the particular theory you are covering that week, although that is obviously the most significant reason for reading and attending lectures and seminars. Active learning actively means reflecting on a host of related issues. For example, think about the questions that spurred the authors you read to put pen to paper – why did they decide to write their pieces and what do *you* think about their response?

Is their interpretation valid, fair, based on sound evidence and argued effectively? How would *you* prepare an answer to the question they set themselves and where would *you* look for evidence? Break down the various segments of their books and articles to help you understand how they did it and that can inform your view on the appropriateness of their position. What issues would *you* have thrown into the mix to perhaps help that author make his/her argument more effectively, or to help the author knock down rival theories? Are there any case studies from the contemporary world of politics and international affairs that shed light on the theoretical problems being explored? Consciously applying theory to present problems is a valuable skill to develop.

At the end of each chapter I suggest a few questions that arise from the theoretical terrain it traverses. I suggest some ways in which you might approach answering them but I leave it up to you to flesh out my suggestions with further detail. These questions are designed to encourage you to engage with the issues discussed and to help you see how important it is to be an active consumer of academic literature rather than a passive receiver. Learning to take an active approach to reading and digesting this material will help you, not just on your course in IRT, but on all the modules you study at university.

REFERENCES TO MORE INFORMATION

Your course tutor will recommend a series of textbooks, journal articles and other resources to help you learn about theories of IR. Different tutors organize course material differently. On the one hand, you might have a reading list that is divided up theory by theory, lecture by lecture, or seminar by seminar, making it easy for you to locate the relevant reading for each week. On the other hand, some tutors prefer to give you a long list of readings and let you choose from them which sources you want to read in preparation for each of the lectures and seminars. On top of your general lecture reading, some tutors might invite you to dissect one or two specific readings in advance of seminars, as a basis for discussion within the group on the day.

All approaches to course design and delivery have their strengths and weaknesses. The first approach puts the readings on a plate, so to speak, speeding up your search for the appropriate texts by saving you having to root around in the library to find the relevant material from an aggregate course list. The second approach puts more onus on you to find the relevant sources for each week, so while it takes more time, it enhances your information retrieval and wider research skills. Directed seminar reading is good for promoting seminar discussion but can, it is said, limit the opportunities for better students to explore from the list the readings that interest them the most.

However your course reading lists are designed there are certain core textbooks that are absolutely invaluable aids to the study of IRT and I frequently refer to them in this book.

These textbooks come with online resource centres and are aimed directly at undergraduate students:

Baylis, J., Smith, S. and Owens, P. (eds) (several editions, 5th edn 2010) *The Globalization of World Politics: An Introduction to International Relations*. Oxford: Oxford University Press.

Dunne, T., Kurki, M. and Smith, S. (eds) (2010) *International Relations Theory: Discipline and Diversity*, 2nd edn. Oxford: Oxford University Press.

Jackson, R. and Sørenson, G. (several editions, 4th edn 2010) *Introduction to International Relations: Theories and Approaches*. Oxford: Oxford University Press.

These books are aimed principally at undergraduates:

Brown, C. and Ainley, K. (several editions, 4th edn 2009) *Understanding International Relations*. Basingstoke: Palgrave.

Burchill, S. et al. (several editions, 4th edn 2009) *Theories of International Relations*. Basingstoke: Palgrave.

Griffiths, M. (ed.) (2007) *International Relations Theory for the Twenty-First Century*. London: Routledge.

Nye, J.S. and Welch, D.A. (2011) *Understanding Global Conflict and Cooperation: An Introduction to Theory and History*. London: Pearson.

Steans, J. et al. (several editions, 4th edn 2010) *An Introduction to International Relations Theory: Perspectives and Themes*. London: Longman.

These books are pitched at undergraduate and postgraduate students:

Brown, C., Nardin, T. and Rengger, N. (eds) (2002) *International Relations in Political Thought: Texts from the Ancient Greeks to the First World War*. Cambridge: Cambridge University Press.

Carlsnaes, W., Risse, T. and Simmons, B.A. (eds) (2006) *Handbook of International Relations*. London: Sage.

Der Derian, J. (ed.) (1995) *International Theory: Critical Investigations*. London: Macmillan.

Griffiths, M. (ed.) (2011) *Rethinking International Relations Theory*. Basingstoke: Palgrave Macmillan.

Groom, A.J.R. and Light, M. (eds) (1994) *Contemporary International Relations: A Guide to Theory*. London: Pinter.

Holsti, K.J. (1995) *International Politics: A Framework for Analysis*, 7th edn. Englewood Cliffs, NJ: Prentice Hall.

Jørgensen, K.E. (2010) *International Relations Theory: A New Introduction*. Basingstoke: Palgrave Macmillan.

Little, R. and Smith, M. (eds) (2006) *Perspectives on World Politics*. Abingdon: Routledge.

Nardin, T. and Mapel, D.R. (eds) (1993) *Traditions of International Ethics*. Cambridge: Cambridge University Press.

Nicholson, M. (2002) *International Relations: A Concise Introduction*, 2nd edn. Basingstoke: Palgrave Macmillan.

Smith, S., Booth, K. and Zalewski, M. (eds) (1996) *International Theory: Positivism and Beyond*. Cambridge: Cambridge University Press.

Sterling-Folker, J. (ed.) (2006) *Making Sense of International Relations Theory*. Boulder, CO: Lynne Rienner.

Vasquez, J.A. (eds) (1996) *Classics of International Relations*, 3rd edn. Upper Saddle River, NJ: Prentice Hall.

Viotti, P.R. and Kauppi, M.V. (eds) (1999) *International Relations Theory*, 3rd edn. New York: Macmillan.

Weber, C. (several editions, 3rd edn 2010) *International Relations Theory*: A Critical Introduction. London: Routledge.

When studying IR it is useful to have a working knowledge of international history, at least since 1945 and preferably back to 1900. The following books will give you the gist of the story:

Best, A., Hanhimaki, J.M., Maiolo, J.A. and Schulze, K.E. (2004) *International History of the Twentieth Century*. London: Routledge.

Calvocoressi, P. (2009) *World Politics Since 1945*, 4th edn. London: Longman.

Gathorne-Hardy, G.M. (1964) *A Short History of International Affairs 1920–1939*. London: Oxford University Press.

Keylor, W.R. (2001) *The Twentieth Century World: An International History*, 4th edn. Oxford: Oxford University Press.

Martel, G. (ed.) (2007) *A Companion to International History 1900–2001*. Oxford: Blackwell.

Reynolds, D. (2000) *One World Divisible: A Global History Since 1945*. New York: W.W. Norton.

Young, J.W. and Kent, J. (2004) *International Relations since 1945: A Global History*. Oxford: Oxford University Press.

If you want more general guides to settling in and succeeding at university try:

Becker, L. (2003) *How to Manage Your Arts, Humanities and Social Sciences Degree*. Basingstoke: Palgrave Macmillan.

Davey, G. (2008) *The International Student's Survival Guide*. London: Sage.

Rugg, G., Gerrard, S. and Hooper, S. (2008) *The Stress-Free Guide to Studying at University*. London: Sage.

Textbooks naturally concentrate on some theories at the expense of others and treat the theories they do cover slightly differently. That said, they all consider core sets of issues associated with the nature of theory, the strength of their claims to knowledge about IR, and their overall contribution to the development of the discipline. They tend to use examples from the 'real world' of politics and international affairs to bring the theories to life. This book is a companion to your textbooks rather than a replacement for them, so make sure you use your textbooks to put the flesh on the bones of what I say here.

There are lots of journals devoted to the study of IR and IRT. Here are some of the most popular. Increasingly, you can access electronic versions of these articles online through your university library: *Alternatives, American Political Science Review, British Journal of Politics and International Relations, Cambridge Review of International Affairs, Ethics and International Affairs, European Foreign Affairs Review, European Journal of International Relations, International Affairs, International Feminist Journal of Politics, International Organization, International Relations, International Security, International Studies Perspectives, International Studies Review, International Studies Quarterly, Journal of International Affairs, Millennium: Journal of International Studies, Political Studies, Review of International Studies* and *World Politics*.

SUMMARY

There is a lot of reading out there about IRT. Don't let this make you apprehensive; one of the most frequent reasons for students not engaging with IRT is fear that because they can't know everything about a theory they are wary of taking those first vital steps to understanding it. A way around this potential pitfall is to read widely from day one of your course and it then becomes routine (we will return to this in the skills section of the book). Target your reading by parcelling up what you need to do week by week. Every student reads differently, works differently and thinks differently, and there are no hard and fast rules on how much preparation is enough for each of the seminars and coursework assignments you will do on your course.

When you are comfortable and up to speed with the basics of IRT, a complementary skill you need to develop is that of knowing when you have done enough to understand the basics of each theory and how you might critique that theory. Make sure you have a thorough knowledge of your module guide and attend all the course lectures and seminars because they will give you a good insight into what your tutor expects from you. It is important that you work out for yourself as soon as you can in your university studies how *you* work best and how you best prepare for handing in assignments and revising for exams. This book will help you develop these transferable skills, as well as helping you come to terms with the diverse, sometimes infuriating and always enjoyable world of IRT.

PART I

INTRODUCTION TO YOUR COURSE IN IR THEORY

No two courses in IRT I have experienced as a student or delivered as a tutor look the same. In the module guide for your course your tutor will explain the topics you will be studying and the expectations he/she has of you in terms of workload, attendance, seminar participation, coursework assignments and exams. It is important to orientate yourself to the demands of your particular course as soon as you can, and your first task will therefore be to read everything about the course as soon as it is available to you – online and/or in hard copy form. Most universities use Virtual Learning Environments (VLEs) such as Blackboard or Learn, and that is where you will most likely find the course materials and supplementaries such as discussion forums, and so on.

   The manifold differences between IRT modules make it impossible to write a book that speaks directly to all of them and this book has been written at one remove from the specifics of your module organization and lecture/seminar schedule. Instead, it moves up a level to guide you through the general field of study with which you will be engaging on your course, and to the big questions that have animated so many writers over the years to put pen to paper on this complex subject. It is useful to try and think about the key points of dispute and debate between scholars working in the same discipline because understanding the intellectual context within which academics work helps you get inside their heads. Academics like students to do this, first, because it helps you understand what points of friction have driven the discipline forward over the years, and, second, it equips you with the weaponry to critique scholarly ideas and opinions on their terms rather than with the benefit of hindsight. Reading this book will encourage you to develop both these skills: understanding academic theories and critiquing them.

This part of the book is organized around underlying disciplinary debates about IRT. In Chapter 1.1 we introduce the hotly contested subject matter of IR. In Chapter 1.2 we add in the contested issue of theory. Chapter 1.3 makes some general remarks about tutors' expectations of students taking IR courses. Chapter 1.4 returns us to the central theme of the book: theoretical disputes about IR. We emerge the other side with a whole host of uncertainties: this is a field of study in which no one can really agree either on the appropriate subject matter, or on how best to study it. If you can grasp the reasons for these disputes and offer up convincing evidence that you have taken a position on them, you are likely to succeed at your course because you will have been engaging actively with each theory at quite a sophisticated level.

CORE AREAS

1.1 Introduction to International Relations
1.2 International Relations Theory
1.3 Your course in IRT
1.4 Theoretical Debates

1.1 INTRODUCTION TO INTERNATIONAL RELATIONS

Even by those who have authored them, the emergence of theories cannot be described in other than uncertain and impressionistic ways. Elements of theories can, however, be identified. (Waltz 2010: 10)

It is difficult to build a **theory** about any academic subject, whether it be in the social sciences like IR or in the natural sciences like physics, biology or chemistry. Theories by their nature are simplified versions of a complex reality. As Kenneth Waltz goes on to argue in the passage quoted above from his path-breaking *Theory of International Politics* (originally published in 1979), it is a big step to go from causal speculation based on factual studies to the construction of theoretical formulations that enables one to arrange newly observed facts through theoretical lenses. 'To cope with the difficulty, simplification is required' (Waltz 2010: 10).

In the process of theory development we are trying to comprehend the complexity of relations between, say, State X and State Y by breaking down into manageable chunks the elements of their inter-relationships that most intrigue us. Necessarily, theories fall prey to criticisms about their coverage, their depth and their relevance to the 'real world' they are trying to explain. It is worth remembering, therefore, that all theories come with a health warning: no theory can explain everything about the world and nor should we expect it to. Even the most ardent supporter of theory development has to admit limitations: '… in order to have a theory, you'll have to have a subject matter, because you can't have a theory about everything. There's no such thing as a theory about everything' (Waltz, quoted in Kreisler 2003). In other words, a theory about everything is a theory about nothing.

Theoretical disputes are common even in disciplines where scholars are trying to theorize the same event or set of events which they agree are happening, or have happened, in the 'real world'. What, then, if scholars disagree on the essence of the 'reality' they are trying to explain? What if they can't come to a basic consensus on what makes the world go round, or on why humans behave the way they do? What then for supposedly comprehensive theories which enable us to make predictions about what might happen in the future on the basis of our existing theoretical knowledge about the world?

Engaging with underlying concerns about the construction, function and value of theory will help you appreciate the nature of the scholarly enterprise in IRT because:

- It helps you see the problem through the eyes of the authors you study
- It enhances your ability to critique each theory
- It helps you 'think' like an IR theorist.

On your IRT course you may well have the chance to study these kinds of **metatheoretical** issues in some detail. 'Metatheories take other theories as their subject' (Reus-Smit 2012: 530). For example, you may have timetabled lectures and seminars on the constituent elements of theoretical work at the start and end of your course, and seminars will doubtless incorporate discussion not only about the substance of each theory that has been developed about IR, but also the convenient assumptions theorists make about how the world works.

Certainly many of the textbooks you read will, usually in the introductory and concluding chapters, engage with metatheoretical issues in some detail, so being aware of them from the off will help you begin to think like an IR theorist (for instance, Dunne et al. 2007; Jackson and Sørensen 2007). In this chapter I try and answer three big questions that have motivated scholars to theorize IR over the years. First, what is 'the world' of international relations that we are studying? Second, what are 'International Relations' as a discipline? Third, who or what are the major **actors** we need to study in IR? Answering these questions helps us understand more about the role of theory in studying a subject like IR, and we cover that in the following chapter.

Metatheory 'quite simply means theoretical reflections *on* theory' (Jørgensen 2010: 15, original emphasis). Metatheory considers the nature, role and practice of theorizing. Metatheorists look upon all the competing theories about a certain topic and try to understand how all the theorists they study are making sense of their subject. This then helps them come to a considered assessment on the nature and significance of theoretical contributions in a given field.

WHAT IS THE WORLD?

Accurate and reliable measurements are of little value unless they measure the proper variables; and, unfortunately, our speculations about changing global structures involve variables that are not readily observed. (Rosenau 1976: 8)

Every academic discipline requires a subject that practitioners agree is the focus for study. This statement might seem obvious, but it has many intriguing ramifications for social science subjects such as politics, history, media and communications and sociology, because looking across these endeavours we do not find a huge amount of agreement on what the 'core' of each discipline is, or should be. So when I ask 'what is the world?', I am trying to alert you to what I like to call the problem of the subject matter of IR: what are we actually theorizing in this discipline? As A.K. Ramakrishnan rightly points out, 'Generating knowledge requires the knower to identify and speak about an object' (Ramakrishnan 1999: 132). In IR this proves contentious because, as R.B.J. Walker astutely observes (1995: 314), most of the debates we engage in 'arise far more from disagreements about what it is that scholars think they are studying than from disagreements about how to study it'.

To this end we can take a cue from literature on the philosophy of social science by comparing the study of the social (or behavioural) sciences on the one hand with the study of the natural (or physical) sciences on the other (see Scriven 1994). This will enable us to draw some preliminary conclusions about the problematic nature of the subject matter of IR and gain insights into the reasons why theoretical disputes recur in the discipline, helping to drive forward the search for knowledge about contemporary global politics.

> If you have friends at university studying in different departments (social or natural sciences) try asking them about their respective disciplines: what do they study and how? Is the subject matter of their discipline and how to study it generally well recognized, or is it contested? Who decides these things? Compare their experiences to your experience of studying International Relations.

Let us start with simple, dictionary-style definitions of the principal natural sciences, biology, chemistry and physics:

- Biology – the study of living organisms
- Chemistry – the study of the composition, properties and reactions of substances
- Physics – the study of the properties of matter and energy.

These disciplines are clearly not monolithic. That is to say, they are divided into communities of scholars working across various specialized sub-disciplines, each with their own scope for inquiry. For instance, physics breaks down into astrophysics, nuclear physics and quantum physics; engineers can be electrical, chemical or biomedical. Nor are the natural sciences immune from some pretty fevered debates about disciplinary development and cohesion. These are especially marked around novel findings or approaches that challenge existing paradigms and claim the status of 'mature' research to sit alongside more established ways of studying a subject. For example, in engineering, Allen Cheng and Timothy Lu (2012) have studied the emergence of 'synthetic biology' which challenges entrenched disciplinary boundaries by reaching out to biology, offering a quite different perspective on what it means to 'do' both biology and engineering in this new subfield.

Although natural science disciplines might be fragmented and have different 'wings', there is usually quite a robust consensus among biologists, engineers, chemists and physicists on essential aspects of their work: on their object of study (or the problem to be solved by a given wing of the discipline), on how to study that problem, on what counts as evidence about the problem, and on when theories or explanations for a given phenomenon have become obsolete. As Martin Hollis and Steve Smith describe the natural science model, 'the broad idea is that events are governed by laws of nature which apply whenever similar events occur in similar conditions. Science progresses by learning which similarities are key to which sequences' (Hollis and Smith 1991: 3). Nicholas Onuf likewise insinuates that the idea of modern science is 'institutionalized through general acceptance of the procedural rules (*the scientific method*) for checking theoretical models (*models stipulating causal relations*) against evidence taken to represent some feature of "the real world" and refining these models accordingly' (Onuf 2009: 187, my emphasis).

This process of disciplinary development is shown in Figure 1, which assumes that the wheels of a discipline turn when scholars come to agree on: (1) the object/phenomenon/event/process to be studied; (2) how to study the object/phenomenon/event/process; (3) what counts as evidence about the object/phenomenon/event/process; and (4) when theories about the object/phenomenon/event/process have been disproved, or proven so untenable that new theories are needed to provide more adequate explanations.

Having established what the disciplinary wheel looks likes for natural scientists, the question for us students of IR is: can we replicate this approach for disciplines in the social sciences? I am not sure we can for the very simple reason that the subject matter of IR is **essentially**

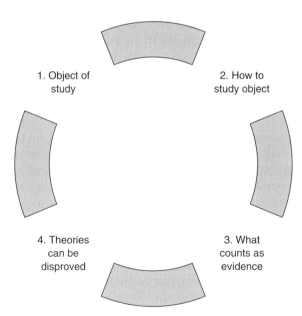

Figure 1   How the wheels of a scientific discipline turn

contested – there is no agreement on what constitutes the basic subject matter of IR.

> As you progress through your IRT course make a list of all the essentially contested concepts, objects and ideas you come across. Why are they essentially contested and what does this mean for the scholarship about them and our grasp of them?

In the natural sciences the objects we study tend to be physical things we can pick up, pin down, observe and measure, either with our own eyes or with the help of measuring devices such as blood pressure gauges for medics or speedometers for automotive engineers. A chemist can don a pair of safety goggles and drop a chunk of potassium into a basin of water to observe the violent reaction. A physicist can monitor the impact of temperature on solids by heating a strip of metal and watching the atoms vibrate faster and faster under a microscope. A biologist can test the impact of light on plant growth by measuring the relative speed of growth of the same plant in lighter and darker conditions.

Hence, as Kal Holsti rightly observes (1985: 7), 'To develop theory, before we can discuss technique, there must be some consensus on what we want to examine'. In the natural sciences the tangibility of the subject matter helps researchers agree on the problem or object to be studied, on how to study it, on what counts as evidence, and to agree finally on when theories have become flawed or obsolete. Natural scientists can put things that interest them under a microscope and study their properties and behaviour in order to generate theories.

If they are unable to 'see' what interests them at first hand (the speed of light for example) they have developed instruments which can measure them accurately in the absence of the visual evidence itself. Importantly, all such measures come to be validated over time through consensus building in the scientific community. Experiments can be replicated by other scientists who can confirm the accuracy of the results and share ideas on what to study next. This process of **falsification** relies on each scientist's work being constantly tested and challenged by other scientists, and this is made easier by the existence of the physical objects that form the basis for experimentation in the natural sciences. We could say in very simple terms, therefore, that natural scientists generate knowledge the **empiricist** way. Like David Attenborough studying the behaviour of tree frogs in the Amazonian rainforest, natural scientists rely on having direct access to a 'real world' which they move through with the help of the scientific instruments to help them see, measure and interpret the world around them.

To put it in formal terms, knowledge in the natural sciences is held to be accurate and reliable when it:

- has a grounded **ontology** – theory connected with the things, properties and events that exist in the world; what is held to be 'out there' and in need of investigation.
- is rooted in empiricist **epistemology** – theory about how we know things and what is regarded as valid/reliable/legitimate knowledge in a given discipline.
- flows from a robust **methodology** – rules and guidelines on how to set up experiments and interpret and record the data collected.
- is subject to **falsification** – a statement, theory or explanation might never be proved undoubtedly true but should be rejected when predictions derived from it turn out to be false.

Empirical scientific investigation tends to be the benchmark by which our claim to produce hard and fast knowledge about the world is judged. Do you think it is fair to judge social scientific knowledge production in this way? Studying IRT will give you lots of ground on which to come to a judgement.

We can now add these formal labels to the disciplinary wheel in Figure 2.

By now you will have twigged why I asked the question 'what is the world?' It is because the discipline of IR is centrally concerned with investigating relationships between 'things' in the world … and yet there is no agreement amongst theorists on what precisely it is that the discipline should study, on how to study it, on what counts as evidence, and on when theories have been proved false. This is why courses in IRT cover so many theories – none of their authors ever admit they are wrong because evidence can always be found to support an updated version of the theory. They cannot even all agree on what it is that they are studying.

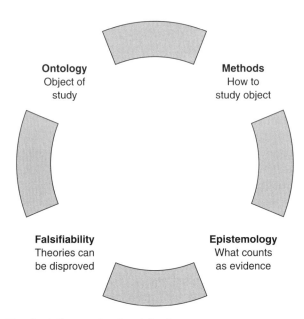

Figure 2 The disciplinary wheel revisited

Think about the differences between disciplines that study 'tangible' things and those that study 'intangible' ones. What does this imply for the reliability of the theories developed in each field, and what steps do you think we can take to develop methods of explaining the relationships between intangible things more accurately?

Unlike in the natural sciences where we can pick things up, put them down, throw them around and see what happens, how can we possibly do this with 'the world', which is what scholars of IR necessarily try to do? In the following section we will start to see how this problem of the subject plays out in the study of IRT by exploring competing definitions of 'international relations'.

WHAT ARE 'INTERNATIONAL RELATIONS'?

In his book *Understanding International Relations*, Chris Brown explains why it is important to identify the scope of the field:

> The reason definitions matter in this way is because 'international relations' do not have some kind of essential existence in the real world of the sort that could define an academic discipline. Instead, there is a continual interplay between the 'real world' and the world of knowledge. (Brown 2001: 1)

Brown adopts the same approach to the problem of the subject in IR that we did in the last section. His logic proceeds as follows:

- The development of academic disciplines is predicated upon there being a well-defined subject matter which organizes and focuses enquiry within that field.
- IR theorists engage with a subject matter that does not necessarily exist in the 'real world' of observable (physical) things. We cannot pick 'states' up and slide them under a microscope.
- Therefore the subject matter of IR is in dispute.
- The subject matter of IR is made doubly hard to pin down because it is so bound up with contemporary developments in global politics and the *study* of global affairs.
- To put it another way: the world which scholars of IR are studying is constantly in a state of flux.

Common Pitfall

In essays and exams you will be expected to be able to summarize key ideas in the field of IR. Too often students do not show the patience to explain interpretations writers arrive at and why. Introducing scholars as 'renowned Professor of IR' is irrelevant except to their pay-packet. Telling readers how they interpret IR is the crux. Note how we have taken Brown's argument apart step by step by examining his assumptions and the conclusions he derives from them.

Brown (2001: 1) goes on to suggest that the field of IR encompasses the study of some or all of the following:

1 **Diplomatic-strategic relations of states** – with a focus on war and peace, conflict and cooperation. This was the 'classical' subject matter of the discipline, also well described by Kal Holsti: 'the consequence of a world made up of states, each possessing the capacity to make war against each other' (Holsti 1985: 10).

Alan James is another who equates IR with the study of 'inter-state relations'; we should only account for the influence of non-state actors as and when they impinge on what goes on between states (James 1993: 270).

2 **Cross-border transactions of all kinds** – meaning the whole gamut of political, economic and social exchanges between states.

3 **Globalization** – of world communications, transport and financial systems, multinational corporations.

You can see from this all-embracing definition that when looking at international relations we are potentially looking at anything and everything that happens anywhere in the world. It is as difficult to nail down the subject matter of IR as it is to nail jelly to a wall!

Other writers who try to solve the problem of the subject in IR by defining the scope of the discipline include Scott Burchill and Andrew Linklater. In their Introduction to Burchill's collection on theories of IR (Burchill and Linklater 2009) they remark that there is more to the study of IR than accounting for diplomatic, strategic and economic relations between **nation-states**. For Burchill and Linklater the study of IR has four dimensions:

1 **Dominant actors** – nation-states, transnational corporations (including business empires such as Adidas and media empires such as Rupert Murdoch's News Corporation), financial markets such as the bonds and futures markets, nongovernmental organizations, **supranational** political communities, **subnational** actors based on ethnic, religious or cultural affiliations, and **international organizations** such as the North Atlantic Treaty Organization (NATO), the Red Cross/Red Crescent and the World Bank.

2 **Dominant relationships** – yes, those between states, but also those that cut across state borders both above and below the purview of the state. Such relationships include those flowing from economic **interdependence**, the global credit crunch, Third World debt, international trade and the spread of multinational corporations, inequality in all its forms, and regional economic and political associations such as the EU, the Organization of African Unity (OAU), the Association of Southeast Asian Nations (ASEAN) and the Gulf Cooperation Council (GCC).

3 **Empirical issues** – here we come to specific themes and issues that are important enough in a global context to warrant understanding and explaining by IR scholars. They highlight the distribution of military power, globalization, human rights, intervention and sovereignty, aid, refugees, ethnicity, women's issues (gender), the environment, HIV, drugs and organized crime. The global economic downturn will no doubt attract a lot of attention from scholars in the coming years.

4 **Ethical issues** – just war, the rights and wrongs of humanitarian intervention to alleviate human suffering, poverty and wealth distribution, respect for cultural differences and our human duties to the environment and future generations, well covered now by Green theory (see Chapter 2.11 of this book).

5 **Philosophical issues** – all the questions we considered above about how to theorize IR, including those surrounding ontology, epistemology, methodology and why writers from different theoretical traditions disagree with each other on the explanation of state and other actors' behaviour in the international system.

6 **The prospects for multidisciplinarity** – how the discipline of IR 'reaches out' to cognate disciplines and is in turn shaped by new developments on its porous disciplinary borders.

Brown and Burchill/Linklater have slightly different views on the field of IR; this is largely down to the goals of their respective books. On the one hand, Brown's is a general introduction to the study of IR which he takes to mean the study of things 'out there' (empirical things) in the world of international affairs. On the other hand, Burchill and Linklater's theoretical focus fits empirical issues into a wider framework. Using the heading 'philosophical issues' allows them to consider the type and quality of the theoretical knowledge that has been generated about issues and actors in the international system.

> As you progress through your course reading, think carefully about the particular focus of the texts you read because this will help you understand the way authors approach the 'problem of the subject'.

Burchill and Linklater's inclusive approach is now quite common. To take another example, in their edited collection *Handbook of International Relations*, Walter Carlsnaes, Thomas Risse and Beth Simmons (2006) split their work into three parts. Part I is on 'historical, philosophical and theoretical issues'; Part II is on 'concepts and context', including chapters on state sovereignty, power, diplomacy, bargaining and negotiation, interdependence and the link between domestic politics and international relations. Part III is on the substantive issues Brown majors on and which Burchill and Linklater incorporate into their broader study: things such as war and peace, nationalism and ethnicity, international trade and finance, international development, the environment, law and human rights.

The upshot of all this is that there is no agreement on what constitutes either the subject area of IR, or how to study this subject; it potentially 'encompasses all phases of human experience because its scope is global and its foci as diverse as the values, preoccupations, and practices of people everywhere' (Rosenau 2002: 545). Grayson Kirk's 1947 comment on the state of the discipline is as relevant now as it was then:

> the study of international relations is still in a condition of considerable confusion. The scope of the field, the methods of analysis and synthesis to be followed, the proper administrative arrangements to be made in college curricula, the organization of research – all these are matters of continuing controversy. (Quoted in Schmidt 2006: 3)

TAKING IT FURTHER

International Relations or World Politics?

In their textbook *The Globalization of World Politics* John Baylis, Steve Smith and Patricia Owens begin by outlining why they put the term 'World Politics' rather than 'International Politics' or 'International Relations' in their title.

'World Politics', they say, suggests something 'more inclusive than either of the alternatives. It is meant to denote the fact that our interest is in the *politics* and *political patterns* in the world, and not only those between nation-states (as the term international politics implies)' (Baylis et al. 2008a: 3). Their opinion on the best title for their book shows the power of language and labels, and why it is important for us to take both seriously when studying at university level. Let us break down their argument into its constituent parts.

- 'International Relations' implies the study of relations between nation-states. For greater accuracy we might rewrite it 'Inter-national Relations'.

- 'International Politics' is similarly limited: 'Inter-national Politics'.

- Neither signifier does justice to what Baylis, Smith and Owens consider to be the essence of the field, which is both wider and deeper than the relations between nation-states.

- IR for Baylis, Smith and Owens is about the study of *politics* and *political patterns* in the world. To use Burchill and Linklater's terminology from earlier in the chapter, Baylis, Smith and Owens are interested in explaining the web of connections and *relationships* between *all* actors in the world.

- Nation-states undoubtedly retain an immensely important place in the study of IR, but they do not play the only or even most decisive part in global politics today. 'World politics' is more comprehensive and a more apt description of the realities of contemporary global political interactions.

Other textbooks that opt for 'World Politics' indicate the stretch in meaning the term implies. For example, Jeffrey Haynes et al.'s (2011) *World Politics* begins with theories and moves on to an array of themes and issues in IR, such as democratization, 'new wars' and terrorism. Karen Mingst and Jack Snyder's (2011) *Essential Readings in World Politics* includes some specifically theoretical interventions but many more which talk to the 'themes and issues' agenda. Shawn Smallman and Kimberley Brown's (2011) *Introduction to International and Global Studies* is broader still. Theory is conspicuous by its absence with the emphasis firmly on the origins and evolution of contemporary global problems such as war, energy security and global underdevelopment. As with the Baylis, Smith and Owens book, nation-states are nowhere near as central to the presentation of IR in these books. The emerging consensus is well put by Peter Sutch and Juanita Elias (2007: 2) who write that the study of international relations 'does not tell us very much about our subject' because 'the agents of international relations that make up the political landscape of our subject area, are not nations at all'. You pay your money, you take your chances!

SOME GOOD NEWS!

Happily, to succeed at a course in IRT you do not need to become a fervent historian of the discipline. Nor do you have to develop a particularly expert knowledge of the ways in which writers and teachers carve up the discipline for their students. However, it is useful for you to be aware of debates arising from the 'problem of the subject' because they will shape the theories you encounter on your course and how those theories generate and apply knowledge about the 'real world'. Ask yourself why it is that some actors and methods have conventionally been 'held largely silent' by the discipline, while others have flourished and come to dominate the agenda (Watson 2006: 237). Forming an opinion on this question will first of all help you understand the theories you cover on your course and, second, help you analyse the strengths and weaknesses of their respective claims to produce hard and fast knowledge about the world of international relations.

QUESTIONS TO PONDER

'Can social scientists claim to produce the same kind of knowledge as natural scientists? Should they try?'

The first thing to do with this question is to consider some key definitional issues: how do we define 'natural' and 'social' sciences? Give examples of fields or disciplines you consider to belong in each category. Maybe even include a small two-column table listing 'social' disciplines on the left and 'natural' disciplines on the right. Think about defining the 'kind of knowledge' produced by each set of scholars: what are the similarities and differences? Is one more 'grounded', more certain, more reliable than the other, and if so why? A simple way to introduce the differences would be to use ideas about the 'problem of the subject' in IR and the 'tangible/intangible' divide explored in this chapter. If we can't pick a piece of evidence up and throw it against a wall to test its properties it is probably not amenable to methods of investigation used by natural scientists.

Your second task is to come up with some way of judging the implications of what you say in the first part. Assuming social sciences do produce different forms of knowledge, do you think this is a good thing or a bad thing – and what do you mean by 'good' and 'bad'? Do you think the social sciences should try and emulate the natural sciences at all? Certainly many social scientists would claim to produce 'objective' and non-biased knowledge – is that the same as being 'scientific', and how do they validate their approaches? The better students might throw into doubt the whole idea of the natural sciences being a paragon of virtue as far as scientific knowledge production is concerned.

Common Pitfall

When a question has two parts to it, students sometimes forget to answer the second part, especially when under pressure in exams. In the above, the second question 'should they try?' invites you to consider the knock-on (ethical) implications of your answer to the first part. Not bothering with the evaluative element of the question component will severely limit the mark you obtain, however good your answer to the first part.

'Why is the subject matter of IR essentially contested?'

This is slightly harder to structure than the first answer because it is open ended, inviting you to consider any and every reason why writers disagree about the most appropriate focus for IR. You have to be absolutely focused on narrowing your essay to just a few points, framed at the outset by the use of a simple, clear argument that outlines what you go on to say in the rest of the answer. Given that you inevitably have time limits (in an exam) and word limits (in an essay), one useful approach is to list all the reasons you can think of and then concentrate on, say, the three or four that you consider the most compelling. You can then structure your answer around each of the points in turn. A possible list might include:

- Labels: 'Inter-national Relations' (narrower remit) or 'World Politics' (wider remit)?
- Which actors?
- What is 'the world'?
- The subject is ever-changing because the world is constantly changing.
- Events or issues seen as important in one era will not necessarily seem so in another.

'"… there is a continual interplay between the 'real world' and the world of knowledge" (Chris Brown). Discuss the implications of this statement for the study of IR.'

This question is a slightly more specific take on the previous one. Your first job is to clarify what you think Brown is saying in the quote. What does he mean by the 'real world' and why has he put it in speech marks? What is the 'world of knowledge'? Are they two separate entities or do they overlap in some respects?

Useful tip: when a word or phrase appears in speech marks in an exam or essay question, it is a cue for you to define what you think the term means, so your tutor understands how you use it in your answer. Debating the merits of competing definitions and then arriving at your preferred definition shows critical skills.

It obviously helps to know the wider context within which Brown makes this remark, so hopefully you will have read that chapter of this book and can summarize what he believes the implications are. You can then weigh up the strengths and weaknesses of his opinion.

You can get analytical purchase out of this question by exploring how the study of IR closely follows events 'on the ground' out there in the real world of international politics, using case studies (as I do with David Cameron and William Hague on Realism in Chapter 2.2) and/or examples of theories which are built on evidence from this 'real world'. You could, for instance, use Steve Smith's argument (2007: 4) that the dominance within the discipline of a theory like Realism flowed directly from 'often unstated, "common-sense" assumptions about the content of world politics'. Note also how the end of the Cold War in 1989 inspired many new theorists to take an interest in this field, some of them with radically different takes on what IR is and how to study it (see Chapter 2.5 and onward in this book).

REFERENCES TO MORE INFORMATION

Generally, on the problems of studying Politics and IR:
Shimko, K.L. (2008) *International Relations: Problems and Controversies*, 2nd edn. Boston, MA: Houghton Mifflin Company.
A good introductory text which shows you where theory fits into the wider study of IR.

Bleiker, R. (1997) 'Forget IR Theory', *Alternatives*, 22(1): 57–85.
Critical evaluation of the methods, practices and limitations of orthodox IR.

Halliday, F. (1995) 'International Relations: Is There a New Agenda?', *Millennium*, 20(1): 57–72.
Examines the interplay between the global political agenda and how developments in the 'real world' of international relations affect the academic study of IR.

Walt, S.M. (2006) 'International Relations: One World, Many Theories', in R. Little and M. Smith (eds) *Perspectives on World Politics*. Abingdon: Routledge, pp. 386–94.
Reviews the impact of the end of the Cold War on theorizing IR.

Hoffman, S. (2001) 'An American Social Science: International Relations', in R.M.A. Crawford and D.S.L. Jarvis, *International Relations: Still an American Social Science?: Towards Diversity in International Thought*. Albany, NY: State University of New York Press, pp. 27–51.

Tansey, S.D. (2004) *Politics: The Basics*, 3rd edn. London and New York: Routledge.
Chapter 1 provides a good introduction to the varieties of approaches and methods, while Chapter 2 introduces you to IR by exploring states and international institutions.

Goodwin, G.L. and Linklater, A. (1975) 'Introduction', in G.L. Goodwin and A. Linklater (eds) *New Dimensions of World Politics*. London: Croom Helm.
Has some useful words at the start on the distinction between 'International Relations' and 'World Politics'.

Waltz, K.N. (2003) 'Conversations with History: Kenneth Waltz', 10 February, available at the University of Berkeley's website, Conversations with History, http://conversations.berkeley.edu/content/kenneth-waltz and on Youtube, www.youtube.com/watch?v=F9eV5gPlPZg
Discusses theory, international politics and the US role in global affairs.

More advanced texts on the nature and role of theory:
Hollis, M. and Smith, S. (1991) *Explaining and Understanding International Relations*. Oxford: Clarendon Press.
Very good on empiricism and its implications for theoretical development.

Singer, J.D. (1961) 'The Levels of Analysis Problem in International Relations', *World Politics*, 14(1): 77–92.

Buzan, B. (1995) 'The Level of Analysis Problem in International Relations Reconsidered', in K. Booth and S. Smith (eds) *International Relations Theory Today*. Cambridge: Polity Press, pp. 198–216.

Martin, M. and McIntyre, L.C. (eds) (1994) *Readings in the Philosophy of Social Science*. Cambridge, MA: MIT Press.

A series of excerpts from key writings in the field. Particularly recommended are Chapter 6 by Scriven, Chapter 9 by McIntyre, Chapter 18 by Lukes and Chapter 27 by Durkheim.

Herrman, R.K. (2006) 'Linking Theory to Evidence in International Relations', in W. Carlsnaes, T. Risse and B.A. Simmons (eds) *Handbook of International Relations*. London: Sage, pp. 119–36.
A defence of positivist thinking in IR together with a consideration of other approaches to connecting theory with evidence.

More general issues raised in this chapter:
Becher, T. and Trowler, P.R. (2001) *Academic Tribes and Territories*, 2nd edn. Buckingham: The Society for Research into Higher Education and Open University Press.
See Chapter 3 for an account of how academics from across disciplines see their work and how this helps us define the concept of a 'discipline'.

Kuhn, T.S. (1996) *The Structure of Scientific Revolutions*, 3rd edn. Chicago: The University of Chicago Press.
Ostensibly about the natural sciences, this path-breaking book boasts a wealth of information about the ideological foundations of all academic knowledge.

Neuman, W.L. (2007) *Basics of Social Research: Qualitative and Quantitative Approaches*, 2nd edn. New York: Pearson Education.
In Chapter 1, Neuman argues that knowledge generated by 'scientific' research is more reliable than knowledge gained by other means.

Barnett, M. and Duvall, R. (2005) 'Power in International Politics', *International Organization*, 59(1): 39–75.
Gives you an idea of how to map disagreements between different IR traditions and explains the causes of some of their disputes.

1.2 INTERNATIONAL RELATIONS THEORY

[W]e are all theoreticians and the only issue is what kinds of theories should we adopt to guide us in our attempts to understand the subject matter. (Joynt and Corbett 1978: 102)

What *is* theory? Why do we have to bother with theory – can't we study IR on its own terms? Why not just look at the facts? These are just some of the questions you might legitimately be asking yourself as you embark on your journey through your course in IR. I want to answer them now by way of introduction, and then in Chapter 1.4 we will return to some of the core issues raised and develop them using the language and tools as they might appear in your course lectures, seminars and assignments.

WHAT IS THEORY?

Theories have to rely on some principles of selection to narrow their scope of inquiry; they discriminate between actors, relationships, empirical issues and so forth which they judge most important or regard as trivial'. (Burchill and Linklater 2009: 13)

We saw in the last chapter that the subject matter of IR is essentially contested, meaning that all scholars bring to the field different yet sometimes overlapping opinions on what constitutes the 'essence' of IR. Disputes run even deeper than that, however. Not only do experts disagree on what to study, they differ on how to study IR and what counts as appropriate evidence in the discipline. With all this complexity and dispute in mind, it seems logical for rational human beings (assuming that's what academics are!) to seek to navigate some sort of logical path through this mire of uncertainty. This is where IRT comes in.

> Think about previous occasions when you encountered a theory or
> theories in your studies at school or college. What was the purpose of
> those theories? What did theorists try and achieve by developing
> them? Did they help you understand more about the subject and how?
> What were their strengths and weaknesses?

Burchill and Linklater's neat summary, above, of the part theory plays
in the study of IR will be the starting point for our consideration of
what theory actually is. The telling words they use are 'principles of
selection'. Theories take complexity and try to simplify it. How theorists
do this, and the success they have trying, is less important to us at this
stage than recognizing the goals theorists set themselves. Let us take a
range of opinions from across the discipline (and see Jørgensen 2010:
8–9 for a useful text box called 'Ten perspectives on the function of
theory'):

- **Martin Wight** (1995: 15): 'By "international theory" is meant a tradition
  of speculation about relations between states'. You can see here how
  Wight solves the problem of the subject by taking a popular line on the
  appropriate subject matter of IR, reflecting its original date of publication
  (1966): it is nothing more, nothing less than a study of relations between
  states.
- **Hans Morgenthau** (1985: 3): theories 'bring order and meaning to a mass of
  phenomena which without it would remain disconnected and unintelligible'.
- **Kenneth Waltz** (2010) 'Theories explain laws', making them parallel 'to
  the definition of the term in the natural sciences'. Laws illustrate associations between variables, while theories explain the causal connections.
  Popular in US IR scholarship the natural science rendering of theory is as
  follows (Rosato 2003: 585): a theory comprises a hypothesis stipulating
  an association between an independent and a dependent variable and a
  causal logic that explains the connection between them. The hypothesis
  is supported if it can be demonstrated experimentally that A (independent
  variable) causes B (dependent variable) because A causes x, which
  causes y, which causes B.
- **Hollis and Smith** (1991: 62–3): Theories perform three functions. They
  abstract (group together events, situations or objects which are not identical). They generalize (identify what these things which are not identical
  have in common by virtue of analysis of the available facts). And they
  connect (identify cause and effect). This definition starts to move us away

from considerations of how 'scientific' theory should or should not be and into the realm of how we *perform* theoretical work by putting them to work. Abstraction, generalization and connection are, for Hollis and Smith, the basic prerequisites of theory in any academic discipline.

- **Buzan** (2004: 24) picks up regional dimensions to how we comprehend the nature and purpose of theory by writing 'Many Europeans use the terms theory for anything that organizes a field systematically, structures questions and established a coherent and rigorous set of interrelated concepts and categories. Many Americans [see Waltz and Rosato above], however, often demand that a theory strictly explains and that it contains – or is able to generate – testable hypotheses of a causal nature'.

- **Hooghe and Marks** (2008: 2): these scholars from a different field, European Studies, show that you can find speculation about the nature of theory across the social sciences and humanities, and that you can be creative about where you look for this kind of material. They suggest that: 'Every theory is grounded on a set of assumptions – intellectual short cuts – that reduce complexity and direct our attention to causally powerful factors'. It is reminiscent of the next authors' use of the term...

- **Baylis, Smith and Owens** (2008a: 4; emphasis in original): '*a kind of simplifying device that allows you to decide which facts matter and which do not*'. This definition undermines those who believe processes of theorizing in IR can or should mimic processes of theorizing in the natural sciences. Theory, they assert, is not simply 'some grand formal model with hypotheses and assumptions' (Baylis et al. 2008a: 4). Instead, we should be modest about what we can expect theory to deliver, and more aware of the presuppositions and biases we bring to the study of the social world.

- **Robert Jackson and Georg Sørensen** (2007: 54): 'We always look at the world, consciously or not, through a specific set of lenses; we may think of those lenses as theory'. Theory, according to this interpretation, forms a fundamental part of the world we live in; it makes the world and helps construct it for us whether we realize it or not.

- **Cynthia Weber** (2010: 2): 'IR theory makes organizing generalizations about international politics. IR theory is a collection of stories about the world of international politics. And in telling stories about international politics, IR theory doesn't just present what is going on in the world out there. IR theory also imposes its own vision of what the world out there looks like'. Weber pulls us even further from the realms of IR theory as natural science. Look at the language she uses. Words like 'story' imply imagined and imaginative elements to theories developed in the field of IR. Weber is in accordance with writers such as Baylis, Smith and Owens when she collapses the distinction between a 'world' of IR and a separate 'world' of the observer.

So we encounter an array of perspectives on theory. From the formal natural science model outlined by Hollis and Smith to Weber's view that we are ourselves parts of the theories we devise, no two IR authors quite agree on what IR theory is or should be. In Chapter 1.4 we will revisit the debate about the impact of these debates over the nature of theory. For now, all you need to have clear in your mind is that these differences exist and they materially influence the work that goes on in the field of IR. In the next section we will take a step back and consider an even more basic question: why bother with theory in the first place?

Whenever you come across a definition of 'theory' or 'IR theory', make a note of it in a theory checklist as I have done above. It will provide you with a comprehensive list of writers and their respective interpretations which you can get lots of mileage from in essays and exam answers.

WHY BOTHER WITH THEORY?

You are not alone if you doubt the 'value added' theory brings to the study of academic subjects. In this section we will review both sides of the argument by looking first of all at the positions taken by those writers who doubt the utility of theory. We then consider those writers who trumpet the value of theory – not just because they believe it is intrinsically useful to us but because it is inescapably everywhere, always shaping our study of the world whether we care to acknowledge it or not. Several IR textbooks (for instance, Mansbach and Rafferty 2008) include reflections on the nature and uses of theory so you can fruitfully consult these before moving to the more complex treatments.

THE 'TAKE IT OR LEAVE IT' APPROACH TO THEORY

In the discipline of history there is a book by Keith Windschuttle (1996) called *The Killing of History: How Literary Critics and Social Theorists are Murdering our Past*. In the book, Windschuttle describes how the discipline of history, traditionally concerned with the factually-based narration of events in the past using archival documents and other remnants from the period in question, 'is now suffering a potentially mortal attack from the rise to academic prominence of a relatively new array of literary and social theories' which question traditional historical practices and the knowledge produced by them (Windschuttle 1996: 10). There is 'history', Windschuttle implies, and there is 'theory', and it is dangerous for the two to get mixed up because the former deals with the real world of the past while the latter throws up needless conjecture about the reliability of all this knowledge. Too much concern with theory, Windschuttle argues, is dangerous. 'The central point upon which history was founded no longer holds: there is no fundamental distinction any more between history and myth' (Windschuttle 1996: 10).

Windschuttle's opinion is that we can have facts or we can have theory. We do not profit from mixing the two. In IR this 'take it or leave it' approach to theory can be exemplified using the sceptical stance on theory adopted by Raymond Aron, who said that theorizing international politics was more arduous than theorizing economics for a list of reasons including the following: the international system is affected by happenings inside and outside states; states are not unitary actors possessing one single aim; identifying the dependent and independent variables is impossible; supposed equilibria at the systemic level are inherently unstable; and prediction is impossible (Aron's position summarized in Waltz 1990: 25. For an excellent overview of Aron's contribution to international theory more generally, see Hoffman 1985).

As James Rosenau describes this position (2003: 7–8): 'Frequent are the comments that theories are wasted effort and misleading, if not downright erroneous. "Come off your high theoretical perch," say the critics, "come down where the action is and get your hands dirty with real world data'. Rosenau identifies three types of critic of 'theory' from within IR: first, those in government circles who believe 'theory' is removed from the 'real' day-to-day public policy problems that need to be confronted; second, journalists who echo Windschuttle by saying that theoretical language is gobbledygook ('Why don't they write in plain English?'); and third, academics themselves, who propound the notion that theory-based teaching is insufficiently policy-relevant (Rosenau 2003: 7–8).

William Wallace put the case that IRT had become too detached from practice in a 1996 article on 'Truth and Power'. Having warned against the perils of 'scholasticism' and what he saw as IR scholars' increasing tendency to speak to each other rather than the outside world, Wallace opened fire on the 'flippancy' of the postmodernist 'celebration of theory at the expense of empirical work' (Wallace 1996: 311). Scholastic word games, he argued, are all very well but theory 'for its own sake' does nothing to contribute to public debate and certainly will not catch the ear of policy-makers (Wallace 1996: 314). Wallace took the line that IRT needed to re-engage with the normative policy-driven agenda that made it such a fruitful approach to international affairs in its early years. Wallace did not suggest we 'leave' theory in quite the same fashion as Windschuttle, but he certainly gave the discipline cause to reflect on the uses of IRT.

THE 'THEORY IS INESCAPABLE' APPROACH

Many writers disagree with the 'take it or leave it' approach to theory exemplified by Windschuttle, Aron and Wallace. Writers subscribing to the interpretation that 'theory is inescapable' push the idea that theory is everywhere, and therefore that understanding theory is not an option but is rather forced on us by the conditions of our human existence.

A review of the literature in this area reveals two interconnected propositions about the role and value of theory. The first and arguably best known is associated with writers such as Steve Smith and Ken Booth, and features in some form in all their books and articles on IRT you will cover on your course. The clearest rejection of the 'take it or leave it' line comes in Baylis, Smith and Owens' Introduction to *The Globalization of World Politics*:

> It is not as if you can say that you do not want to bother with a theory, all you want to do is to look at the 'facts'. We believe that this is simply impossible, since the only way in which you can decide which of the millions of possible facts to look at is by adhering to some simplifying device which tells you which ones matter the most. (Baylis et al. 2008a: 4)

Contrary to what the theory-sceptics say, argues Rosenau, the element of choice implied by the proposition that we can either embrace theory *or* ignore it simply does not exist:

> Being theoretical is unavoidable! Why? Because the very process of engaging in observation requires sorting out some of the observed phenomena as important and dismissing others as trivial. There is no alternative. The details of situations do not speak for themselves. Patterns are not self-evident. Observers must give them meaning through the theories they bring to bear. They must, to repeat, select out from everything they observe those aspects that seem significant and discard those they deem as inconsequential. (Rosenau 2003: 8)

Fred Halliday takes a similar position, contending that theory performs three functions with respect to facts: it helps us decide which facts are significant and which are not; it helps us explain how the same fact can be interpreted differently; and it helps bring to the fore questions of morality which cannot be decided by an appeal to the facts alone (summarized in Burchill 2001a: 13). Whether you are member of a governing coalition, journalist or academic you will use theory daily to come to a view on pressing political matters.

> When watching television, listening to the radio and reading newspapers think about the number of times you hear the words 'fact'. Why are the 'facts' of a story prized so highly? What is it about 'facts' that makes them so important to us? What, at root, are 'facts'?

Why do these writers see a world in which theory is inescapably everywhere? The answer lies in a second assumption about the role theory has played, unwittingly or not, in the actual conduct of international relations. As Stephen Walt puts it:

> Even policymakers who are contemptuous of 'theory' must rely on their own (often unstated) ideas about how the world works in order to decide what to do. It is hard to make good policy if one's basic organizing principles are flawed, just as it is hard to construct good theories without knowing a lot about the real world. (2006: 386)

It is only by knowing theory that we can improve practice and by the same token theoretical sophistication comes from knowing about the world policy-makers inhabit. Scholars engage in theoretical speculation, but so do policy-makers. As Martin Wight explains: 'The political philosophy of international relations is the fully-conscious formulated theory, illustrations of which you may find in the conduct of some statesmen, [Woodrow] Wilson, probably [Winston] Churchill, perhaps [Jawaharlal] Nehru' (Wight 1987: 221).

Our goal here is not to evaluate the persuasiveness of this argument (I leave that up to you as you progress through this book and your course), but rather to set out a range of opinions which you might find interesting points of departure. Steve Smith (1995: 3) puts the theory–practice overlap in its sharpest relief by writing that 'international theory has tended to be a **discourse** accepting of, and complicit in, the creation and recreation of international practices that threaten, discipline and do violence to others'. He points to the role that theoretical assumptions associated with the Realist tradition (explored in Chapter 2.2 of this book) played in moulding superpower foreign policies during the Cold War from 1945–89, particularly in terms of the nuclear arms race. Playing an active part in the development of aggressive American and Russian foreign policies, this suggests, Realist IRT can be held partially accountable for some of the many horrors and catastrophes the world witnessed during that period. Smith has therefore entered into dialogue with William Wallace over the alleged 'theory–policy' divide, which he sees as a misnomer. Theory and practice are not separate spheres of activity, Smith argues: 'theory is already implicated in practice, and practice is unavoidably theoretical' (Smith 1997: 515); the world is theoretical 'all the way down'.

Tim Dunne and Brian Schmidt agree that policy and theory are interconnected, especially as far as Realism goes: 'From 1939 to the present, leading theorists and policymakers have continued to view the world through realist lenses' (Dunne and Schmidt 2008: 92). Francis Fukuyama likewise suggests that Realism has provided 'the dominant framework for understanding international relations and shapes the thinking of virtually every foreign policy professional today in the United States and much of the rest of the world' (quoted in Little 1995: 71). Martin Hollis and Steve Smith give us an excellent summary of the 'theory is inescapable' approach:

> [M]any International Relations scholars are directly involved in the US foreign and defence policy community. They try to use their theories to improve policy-making and they search for theories which will be relevant and useful for this purpose ... Hence the truth of International Relations theories has something to do with which theories are known and applied in the process they purport to analyse. (Hollis and Smith 1991: 70–1)

We come to discuss the tenets of Realist theory later. The salient point for now is that Realism is the theory most frequently cited by writers seeking examples of the theory–practice overlap.

Is it just coincidence that Realism is so often used as an illustration of the interplay between the theory and practice of international relations? As you go through your course see if you can find other examples from the literature where writers cite a direct connection between theory (any theory) and practice.

In sum, contrary to the 'take it or leave it' approach, writers in the 'theory is inescapable' school are very clear about the pervasiveness, the 'everywhere-ness' of theory. For them, there is no such thing as choosing to use a theory or not because it is a fundamental part of life. And if that is not enough, they argue, look at the reasons why IR was founded as an academic discipline (explored further in Chapter 1.4 below). It was set up in the aftermath of the First World War (1914–18) to help us understand and explain (theorize) the relations between states, so that the futile carnage of the Great War could be avoided in the future. The theory–practice overlap has not just come about by chance, but by design. As Scott Burchill (2001a: 6) explains: 'The very purpose of intellectual endeavour was to change the world for the better by eradicating the scourge of war. This was really the only function international theory had'. If we accept the 'theory is inescapable' approach in general, then in the field of IR its ramifications are doubly important because it is a discipline and a practice that deals directly with war, conflict, death and destruction.

Ray Winstone on facts and theory

TAKING IT FURTHER

In 2009 a UK advertisement for a new cereal ran on television and in the cinema, featuring British actor Ray Winstone. In the cereal advert Winstone complained that 'When it comes to food there's a bit of a nanny culture thing going on. Don't do this. Don't do that. That is very bad for you. This is for your own good.' He argued that we should be free to choose for ourselves how we live and what we do to our bodies – the state should butt out. 'We're old enough and wise enough to just be given the facts, so this is a new cereal called Optivita. It contains oatbran which can help actively reduce cholesterol. Now, it's up to you to reduce cholesterol – or not.' In the final scene Winstone made clear he was not trying to bully us into making a decision. 'Well don't look at me: I'm not gonna tell you what to do.' The decision, it seems, was ours – to Optivita or not to Optivita.

There are many interesting points about this advert, not least the idea that you might choose to ignore the advice of a well-known 'hard man' such as Winstone. But the crucial point for us lies in the moves the advert made to convince us to buy this product. Winstone tells us that there is a 'bit of a nanny culture thing going on' when it comes to food. This is asserted as the truth (a 'fact' if you like) but the nature of that 'nanny culture' is neither defined nor elaborated upon – as if we all plug into what he is talking about straight away. There is an extensive British libertarian tradition of railing

(Continued)

(Continued)

against an overweening 'nanny state' which unnecessarily interferes in the daily lives of 'ordinary people'. The advert was broadcast at a time when then British Prime Minister Tony Blair was promoting the idea of 'social marketing' which relied on food companies giving the public more information on health and diet because he felt that consumers were more likely to believe companies than the government and untrustworthy politicians (Wainwright and Carvel 2006). The 'fact' of the matter was that Britain was becoming *less* of a 'nanny state' just when the advertisers told us it was becoming *more* of one.

Thus, the 'nanny culture thing' was not a fact about the world, but a theory. It was one interpretation or 'take' on the government's policy to promote corporate and social responsibility for healthy living. If we do not accept the theory of the nanny state as far as healthy eating goes, then the rationale for both the cereal and the advert go out of the window. The idea that there are theory-free 'facts' about the world might not be as accurate as we might wish to believe.

Can you think of other advertisements which rely on theories about how the world works presented as straightforward facts about how the world works?

INTERNATIONAL RELATIONS THEORY ON FILM

Scholars of IR are not alone in debating the value – or otherwise – of theory, and in doing so they show how deeply interconnected IR as a discipline is with the wider cultural context within which scholarship is practised and disseminated. If we take this view seriously it has potentially radical consequences. Gone are the days of the lonely scholar sat under a wodge of papers and books in an ivory tower writing huge tomes which only get read by a handful of other professors working in the same field, but of marginal importance to society as a whole.

There is a popular phrase 'it's only academic', used to refer to something that has theoretical relevance but no practical relevance. In the study of IR is it feasible to say that the books and articles we read are ever only of 'academic' relevance?

Two writers who make this point very effectively are Cynthia Weber (2010) and Dan Drezner (2011), who show us how we can use popular films and characters to understand and critique key IR theories. At first sight this might seem a strange thing to do. Is not IR a distinct discipline of study with its own language, ideas, set of concepts, and 'great debates'? Is it not the case that early IR theorists and their successors today pride themselves on working in a separable, if not separate, social scientific discipline which they have worked for years to demarcate from history, law, philosophy, politics and economics (see Chapter 1.4)? What can Weber's films and Drezner's zombies tell us about a theoretical, sometimes abstract subject like IR?

How you answer this question depends on your view of what makes an academic discipline and what makes for a valid approach to studying IRT. Let us take a look at the reasons why Weber believes it is possible and enlightening to study IR through film using two quotes from her book:

> IR theory can be studied as a site of cultural practice. IR theory is an 'ensemble of stories' told about the world it studies, which is the world of international politics. Studying IR theory as a site of cultural practice means being attentive to how IR theory makes sense of the world of international politics. (Weber 2010: 4)

> Popular films provide students with answers to the question, How does an IR myth appear to be true? In so doing, popular films point to how politics, power, and ideology are culturally constructed, and how the culture of IR theory might be politically reconstructed. (Weber 2010: 20)

The moves Weber makes here are fascinating.

First of all, like Holsti (1985) she argues that the development of IRT reveals a good deal about the cultures within which those theories have developed (and vice versa), particularly the 'Westernized' bias within the discipline. IR is assumed to be a site of 'cultural practice' which reveals theorists' unspoken assumptions about how the world operates. Second, the 'stories' IR theorists tell us about the world rely on the same plot lines we find in 'stories' told to us by novelists and filmmakers. Third, theories have to rely on hidden assumptions to make them 'work'. They are 'mythical' in the sense that they purport to describe aspects of the 'real world' whilst simultaneously constructing aspects of that 'real world' for us (this is what goes on in the Ray Winstone advert in the 'Taking it further' section above). Finally, since IR, like novels and films, is composed of 'stories' about international politics, uncovering the assumptions and ideologies behind the narratives IR tells enables us to rethink the basis of IR theories themselves.

This strategy for studying IR is enlightening because:

- It helps us better understand IR theories by making a complex set of ideas and language more accessible to us as students.
- It helps us critique the theories as well us understanding them. Being able to critique theories is likely to be a vital part of the assessments you undertake on your course in IR theory. Criticizing a theory in an academic way is not undertaken to say it is 'wrong', but to unpack its assumptions (explicit or implicit), empathize with the evidence it presents, and then to read down into the theory to expose its explanatory and/or factual limitations.
- It provides us with a new dimension to the 'facts versus theory' debate. By arguing that theory is everywhere, even in Hollywood blockbusters such as *Independence Day*, these scholars encourage us to think about theory's role in our efforts to explain international relations today.

You might be lucky enough on your course to spend time exploring how Weber uses film to deconstruct IR theory in timetabled sessions. If not, you can still get full value for money by renting or buying the various films, watching them, and then seeing how Weber makes use of them in her work. You could incorporate the films as case studies in assessed work on the respective theories.

QUESTIONS TO PONDER

'Why do we need theories about international relations when we can look at the facts?'

There are two promising ways to approach this question. The first is to think about it in 'for and against' terms. You would begin by setting out the case 'against' theory and 'for' facts, looking at writers who question the utility of theory. You should mainly concentrate on writers from within the discipline of IR who posit the 'take it or leave it' approach to theory. You might show knowledge of the wider social scientific debates by referring to writers from outside the discipline, such as historians, who question the value or utility of theory. In the second part of the essay you would consider the case 'against' facts and 'for' theory, using any of the key points about the 'everywhere-ness' of theory raised by writers such as Steve Smith and Cynthia Weber. All this would be framed by your own view on which body of writing you find most persuasive.

A second approach would be to present a numbered list of reasons why you believe we should bother with theory and deal with each in turn in a 'fat paragraph' (of approximately 250 hundred words). Taking this route makes it slightly harder to achieve balance in the essay because your tutor would presumably want to see some consideration of the 'take it or leave it' approach and you would have to think hard about where and how far to explore that interpretation. It might, for example, be useful to have a long introduction setting out the rationale for the assertion made in the question and then arguing that you intend to knock it down by exploring a series of points from the literature on the value of IR theory.

'How do IR theorists make sense of the world?'

Vague or open-ended questions can be both a curse and a blessing. To put it another way, they can be deceptively difficult to answer despite on the surface appearing to be fairly straightforward. The place to start is to try and pin down for your tutor what you take the different bits of the question to mean:

Which IR theorists? Can they all be lumped together? Do all of them view 'theory' in the same way? Are there differences between, say, a Realist and a postmodernist take on theory and if so how is this expressed in their ontological, epistemological and methodological approaches to studying IR?

What does 'make sense of the world' mean in this context? It seems fair to take it to mean 'how do the theorists you have chosen study the world of IR?' That is, how do they make it intelligible to us as fellow students of international affairs? Here we get into issues raised in the previous chapter about how different IR theorists define their field of study.

One thing you might then do is choose a case study which exemplifies how academics from obviously different theoretical traditions 'make sense' of 'their world' of IR and draw conclusions from that. Weber's films could be used here, amongst other cases.

The use of case studies can provide you with valuable ways of comparing and contrasting different theoretical approaches to IR. Always make it clear why you choose particular cases and make sure to tell the reader after presenting case study material what conclusions you draw from it. Do not expect your tutor miraculously to be able to infer from your case studies why you chose them: make it explicit in the essay.

REFERENCES TO MORE INFORMATION

Lepgold, J. (1998) 'Is Anyone Listening? International Relations Theory and the Problem of Policy Relevance', *Political Science Quarterly*, 113(1): 48–62.

Booth, K. (1997) 'Discussion: a Reply to Wallace', *Review of International Studies*, 23(3): 371–7.
Backs Steve Smith (1997) in his counter attack on William Wallace's views on 'truth and power'.

Reus-Smit, C. (2012) 'International Relations, Irrelevant? Don't Blame Theory', *Millennium: Journal of International Studies*, 40(3): 525–40.

Carr, E.H. (1990) *What is History?* Harmondsworth: Penguin.
There are various reprints of the 1961 original. Especially thought-provoking is the opening chapter which rethinks the idea of 'facts'.

Goldstein, J.S. and Pevehouse, J.C. (2008) *International Relations*, 8th edn. New York: Pearson Education.
Usefully, from a student's point of view, the book is liberally sprinkled with 'thinking theoretically' text boxes which help you think through theoretical explanations for different outcomes in the cases covered.

Hay, C. (2002) *Political Analysis: A Critical Introduction*. Basingstoke: Palgrave.
The opening two chapters introduce you to the problems of defining the field of Political Science (including the subfield of IR) and to the problems we encounter in trying to study this subject 'scientifically'.

Burnham, P., Gilland, K., Grant, W. and Laytonhenry, Z. (2004) *Research Methods in Politics*. Basingstoke: Palgrave Macmillan.
Chapter 1 outlines big debates about how to study Politics which filter into discussions about how to study IR.

Axford, B., Browning, G.K., Huggins, R. and Rosamond, B. (2006) *Politics: An Introduction*, 2nd edn. London: Routledge.

Chapter 14 by Rosamond introduces ways of thinking about IR and shows how the borders between domestic and international politics are in the process of dissolving.

Nexon, D. and Neumann, I.B. (eds) (2006) *Harry Potter and International Relations*. Lanham, MD: Rowman and Littlefield.
For fans of the novels and/or the films of J.K. Rowling, this book helps us see the parallels between the 'real world' of international relations and the fictitious world of Harry Potter.

Sterling-Folker, J. (2006) 'Making Sense of International Relations Theory', in J. Sterling-Folker (ed.) *Making Sense of International Relations Theory. Boulder*, CO: Lynne Rienner, pp. 1–12.
This short chapter usefully introduces you to the main contours of the debates about 'theory' and works by using different theoretical takes on the same case: the Kosovo intervention of 1999.

Jabri, V. (2000) 'Reflections on the Study of International Relations', in T.C. Salmon (ed.) *Issues in International Relations*. London: Routledge, pp. 289–313.
Good on the nature of theory and the problems of defining the scope of IR as a subject area.

Hall, I. (2006) *The International Thought of Martin Wight*. Basingstoke: Palgrave Macmillan.

Neuman, W.L. (2007) Basics of Social Research: *Qualitative and Quantitative Approaches*, 2nd edn. New York: Pearson Education.
Chapter 2 covers general issues to do with the nature of theory.

Harding, S. and Hintikka, M.B. (eds) (2003) *Discovering Reality: Feminist Perspectives on Epistemology, Metaphysics, Methodology, and the Philosophy of Social Science*, 2nd edn. Dordrecht: Kluwer Academic Publishers.
See especially the chapters by Eve Keller on gender and science.

Roskin, M.G., Cord, R.L., Madeiros, J.A. and Jones, W.S. (2006) *Political Science: An Introduction*, 9th edn. Upper Saddle River, NJ: Pearson Prentice Hall.
Part I introduces the 'science' debate and introduces basic concepts useful for the study of domestic and international politics.

1.3 YOUR COURSE IN IRT

COURSE STRUCTURE

No two university courses on the same subject look quite the same for a variety of basically practical reasons. First of all, universities tend to carve up their teaching time differently. Some still use the three-term system, but increasingly UK universities have moved to a two semester system, the first running roughly from September to December and the second from January to May. Within these semesters some universities offer reading weeks mid-way through, others do not. Even within the same Faculty at a given university, departments differ on whether or not to give students reading weeks. An IR course spread over 10 weeks will look very different from one spread over 12 or more weeks.

Second, because university courses are designed, written, administered and taught by individual members of staff (sometimes pairs or small teams of staff share the workload), you will usually be taught by more than one person. The module convenor will likely deliver the lectures but the seminar element might be delivered by another tutor. Exposure to different personalities and teaching styles is part and parcel of learning at university level. In a field like IR where the subject matter is in dispute, it is only to be expected that different tutors will want to cover some topics and not others and order them in a variety of ways, and will expect students to achieve varieties of learning outcomes from the course. Whilst universities and outside agencies routinely regulate academic teaching quality and practice, it is still up to the individual tutors to put the courses together and therefore those courses are infused with, and representative of, tutors' varying research interests, teaching styles and, yes, personal hobby horses.

You will be given a variety of materials when you begin a new module. Traditionally these are delivered to you as hard copies, but most universities are now choosing to present course material electronically in a Virtual Learning Environment (VLE) such as Learn or Blackboard. Be sure to read everything your tutor gives you at the start of the course and refer back to it as often as you need throughout the course to keep up to date on where you need to be for lectures and seminars, what reading you are expected to be doing, and when assessments are due in so you can plan your preparation effectively.

A third reason relates to the amount of theory on courses in IR. Some will cover a few theories but, like many popular textbooks (for example, Baylis et al. 2008b), will also cover various 'themes and issues' in global politics today. Even on courses where IR theory is the sole focus, it is unlikely, given the proliferation of theories, that your course will cover all the theories included in this book. Your tutor will have developed the course content with specific aims and learning outcomes in mind and will have designed a lecture/seminar programme to help you achieve them. From courses where theory plays a 'walk-on' or cameo role to those majoring on IRT you can be sure that you will need to develop all of the thinking and practical skills explored in this book to get the best out of your course.

The aim of this chapter is to provide you with a very brief introduction to the world of academic course design. I have written it to show you where courses come from (not thin air!), and to try and convey how important it is for you to be attuned from the very start of each and every course you study at university to exactly what the course aims are, and how your tutor expects you to achieve those aims through the lecture, seminar and assessment schedule. If you would rather concentrate on the IRT-specific material feel free to jump straight to the next chapter on theorizing IR.

COURSE AIMS AND LEARNING OUTCOMES

What is the point of studying IRT? Your tutor's answer will be contained in the aims and learning outcomes they set out for the course. Here I will write from my own experience of teaching a course specifically on IRT, but be sure to check the module specification for your particular course before it begins so you are comfortable from the outset about what your tutor expects you to be able to achieve by its close.

Every unit you study at university has what is usually called a 'module specification' explaining in one or two pages the main aims of the course, the student learning outcomes to be achieved, assessment details and an overview of course content and structure. These are usually available electronically on your departmental website and in hard copy. Be sure you know where to find these specifications and read them thoroughly before the start of your studies so you are absolutely clear about what you can expect of the course.

AIMS

The aims of an undergraduate course in IR that incorporates a theoretical component are likely to be:

1 To understand the interpretation of IR put forward by each theory covered.

2 To understand, compare and contrast the simplifying assumptions made by each school of theory.

3 To evaluate the strengths and weaknesses of each theory.

There are two points to note about these aims. First, you can see that they are pretty general building blocks for the course, helping tutors identify what they want students to achieve when they have successfully completed it. Plus, there is a key word here: by saying that the first aim is to cover the 'main' theories of IR, I am stressing that tutors are unlikely to cover each and every theory. Tutors will actively encourage you to explore other theories not covered on your particular course should you wish to do so.

Students who read about other theories not specifically covered on their IRT course usually gain vital additional subject matter expertise and get into good habits of wider reading.

The second point is that these aims are designed to facilitate robust and fair assessment. An average student (achieving marks in and around the 2:2 classification, so 50–59 per cent) will demonstrate in an exam answer or coursework essay that they can achieve the first two aims: understanding the interpretations and assumptions of the theories. Higher achieving students (those achieving marks into the 2:1 and first bandings) will demonstrate a solid appreciation of a particular theory or theories *and* will be able to dissect the assumptions of the theory and to evaluate their relative merits by critically appraising them.

LEARNING OUTCOMES

Student learning at university is themed around discrete modules where you explore themes and issues relating to given events, historical periods, ideas and concepts relating to the subject matter of the module. But the whole idea behind university education is to encourage you to develop a range of what are known as **generic skills** or **transferable skills** – skills to do with writing clearly, communicating effectively, presenting an idea, and constructively criticizing different sides of an argument. All of these skills will improve your employability prospects and will be valuable in your later career; universities are the ideal place to learn how to enhance them, and keeping a log of the skills you develop, and when, can be useful down the line in many regards.

The wider aims of your degree programme should be set out in your departmental handbook: look for the section on generic or transferable skills.

The skills you can expect to learn will be identified in the Learning Outcomes for each module (Figure 3).

Part A covers the subject matter skills, but the bulk of the learning outcomes relate to the generic intellectual and personal transferable skills in Parts B and C. University tutors always appreciate students performing well in coursework and exams, but even more than that, they like to see students making the best of their individual abilities across the board. If you treat each module as an opportunity to develop good working, organizational and time management habits you will not go far wrong in terms of the overall impression you give your tutor of your personal qualities as well as your subject matter expertise.

A. *Knowledge and understanding*

On completion of this module students should be able to:

1 Understand the importance of theory to the study of International Relations as an academic discipline.
2 Identify the central tenets of a number of International Relations theories.
3 Analyse the points of debate between these theories.
4 Apply theoretical positions to the 'real world' of international relations.

B. *Generic intellectual skills*

On completion of this module students should be able to:

1 Gather, organize and deploy evidence, data and information from a wide variety of secondary sources.
2 Construct reasoned argument.
3 Synthesize and analyse relevant information.
4 Exercise critical judgement in relation to issues in IR theory and world politics.
5 Reflect on their own learning and make use of constructive feedback.

C. *Personal transferable skills*

On completion of this module students should be able to:

1 Communicate effectively in speech and writing.
2 Use communication and information technology for the retrieval and presentation of information.

Figure 3   Typical learning outcomes for a course in IRT

Thinking long term from your first year is a good skill to develop. One attraction of putting everything into every module you study is that tutors tend to remember the names of hardworking students. This can be useful when you want references for jobs and/or to enable you to go on to postgraduate study after your final year.

THE SKILLS YOU WILL NEED

Having explained the lecture programme, the rationale behind it, and how we are going to progress from start to finish I put up this slide in the first lecture on IRT (Figure 4). Let us take them one by one:

What do I need to succeed?

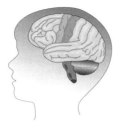

- Communication skills
- Willingness to take intellectual risks
- Openness to new concepts
- A willingness to work …
  … hard!
- Reading/thinking/participation/reflection

Figure 4   The skills you will need

- **Communication skills.** Developing your communication skills at university is essential. By 'communication' we are thinking of both oral (talking), aural (listening) and written (note-taking and referencing, structure, logic, clarity, use of evidence, good English). Almost everything you do at university requires you to talk to people (for example, in seminars and individual or group presentations), to listen to people (in those same environments, plus in lectures) and to write clearly and persuasively from an informed perspective (in exams and coursework assignments). This process of contributing a point, listening to others' contributions, discussing and being able to communicate your ideas in clear written English will underpin your success at your course in IRT, as in all the courses you take at university. That is why these skills are called 'transferable'.
- **Willingness to take intellectual risks.** What are 'intellectual risks'? It is tempting when first attending university lectures and seminars to fall back on what you know – from your A-Level or International Baccalaureate, for example. It is equally tempting to re-hash essays you did in your secondary education as a way of saving time and presenting arguments with which you are comfortable, having rehearsed them several times before. The whole point about university education is that you throw yourself into new subject areas, expose yourself to new ideas, assimilate new concepts and theories, and evaluate provocative ways of viewing the world. Students who take intellectual risks willingly plough through the essential and desirable course readings, even if they have never studied the subject before. They,

in fact, go beyond the core readings and actively seek out wider reading on a given topic. This tends to show through in the clarity of their thinking and the extensive evidence on which they are able to draw in exams and essays.

The word 'risk' has negative and positive connotations; humans tend in the main to be risk averse. Rather than worrying about the possible negatives, think instead about the potential payoffs in terms of marks and intellectual development if you throw yourself wholeheartedly into a course. Tutors will always reward a student they believe to be going that extra mile.

- **Openness to new concepts.** This follows on from the last point about being open to new challenges rather than shying away from them – it relates to your mindset regarding studying at university. At this level you will be constantly confronted with ideas, bodies of knowledge and sets of literatures with which you will be unfamiliar. There are no 'model' answers and this should not frighten you. Challenging yourself to read a tough book or journal article, and getting used to meeting those challenges on a regular basis is part of what higher education is all about. It will sometimes be the case that you find a core text really slow going the first time around, in which case do not be afraid to read around the subject and then reread it at a later date, either later the same week, later in the course or during the revision period. Self-directed reading over the summer break never hurt anyone either. You might be surprised how much you grasp of that difficult text the second or third time around as you develop a better working knowledge of the field.
- **A willingness to work ... hard!** The key difference between the school/college environment and the university environment is that at university your learning is mostly self-directed. At university you have more time on your hands to do with as you wish so you need to develop sophisticated, motivational time management and organizational skills to see you through each course. If you are taking a degree programme in the broad realm of Politics or International Relations, you will have only limited direct contact time with your tutor – typically one lecture and/or one seminar per week. But try to avoid seeing your courses as lasting for just these two hours every week: the calculations in Figure 5 demonstrate why.

The credit system and total student effort

- Assume an undergraduate IR Theory module carrying a 'core module' credit weighting of 20 credits.
- Each credit equates to an average student effort of 10 hours.
- 20 credits x 10 hours' worth of effort = 200 hours total student effort for the course.

Hours per week on IR Theory

- A 12-week course.
- 2 hours per week contact time.
- Total contact time with tutor: 24 hours per course.
- Total student effort: 200 hours. Take from this the 24 hours contact time = 176 hours.
- 176 hours spread over the 12-week course = 14.66 hours per week.
- Each contact hour for IR Theory entails approximately 7 hours of student preparation time.

Figure 5   The credit system and student effort

- Some basic mathematics shows just how much work is expected of students on a typical core module at university. The direct contact time in lectures and seminars is only the beginning. For each contact hour on this course students are expected to put in seven hours of effort outside of the lecture hall and seminar room. Knowing how to get the best out of this self-directed study time will be crucial to your success.

Total student effort outside of contact hours covers everything from information retrieval, to reading, thinking, reflection and organization of notes. Contact and effort time can further include meeting your tutor in his/her office after hours or out of class, individual essays and group assignments.

- **Reading/thinking/participation/reflection.** These skills are closely intertwined and mutually reinforcing (Figure 6). If you can get into a healthy cycle of reading widely, thinking about that reading before you attend lectures and seminars, actively participating in seminars, and then reflecting seriously on what you learnt from the lectures and seminars, you will be in a strong position to succeed at your IRT course. You will also be developing a good work ethic which will stand you in good stead for your other studies at university.

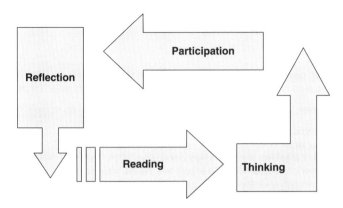

Figure 6   The learning cycle

REFERENCES TO MORE INFORMATION

Here is a selection of the many university study skills books on offer:

Moran, A.P. and Sutton, S. (2000) *Managing Your Own Learning at University: A Practical Guide*. Dublin: University College Dublin Press.

Palmer, S. and Puri, A. (2006) Coping with Stress at University: *A Survival Guide*. London: Sage.

Pritchard, A. (2008) *Studying and Learning at University: Vital Skills for Success in Your Degree*. London: Sage.

Race, P. (2002) *How to Get a Good Degree: Making the Most of Your Time at University*. Buckingham: Open University Press.

1.4 THEORETICAL DEBATES

In this chapter we deepen our understanding of the theoretical debates that have dominated the academic study of IR. In Chapter 1.2 we began by trying to define the problematic term 'theory' and discovered that scholars do not necessarily view theory in the same way. If that did not make life difficult enough, we then encountered the debate that takes place between those scholars who question the utility of theory in explaining human affairs and those scholars who laud the achievements of theoretical perspectives in making sense of a complex world. We labelled the former approach the 'take it or leave it' approach to theory and the latter the 'theory is inescapable' approach.

In this chapter I want to pick up a few loose ends I left dangling in that chapter. In particular, I want to take these general debates about the nature, value and role of theory and show you how they have played out in the study of IRT. In order to do this I want to investigate a fundamental issue IR theorists argue about: the causes and consequences of **anarchy** in the international system. I will move on to explore whether we can tell a 'story' about the evolution of theoretical debates in IR. Finally, I will give an overview of different ways of evaluating the strengths and weaknesses of IR theories and explore the prospect of developing an IR 'super-theory'.

ANARCHY IN IR

> Domestic systems are centralized and hierarchic. International systems are decentralized and anarchic. (Kenneth Waltz, quoted in Onuf 2009: 186)

What do IR theorists argue about, and what animates research in the discipline? This question has partly been answered in Chapter 1.2 where we considered the 'problem of the subject'. The fact that the discipline tries to explain anything and everything that might come under the general headings 'international relations' and 'world politics' means there is little consensus within the discipline on what the subject matter of IR is, or what it should be. The sheer breadth of the discipline today, however, obscures the fact that in the early years of the discipline there was a bit more agreement on what IR scholars and students should study: how to manage interstate relations. Everything else was secondary, if it was on people's radars at all. It seems fair to suggest, therefore, that in its formative years as a discipline the 'agenda' of IR was more limited than it is today.

This had one important influence on the discipline: it placed the study of the condition of anarchy right at its heart, as *the* bone of contention between theorists. As Richard Ashley has observed (1995: 94–5, original emphasis), the obsession with anarchy put three questions to the fore: 'How can there be governance *in the absence of government*? How can order be constructed *in the absence of an orderer*? How can cooperation be facilitated *under a condition of anarchy*?' Part II of this book details how different theoretical traditions deal with each question; for now, we need to clarify what 'anarchy' is and why it is foundational to the study of IR.

If you want to get into the heads of different IR theorists try thinking about how they define anarchy and how they view its consequences for international relations. Is it central to their work, and why or why not?

If you asked 10 friends down the corridor in your hall of residence to define 'anarchy', they would probably give you a range of familiar themes: lawlessness, chaos, disruption, opposition to 'the powers that be' and violence might all feature in some combination in their answers. 'Anarchy' in its IR context picks up some of these themes. So central is it to the study of IR that it is worth briefly exploring its **etymology** before showing how IR theorists have deployed it in their work.

ETYMOLOGY

The word 'anarchy' comes from the Greek and has two components:

1 The prefix *An-* means 'without', 'not' or 'lacking' (Dictionary.com 2007a).

2 The suffix *-archos* (Dictionary.com 2007b) comes from the word *archon*, meaning: one of the nine principal ruling magistrates of ancient Athens, or more generally an authoritative figure, a high official or a ruler.

Putting the two parts of the word together we find that the literal meaning of anarchy can be any or all of the following:

- No ruler.
- Without a high official.
- Lacking an authority.

In the study of IR, this is key because the central unit of analysis has tended to be the sovereign state. **Sovereignty** is another word that can cause problems because of the various layers of meaning it has acquired over the years.

Sovereignty is a politically charged term. UK students will probably know it best from debates about the advisability of British involvement in the European Union's (EU) various proposals for political and economic integration such as the European single currency and the Lisbon treaty. For Eurosceptics, such schemes are said to detract from British sovereignty, which has political and economic dimensions as well as a legal angle, because EU decisions then take precedence over British decisions (for more on sovereignty as seen in Britain's debates about European policy, see Axford et al. 2006: 484–5).

In IR it means that different states in the international system are independent, territorially defined and able to determine their own destinies (Dunne et al. 2007: 340). State sovereignty has internal and external dimensions. A state is internally sovereign 'when it exercises supreme authority over the affairs and people within its territory'; it is externally sovereign 'when it is recognized as such by the international community'; that is, when both its internal sovereignty and territorial integrity are respected and upheld (Jackson and Sørensen 2007: 313). In sum, sovereignty, says Ben Rosamond, is 'about the power to make laws and the ability to rule effectively' (Axford et al. 2006: 485).

We now have definitions of two fundamental terms in IR. Why are they fundamental? Well, it all comes down to the potential problems of having all these sovereign states existing together side by side in the **international system**. If each state is sovereign, who or what has the power/influence/authority/means to shape their behaviour so they can live peaceably together? What if one state, or a group of states, chooses to attack another state or group of states? What if one state or a group of states chooses *not* to recognize the domestic government or territorial integrity of another state? What if the leader of one state turns on his own people and subjects them to crimes against humanity? In the final reckoning, *who regulates state behaviour in an anarchic international system?* It is this question that motivated IR theorists into action, certainly in the founding years of the discipline.

IR scholars take core tenets of the literal meaning of anarchy identified above and emerge with the following formulations:

- **Booth and Wheeler** (2008: 2): 'Under anarchy, the last word rests with governments whose primary responsibility is to promote the interests, and especially the security interests of their own state'.
- **Hollis and Smith** (1991: 7) argue that by calling the international system 'anarchic' we are suggesting 'not that it is chaotic but simply that there is no government above the states which comprise it'.
- **Brown** (2001: 4) likewise suggests that anarchy, in its IR context, 'does not necessarily mean lawlessness and chaos; rather it means the absence of a formal system of government'.
- **Donnelly** (1996: 87): 'Anarchy does *not* imply chaos or the complete absence of order. Rather, anarchy is the absence of political rule, of a "hierarchical" political order based on formal subordination and authority'.
- **Mearsheimer** (2001: 30): 'That the international system is anarchic ... does not mean that it is chaotic or riven by disorder ... it is an ordering principle, which says that the system comprises independent states that have no central authority above them'.
- **Waltz** (2010): 'Among states, the state of nature is a state of war'; the anarchic ordering principle entails 'each state deciding for itself whether or not to use force'.
- **Glaser** (1994/95: 50) follows Waltz and the structural (Neo)realists defining anarchy as: 'the lack of an international authority capable of enforcing agreements'.
- For **Weber** (2010: 14) anarchy 'denotes *lack of an orderer*' (her emphasis) – there is no one or nothing to impose order on the behaviour of states in a top-down way.
- **Holsti** (1985: 34): 'The absence of a universal authority'.
- **Nye and Welch** (2011: 4) sum it up by writing that international politics is 'politics in the absence of a common sovereign – politics among entities with no ruler above them. International politics is a self-help system'.

'Anarchy' is a central term in IRT and will feature in coursework and exam questions on your course. Find a succinct definition from an established IR scholar which you can use as your definition at the beginning of essays and exam answers.

As we move through the various theories in Part II of the book you will see how anarchy and sovereignty play out in the various traditions we explore. For now, all you need to bear in mind is that these are not neutral concepts: they are loaded with meaning. Their implications for IR are constantly in dispute and are as pressing as is the recognition that the theorization of anarchy is what marks IR apart from political science more generally: 'the IR discipline had to insist that there was a significant difference between domestic and international politics. The notion of "anarchy" satisfied this quest' (Guzzini and Leander 2006: 75). Let us now take a look at how the discipline has unfolded over the years to grapple with these issues.

Anarchy personified: the Joker in Batman

The 2008 Batman movie *The Dark Knight* tracks the Heath Ledger characterization of the Joker as he moves through a relatively ordered society in Gotham City wreaking havoc. He does not do this because he is working to some master plan; that's for the mafia, the police, the politicians, 'the schemers', as he calls them. He does it without any real thought for the consequences at all. He just enjoys causing trouble for 'the schemers', who with their 'plans' are trying to manage everything in a world of control and organization. 'Look what I did to this city with a few drums of gas and a couple of bullets' he boasts. 'Introduce a little anarchy … ', he continues, taking a revolver from his pocket, ' … upset the established order, and everything becomes chaos. So, I am an agent of chaos. Oh, and you know the thing about chaos? It's fair' (see the movie clip on Youtube at Joker Scene (2008); the text is at English Daily (undated)).

The Joker could be considered the personification of anarchy, its physical manifestation on earth, the ultimate challenge to the hierarchical relations that, it is supposed, domestic systems and international systems need to function 'normally'. The plot of *The Dark Knight* shows how fragile Liberal notions of order, cooperation and justice can be when society shifts from

(Continued)

TAKING IT FURTHER

(Continued)

hierarchic to anarchic structures. Unfortunately, in IRT, it is the condition of anarchy not hierarchy that is said to prevail. Truces can only ever be temporary. We live in a state of fear.

THEORIZING IR

Narrating a story about the development of a discipline such as IR is complicated, to put it mildly. How do we write the history of an academic discipline? Who are the key actors? What are the key dates and events? How do we track and describe the comings and goings of academic debate over time? It is safe to say that a definitive disciplinary history is more or less impossible, and where it is carried out it will inevitably contain gaps, distortions and simplifications because

> the academic context itself often works as an incentive for over-rationalizing selected ideational threads that, once put together, allow for the orderly presentation of "doctrines" that can be *taught*. An artificial coherence is thus manufactured and projected into quite diverse intellectual sources. (Guilhot 2011: 2–3, original emphasis)

This has not stopped IR scholars from trying, however (for instance Alker and Biersteker (1995) tried to map the discipline in the 1980s). In the literature you read on your course you will find many books and articles telling the story of IR, developing around a series of so-called 'great debates'.

Some textbooks, for example, Jackson and Sørensen (2007) still like to begin with the story of the 'great debates'. Others, for example Dunne et al. (2007), avoid this story until the very end. How does this affect their presentation of the 'story' of IR? What are the key fault lines these writers see running through the discipline today?

These 'great debates' have 'served to organize the discipline' (Wæver 2007: 299), giving it focus and helping it regulate, categorize and 'place' scholarly writing within its borders. I will briefly review the gist of this story and then critique it using the work of Brian Schmidt (2006). From here we will develop a framework for understanding the nature of the theoretical disputes running through the discipline which it will help to have at the back of your mind when you begin your analysis of each theory.

Origins of IR as an academic discipline

The study of IR as a separate academic discipline began after the First World War (1914–18). Until that time, scholars from various disciplinary backgrounds had engaged in the study of international politics. Lawyers, historians, philosophers, diplomats and economists all had something to say about the conduct of international affairs and the relations between states. But there was no discipline devoted exclusively to the study of inter-state affairs. This all changed after the mass death, destruction and devastation of the First World War. Suddenly it seemed more important than ever to try and find answers to three questions: Why do wars begin? What do wars achieve? What lessons can we learn from past wars to prevent future ones? When IR was founded, it was specifically tasked to generate answers to those tricky questions and drew on approaches, ideas and evidence from several other disciplines (Figure 7).

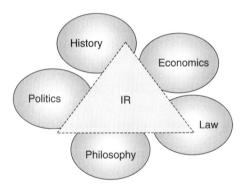

Figure 7 IR's creation as a discipline

IR thus shares an intellectual affinity with many neighbouring disciplines; its disciplinary borders are quite porous. Pick up any IR journal today and you will see a proliferation of approaches, themes, issues and debates. This is a legacy of both its positioning in the academic marketplace and a reflection of changing times, bringing new issues onto the international political agenda.

IR'S GREAT DEBATES

- **Great debate 1: 'Idealism' versus 'Realism'.** This controversy is said to have emerged in the formative years of the discipline between the First and Second World Wars, 1919–39. The 'winners' of the debate were the Realists who managed to depict the Idealists as head-in-the-clouds dreamers – utopians – who gullibly overlooked the true nature of power politics in the modern world. While liberal-minded politicians such as Woodrow Wilson (see Chapter 2.1) worked for global peace and security, the League of Nations collapsed around them and the world plunged into a disastrous second global war in the space of 25 years. It did not take too much effort to convince students (and practitioners) of IR that Realism 'was superior in its ability to rationally explain the persistent and ubiqui- tous struggle for power among nations' (Schmidt 2006: 11. See also Jackson and Sørensen 2007: 31–9).
- **Great debate 2: 'Behaviouralists' or 'scientists' versus 'Traditionalists'.** This debate emerged in the 1960s – after the Realists had 'won' the first debate in and around the period of the Second World War. It pitted beha- viouralists, especially in the US, who believed that IR could best be stu- died using methods drawn from the natural sciences, against traditionalists 'who argued that the study of the social world was not amenable to the strict empirical methods of natural science' (Schmidt 2006: 11). It was a rehearsal, in fact, of the disputes about methodology that have impacted many social science disciplines in recent years. As such, there was no clear 'victor', as in the first debate (Jackson and Sørensen 2007: 40–2).
- **Great debate 3: Neorealists versus the rest?** This is a far harder debate to describe, not least because we are not fully clear about who was involved or what they were arguing about! For Schmidt, the third debate developed out of a crisis within Realism in the 1970s, which found its core assumptions being challenged by events 'on the ground' in international politics, and economic and security concerns. Scholars increasingly attacked the state-centrism of Realism and noted that state relations were charac- terized as much by interdependence between states as by their inde- pendence from one another. Schmidt suggests that it was within the context of a focus on interdependence and economic relations between states that the subfield of International Political Economy (IPE) emerged (Schmidt 2006: 11). Jackson and Sørensen (2007: 42–52) portray the third debate as the product of a range of new theories, notably those inspired by Marx (see Chapter 2.6) and the English School (see Chapter 2.4), coming to feast at the IR table.

- **Great debate 4: 'Post-positivists' versus 'Positivists'.** I have called this the fourth debate, but for some writers (see Schmidt 2006: 12), this is the *genuine* 'third debate'. The post-positivists came to prominence in the 1980s, and they were critical of all prior mainstream approaches to IR. Feminists, Critical Theorists and postmodernists/poststructuralists (all of whom we explore in this book) critiqued the positivist approaches of the dominant theorists in the field. What they effectively say is that the alleged third debate is a non-debate because all the approaches identified above share the same commitments to doing IR the positivist way. This is much more of a divisive debate, therefore, because post-positivists 'address methodological issues (i.e. about *how to* approach the study of IR) ... and substantial issues (i.e. *which* issues should be considered the most important ones for IR to study)' (Jackson and Sørensen 2007: 53, their emphases; Smith 2004).

Having outlined the points of contention in the 'great debates' about IR we can better see the problems of trying to write the history of the field. Everyone agrees that debates about IR have occurred and will continue to occur about all sorts of philosophical, theoretical and empirical questions. But no one can agree on how to capture the essence of these debates over time (Holden 2002). As soon as we try to put chronological boundaries or dividers between the debates, something of the complexity of the field gets lost – and this can present real problems when it comes to educating students about the state of the study of IR today and how it has reached its present state (as it were).

> When doing your course reading, make a note of all the different ways writers tell the story of the discipline. You might even think of different disciplinary histories as different theories about how to tell the story of IR. What does this tell you about the nature and value of theory?

FROM GREAT DEBATES TO THE POSITIVIST–NORMATIVE DISTINCTION

Having told the story of IR's 'great debates', Schmidt sets about critiquing the idea that such a simple story can be told. Most damagingly, he writes, 'it is not evident that all of the three debates actually took place'. Second, he questions whether our contemporaneous 'stylized' versions of the debates can do justice to the contours of the discussions that have been taking place around the global academic community – it seems very much like a 'Western' version of IRT. Third, by focusing on the 'great' debates, he says we ignore other equally important and interesting disciplinary controversies that were taking place at the same time. And, finally, by telling the history of the field as a story of 'this happened then that' we risk giving chronological coherence to it where in fact none was evident (Schmidt 2006: 12).

In this light, is there a framework for studying IR theory within which we might explore key points of contestation amongst its scholars, and which makes it intelligible, but which does not claim to tell a simple chronological history of the field? Any such framework will be open to criticism, but one way I have found useful is to shift away from the idea of three or four 'great debates', and instead present the story of the discipline as an unfolding argument between two approaches: **positivism**, on the one hand, and **normative theory**, on the other. Let us look first of all at what these terms mean and then think about how we might categorize each of the theories you will cover on your course.

- **Kenneth Waltz** (quoted in Onuf 2009: 186): 'A theory, while related to the world about which explanations are wanted, always remains distinct from that world. Theories are not descriptions of the real world; they are instruments that we design in order to apprehend some part of it. "Reality" will therefore be congruent neither with a theory nor with a model that may represent it [theory]'.
- **Steve Smith and Patricia Owens** (2008: 176–7): explanatory (positivist) theory 'sees the world as something external to our theories about it' while constitutive (normative) theory 'thinks our theories help construct the world'. This distinction is unpacked in Suganami (2005).
- **Anthony Langlois** (2007: 152): theory-building aims at explanation and occurs on the back of worldviews which are 'frames through which we see and understand the world. ... they circumscribe what we can see, and thus they give grounds for a particular interpretation of international politics'. Moreover, we see the world not untainted through

frames of our own making but usually through frames which have been set for us by other people – scholars and policy-makers. All theory therefore has normative and ethical implications (see also Griffiths 2011: 6–8).

- **Richard Devetak** (2009a: 161) uses Max Horkheimer's categorization between traditional (positivist) and critical (normative) theory. In traditional theory the theorist is removed from the object of analysis; assumes an external world 'out there'; and achieves objectivity by withdrawing him/herself from the object of study and leaving behind ideology, beliefs and values that would invalidate the inquiry. Critical theories, by contrast, are always embedded in social and political life; they 'allow for an examination of the purposes and functions served by particular theories'. In other words, normative theorists combine conventional theory (a study of an event/process/issue) with metatheory (theory about theory).
- **Jim George** (quoted in Zalewski and Enloe 1995: 299) notes that positivism assumes 'a cognitive reaction to reality' rather than it 'being integral to its construction'. In other words, theory 'takes place after the fact'. For normative theorists, by contrast, 'theory does not take place after the fact. Theories, instead, play a large part in constructing and defining what the facts are'.
- **Steve Smith** (2004: 504): 'scholarship cannot be neutral; it is unavoidably partial, is unavoidably political, and unavoidably has ethical consequences. Crucially, this is the case whether or not the scholar is explicit about these ramifications'.
- **Kimberley Hutchings** (1999: xiii and 1–2): 'the theorist does not operate in abstraction from the object of analysis' (positivism); normative theories are 'concerned with how to criticize, change and improve the world as it is'.
- **Edward Said** (1981, cited in Ramakrishnan 1999: 136; original emphasis): 'there is never interpretation, understanding, and then knowledge where there is no *interest*'.

Taking these definitions together the differences between positivist and normative approaches are summarized in Table 1.

Can we use this distinction between positivist and normative approaches to map IR theories according to their methodological, epistemological and ontological leanings? Quite possibly, if we sketch things as shown in Figure 8.

Table 1 The positivist–normative distinction

Positivism	Normative theory
Also known as explanatory or traditional theory	Also known as constitutive or critical theory
A contested term	A contested term
Empiricist: sensory experience 'provides the only legitimate source of knowledge' (Dunne et al. 2007: 338)	Focuses on: (1) fundamental values of international life; (2) the moral dimensions of international relations; and (3) the place of ethics in statecraft (Jackson and Sørensen 2007: 310)
Naturalist: Social scientists can emulate methods of natural scientists	Critiques positivist belief in naturalism
Belief in separation of facts from values	Collapses fact/value distinction

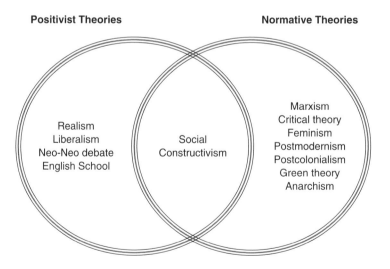

Positivist Theories   **Normative Theories**

Realism
Liberalism
Neo-Neo debate
English School

Social
Constructivism

Marxism
Critical theory
Feminism
Postmodernism
Postcolonialism
Green theory
Anarchism

Figure 8   Mapping theories of IR

MERITS AND FLAWS IN THE THEORY MAP

The merits of this framework are as follows:

- **Avoids history** – By moving away from the story of 'great debates' we do not have to worry about whether or not we can or even need to tell a neatly packaged chronological story about the evolution of the discipline. As Schmidt argues, this approach does a disservice, a violence even, both to the range and the nature of the disciplinary debates in the field at any given moment in its past.
- **Freedom to choose** – The relatively simple positivist–normative distinction gives students scope to make up their own minds about the evolution (the 'story') of the discipline. Rather than us lecturers and professors telling you the story you have more freedom using this model to place the theories where you see fit.
- **Nature of story** – If you do believe there is a story to be told about IR, then how important in your story is the positivist–normative dispute? Or do you think that the great debates capture the story well enough?

At the beginning of your course try starting off with my map in mind, and as you go through the course try and identify writers within each theoretical tradition who might not fit my classification so easily. Use the map as a living document and move individual theorists around within it as you go. You might find some writers appearing in both circles or in the overlapping area. What does this tell you?

Two further questions arise from a consideration of the evolution of IRT over time; it is likely that some or all of them will appear in some form in the course of your lectures, seminars, coursework assignments and exams. The first concerns how we judge the quality of competing theories and the second investigates the possibility of building an IR 'super-theory'.

HOW DO WE EVALUATE IR THEORIES?

> International historians such as [John Lewis] Gaddis stressed that none of the major traditions of international theory predicted the collapse of the Soviet Union and its immediate consequences for Europe and the rest of the world. But many theorists do not believe that their purpose is prediction.... (Burchill and Linklater 2009a: 25)

Burchill and Linklater's comment on the inadequacy of IR theories in predicting 'real-life' events raises serious concerns about our expectations for them. Should they be able to predict the timing and nature of the kinds of seismic international political events such as the end of the Cold War? Or should we have more modest expectations about what theories can offer us by way of predictive capacity? Burchill and Linklater suggest we should have more modest aspirations for theory (2009: 25).

Comparing the relative strengths and weaknesses of theories is also difficult. As Steve Smith puts it, 'they emerge from very different intellectual traditions' (2007: 8), making comparisons between them tenuous at best and vacuous at worst. If all theoretical perspectives emphasize different facets of the world, centre their attention on different actors (in short, 'see' different worlds, or 'read' the world differently), then Smith's point is well made. Choosing between theories comes down to a question of the tastes of the person making the selection because there is nothing inherent in the theories themselves that can make comparison in any way objective; it will be a subjective decision based on **aesthetics** as much as anything else.

Waltz has argued that 'explanation, not prediction, is the ultimate criterion of a good theory'. The more successful theories, he goes on, depict 'the organization of a realm and the connections among its parts' (Waltz 1997: 913). He gives as an example the theory of evolution: it is very good at explaining evolution but doesn't predict anything in particular – but it is no less significant and useful for it.

When evaluating the maze of theories you will encounter on your course it is important to bear in mind the kinds of limitations Burchill and Linklater identify, and which Waltz considers in his article. Were theory simply putting a mirror up to reality, there wouldn't be much point in devising the theory in the first place! Ask yourself, what do I except of theory? How much evidence is enough to prove or disprove this theory? Can I ever come to the conclusion that this theory is 'true' or 'false'? Pondering such questions at the back of your mind while you work through each theory will make you a critical and astute student of IRT.

AN IR SUPER-THEORY?

After my IRT lectures students regularly come and ask me a deceptively simple question. Assuming that no theory is perfect, they say, such that none can score a perfect 10 on the Burchill criteria above, can we take the best bits of each theory and put them together to make an all-in-one, comprehensive super-theory that would explain everything we need to know about world politics?

Smith calls this the 'pick and mix' or 'jigsaw' approach to thinking about IRT. If we lay out the best bits of each theory, and leave aside their flaws, we can fit them together like a jigsaw puzzle which, when finished, gives us *the* definitive IR theory – we might use Realism to explain the persistence of inter-state conflict, Liberalism to explain inter-state cooperation in international institutions and organizations such as the EU, with Marxism coming in to explain global economic exploitation of the underprivileged and **Feminism** accounting for the roles women play on the international stage. Smith comments that this is an attractive idea and one that is extremely comforting for students who want to discover the 'right' answer (2007: 10–11). Like Smith, I tend to think the existence of a super-theory would simplify things, certainly as far as answering the students goes.

Whether you think this a viable way forward turns on how you view the nature of the various IR theories on offer. On one hand, the jigsaw model assumes that all theories are **commensurable** – that they all see the same world but choose to expose and explain different aspects of it; in effect their ontological and epistemological positionings are the same and if we collect enough of them we have a comprehensive appreciation of the 'stuff' of IR. On the other hand, Smith's argument is that we should see IR theories as

> different coloured lenses: if you put one of them in front of your eyes, you will see things differently. Some aspects of the world will look the same in some senses, for example, shapes, but many other features, such as light and shades of colour, will look very different, so different in fact that they seem to show alternative worlds. (Smith 2007: 11)

The problem as Smith sees it is that no two theories are commensurable – they exist in different intellectual universes. Thus, piecing together a picture of the world from all the different theories is quite literally impossible. There is no one 'frame' for the jigsaw and the pieces physically do not interlock.

> The jigsaw model is an alluring way of picturing the ultimate IR theory – the one to beat all others. How valid do you think the model is? As you progress through your course try and note down the best arguments in support of the jigsaw model and key arguments against. You will build up a bank of critical thought about the nature of IRT that will be invaluable when it comes to 'big picture' essay and exam questions.

QUESTIONS TO PONDER

'Can we accurately tell the history of IR as an academic discipline?'

This question invites one of several responses. Either you think we can tell a story about the evolution of the discipline, or we cannot, or that we can tell several stories, in which case your answer is both yes and no. Yes and no answers are not fence-sitting, they are often the best way of setting up academic answers, even if you come down slightly more towards one side than the other. When the world is not black and white but shades of grey it makes sense to provide as many of those shades as is realistically possible in an answer.

If you take either of the first two approaches it is easy just to concentrate on one side of the argument, but do not forget to include analysis of the counter-arguments. Knocking them down can you help make your case more convincing. More importantly, it will show your tutor that you have read around the subject and that you are aware of the broad sweep of the debate. Structuring an essay should not be too difficult because you can theme the opening part around the evidence to support your view; the second part will then be a deconstruction of the counter-arguments. The third answer (yes/no) is slightly harder to structure because you potentially have more to cover in the essay. Simply listing all the different types of story we could tell ('great debates'/positivism versus normative) will take a lot of words and could become merely a description of those stories. Think carefully about how you can fit in a serious engagement with the arguments of writers who challenge the idea of a neat story about the discipline.

Across all three types of response, the better student will show an appreciation of the importance of key words in the question, notably the ideas of 'accurately' telling a 'historical' story.

'How do you think we should judge the quality of different theories of IR?'

The key word in this question is 'quality'. Does it mean accuracy, scope, predictive capacity or empirical soundness? The question invites you to identify how *you* would go about judging such attributes, but do not feel compelled to devise a brand new set of criteria! You can happily draw on existing writers to make your case.

The obvious place to start is with writers such as Burchill/Linklater and Waltz, who dwell on the evaluation of theories in their work. You might either or also (depending on the word limit and/or time in an exam) explore what practising IR theorists say about the nature and strength of their theories, as well as analysing their critiques of other theoretical traditions. Theorists who cleave to a **naturalist** understanding of theory tend to have quite forceful appreciations about the quality of theory. More openly normative theorists who discuss the ways in which we are interminably 'inside' the theories we devise are more modest about what theories can hope to achieve.

REFERENCES TO MORE INFORMATION

Wight, G. and Porter, B. (eds) (1992) *International Theory: The Three Traditions*. Leicester: Leicester University Press.

Booth, K. and Smith, S. (eds) (1995) *International Relations Theory Today*. Cambridge: Polity Press.

Contains a thorough analysis (pp. 8–29) of the various ways in which we might tell the story of the discipline.

Kubálková, V. (1998) 'The Twenty Years' Catharsis: E.H. Carr and IR', in V. Kubálková, N. Onuf and P. Kowert (eds) *International Relations in a Constructed World*. Armonk, NY: M.E. Sharpe.
Includes a fascinating diagram (pp. 42–3) which attempts to map the discipline and considers the problems with doing this.

Morgenthau, H.J. (1972) *Science: Servant or Master?* New York: W.W. Norton.
Explores the tensions between the worlds of academia (science; the pursuit of truth) and practice (the pursuit of power).

Buzan, B. and Little, R. (2000) *International Systems in World History: Remaking the Study of International Relations*. Oxford: Oxford University Press.
Thoroughgoing case for bringing history to the study of IR with an English School emphasis on how we theorize IR as 'international systems' (see Chapter 2.4 of this book for coverage of the English School).

Review of International Studies (2002) Interview with Kal Holsti by A. Jones, 28(3): 619–33.
Holsti bemoans the fragmentation of the discipline of IR and as such acts as a counterpoint to the views of Steve Smith and others who see theoretical diversity as a source of empowerment.

Tauber, A.I. (ed.) (1997) *Science and the Quest for Reality*. Basingstoke: Macmillan.
See especially the editor's introduction and the chapters by Larry Laudan (on theories of scientific knowledge) and Hilary Putnam (on facts and values).

Henry, J. (2002) *The Scientific Revolution and the Origins of Modern Science*, 2nd edn. Basingstoke. Palgrave.

Russell, B. (1948) *Sceptical Essays*. London: George Allen and Unwin.
A work of philosophy which deals, amongst other things, with the value of taking a sceptical attitude to knowledge, 'dreams and facts', the superstitions of science, rationality and the psychology of politics. Particularly useful if you have never read a 'straight' work of philosophy because it helps you think about big issues in the human pursuit of knowledge.

Olson, W.C. and Groom, A.J.R. (1991) *International Relations Then and Now: Origins and Trends in Interpretation*. London: HarperCollins.

Blaikie, N. (2007) *Approaches to Social Inquiry*, 2nd edn. Cambridge: Polity.
Written for a general social science audience, the second chapter is excellent on whether social scientists can or should borrow methods and approaches from natural scientists.

Zima, P.V. (2007) What is Theory? *The Concept of Theory in the Social and Cultural Sciences*. London: Continuum.
An advanced text exploring different understandings of 'theory', including positivist, constructivist and postmodern approaches.

Wight, C. (2006) 'Philosophy of Social Science and International Relations', in W. Carlsnaes, T. Risse and B.A. Simmons (eds) *Handbook of International Relations*. London: Sage, pp. 22–51.
A study of the sometimes uneasy status of philosophical questions within the field of IR.

Waltz, K.N. (1979) *Theory of International Politics*, 1st edn. Boston, MA: McGraw-Hill.
See especially the opening chapter on the nature of theories and how we test them.

PART II
THEORIES OF IR

Part I introduced the big themes that have been debated in the study of IR over its years as a formal discipline of academic inquiry. These range from the philosophical (the kinds of knowledge we think we can produce about IR) to the empirical (what themes and issues IR scholars should study and IR students should be taught). Part II surveys the main IR theories you are likely to encounter on your course. Feel free to dip in and out as you see fit and do not be afraid of looking into theories not directly covered on your unit. The more you can read around the subject, the better equipped you will be to appreciate the debates these writers are engaged in, and the better able you will be to express the disagreements between them succinctly and efficiently in coursework essays and exam answers.

A word of warning: each chapter below tries to summarize in a couple of thousand words theories about which millions of words have been written. I put forward my interpretation of each tradition in the knowledge that it can easily be contested, and in fact that has been part of the challenge for me when writing this book. I have had to answer two central questions that you as students will face when putting together your essays and exam answers. How do I define each theoretical tradition? What do I leave out? So, I present my overview not just in the *expectation* that you will be able to challenge the story I tell you as your reading progresses, but in the *hope* that you might. Bear in mind that this book is as much about how to think about IRT as it is the detailed knowledge of each theory, and it is in that spirit that I have tackled each one.

The chapters in Part II can only give you a very brief introduction to each theory; it is up to you to delve further into them. There is no better way than reading the landmark texts – these give you a real insight into the hopes and ambitions for each theory set out by their leading exponents. Textbooks are useful guides to theories, but consulting the originals is where the real prospect for intellectual development lies.

CORE AREAS

2.1 LIBERALISM

Key Terms

- Anarchy
- State
- Peace
- Progress

- Democracy
- Cooperation
- Interdependence
- Democratic Peace Theory

In this chapter we explore the founding theory of IR, Liberalism, which grew out of a much wider political theory of the state. We will put this theory in context by considering: first, the historical context of the Liberal tradition; second, the impact of the First World War on thinking about IR; third, the Liberal resurgence after the Second World War; fourth, Liberal thinking on international organizations and institutions; and finally, the rise and fall (?) of Democratic Peace Theory from the end of the Cold War to the post-Iraq era.

THE LIBERAL TRADITION

The liberal view of international politics and relations had a pervasive effect on the academic study of the field throughout the first four decades of [the twentieth] century. (Holsti 1985: 29)

Like many theories you will study on an IRT course, Liberalism traces its roots back way beyond the establishment of the discipline in 1919. It draws on centuries' worth of political theory and political/economic philosophy, applying them to the study of relations between states. Inspiration for Liberal IRT has come from various countries and periods and flows from the practice as well as the study of politics. Key Liberal thinkers you might hear about will include Erasmus (1466–1536), Hugo Grotius (1583–1635), John Locke (1632–1704), Adam Smith (1723–1790), Immanuel Kant (1724–1804), Jeremy Bentham (1748–1832) and Abraham Lincoln

(1809–65). A range of thinkers, scholars and policy-makers have helped shape this diverse tradition.

Across the Liberal tradition many themes intertwine and recur over time. To help identify some of the most significant (see Burchill 2009; Dunne 2008: 112–16), we can break Liberal ideas down into three categories (Figure 9). Having done that we will trace how Liberal ideas were moulded into a distinctive theory of IR after the First World War.

Jackson and Sørensen's description (2007: 98) of the Liberal tradition in IR is that it is 'optimistic' about human nature. Liberals suggest that human beings are, if not perfectible, then certainly capable of moral progress, particularly when given the opportunity to express their essentially peaceable ambitions in democratic political structures. Liberals in IR extrapolate up from the domestic (state) level to the level of the international system. They treat states as individual units (like individual human beings living in a national society) and focus on the mechanisms by which states can and do choose to manage the worst excesses of the **security dilemma** in regulating their interaction in international organizations (IOs) and institutions (for an extended treatment of

On war

- War is not the natural condition of international relations.
- Peace is normal.
- National interests safeguarded by more than military means.

On governance

- Democracy is necessary for the perfectibility of human beings to develop.
- States not the main actors on the international stage.
- States not unitary actors.
- Interdependence between states a key feature of international relations.

On human nature

- Human beings are perfectible.
- Faith in the power of human reason.
- Faith in power of humans to realize their inner potential.
- Belief in progress (scientific/technological/moral/social).

Figure 9   The Liberal tradition

the foundational IR concept of the security dilemma see Booth and Wheeler (2008)). These can be established influential global actors such as the United Nations, its Security Council or the World Bank, specialized agencies such as the International Labour Organization or the European Bank of Reconstruction and Development, or newer organizations such as the International Criminal Tribunal for the Former Yugoslavia (for more see Abbott and Snidal 1998: 4).

For Liberals, even though states exist in a condition of anarchy, progress away from a state of perpetual war can be fashioned by creating formal and informal 'institutions' of modernization – of economies, of technology, of human morality and of communication within and between states. Human beings, Liberals assert, possess the power of reason 'and when they apply it to international affairs greater cooperation will be the result' (Jackson and Sørensen 2007: 99). In this context, peace, progress and human advancement are all possible, even in a situation in which there are distinct entities known as states, each with their own languages, traditions, histories and political setups.

As Jennifer Sterling-Folker observes, therefore (2006a: 56, original emphasis), Liberal IR theorists take the same starting assumptions as Realist theorists (see Chapter 2.2), and investigate 'what *prevents* progress from being achieved, with the underlying assumption being that progress could be realized if we could uncover the barriers to collective action and promote their resolutions'. J.D. Bowen (2011) describes the Liberal approach to IRT as follows: 'The international system creates opportunities for cooperation and conflict. It's up to the states and other actors in the international political system to either take advantage of those or not'. The world is not perfect but Liberals argue that we (as individuals and states) can make the best of it, given certain preconditions that help build a sense of community. Liberals focus on the opportunities available to us to manage inter-state relations and why states might or might not take advantage of them at a given moment.

LIBERALISM AFTER THE FIRST WORLD WAR

The study of IR after its emergence as a recognizable academic discipline in 1919 became closely enmeshed with a fertile period in Liberal thought about the relations between states in the aftermath of the Great War. What, people asked, had been the ultimate value to states entering that conflict? How had they marched into such a disastrous war seemingly against their will? Why had these same states persisted in sending thousands of their citizens to their death for apparently minimal gains over the years 1914–18? Early scholars of IR set about trying to find answers to just such questions. As William Wallace rightly suggests (1996: 302): 'International Relations as a discipline grew out of reflections on policy, and out of the desire to influence policy, or to improve the practice of policy'.

A key player in helping Liberal theory become central to the early study of IR was Woodrow Wilson, a former political scientist and President of the US when the country decided to intervene, decisively, in the First World War in 1917. In a speech to Congress in January 1918 Wilson declared that he wanted to make the world

> fit and safe to live in; and particularly that it be made safe for every peace-loving nation which, like our own, wishes to live its own life, determine its own institutions, be assured of justice and fair dealing by the other peoples of the world as against force and selfish aggression. (Wilson 1918)

He proceeded to outline his 'Fourteen Point' programme which provides us with a vivid insight into how Liberals perceive international affairs. Some of the most important of his Points were:

- **Point I. 'Open covenants of peace, openly arrived at'** – a call for transparent and honest diplomacy; this would help get round the problem of secret alliances which entangled states in war apparently against their better judgement. Selecting an astute strategy for the conduct of international affairs is trickier when, as a state, you are bound to the decisions of other states in alliances, and particularly when you are not quite sure which states are in alliance with which other states in the system, and with what degree of certainty they will back each other. This is why Liberal scholars focus on promoting international institutions which set down rules, laws and guard the norms of international behaviour as prerequisites to achieving an open and honest 'game' of international relations.
- **Point III. Removal of economic barriers** – the establishment of free trade among all states consenting to the peace. The deeper the ties between states in trading terms, the less likely they will be to judge it financially effective to make war on their trading partners.
- **Points V–XIII. National self-determination** – incorporating a call for the dismantling of empires, and associated with the push for democratic forms of governance as a force for good in global politics. In its contemporary form it can be seen in Michael Doyle's Democratic Peace Theory.
- **Point XIV. Association of nations** – coming together to guarantee 'political independence' and 'territorial integrity' (Wilson 1918).

Liberal Internationalism is sometimes known as 'Idealism'. You might also find it called Classical Liberalism or Utopian Liberalism. Keep a note of all the different labels you come across and the characteristics writers ascribe to those various theoretical positions.

Wilson was a key player in the establishment of the League of Nations via the Paris Peace Conference of 1919. His view was that there was not necessarily a harmony of interests between states but that international order could be constructed with the help of international organizations, which would promote diplomacy, cooperation and the rule of law. The League of Nations is a concrete example of the widespread appeal and political influence of Liberal thought in the immediate aftermath of the First World War: note the Wilsonian leanings evident in Figure 10.

The high contracting parties, in order to promote international co-operation and to achieve international peace and security

- by the acceptance of obligations not to resort to war

- by the prescription of open, just and honourable relations between nations

- by the firm establishment of the understandings of international law as the actual rule of conduct among Governments, and

- by the maintenance of justice and a scrupulous respect for all treaty obligations in the dealings of organised peoples with one another

Agree to this Covenant of the League of Nations.

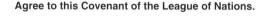

Figure 10   Preamble to the Covenant of the League of Nations

Crucially, the League was helped into existence via 'solid political backing from the most powerful state in the international system at the time': the US (Jackson and Sørensen 2007: 33). When American support for the League ebbed away over the following years it fell somewhat into disrepute, indicating that 'in practice states remained imprisoned by self-interest' (Dunne 2008: 114). It is a huge irony that for domestic reasons the US decided not to join the institution it had created. The League quickly became a 'talking shop' shorn of real international political clout and legitimacy. Adolf Hitler's aggressive diplomacy and Germany and Italy's military expansionism in the 1930s effectively exposed the League's weaknesses and, the story goes, 'dealt a fatal blow to Idealism' (Dunne 2008: 114).

Note the connection between the rise of a theory and the international events occurring at the time it becomes popular. What does this tell you about the normative nature of IRT?

LIBERALISM AFTER THE SECOND WORLD WAR

There is a parallel to be drawn between the real and lasting surge in Liberal thought after the First World War and the resurgence of those same ideas after the Second World War. After 1945 there was a renewed push to create international organizations for the promotion of peace, prosperity and security at the global and regional levels. However, Liberals had learnt that they needed to be a bit more hard-headed about what they said and did to take account of the realities of international politics, so after 1945 they spoke a more 'pragmatic' language of IR (Dunne 2008: 114). We will briefly explore the origins and nature of two such bodies, the United Nations (UN) and the European Union (EU), before showing how these renewed efforts to manage inter-state relations came from, and injected new lifeblood into, Liberal thought.

THE UNITED NATIONS

- **Origins.** Successor to the League of Nations which 'ceased its activities after failing to prevent World War Two' (UN 2005). The UN Charter was drawn up in 1945 by representatives of 50 countries, and the UN officially came into existence on 24 October 1945 when the Charter was ratified by China, France, the Soviet Union, the United Kingdom, the United States and a majority of the other 50 signatories (UN 2005). Compare the preamble to the Charter of the United Nations (Figure 11) with the preamble to the Covenant of the League of Nations (Figure 10).

- **Growth.** The number of states in the international arena has grown rapidly since 1945, helped by the decolonization of former Empires such as the British and the French, and the end of the Cold War in 1989. With the accession of South Sudan in July 2011 the UN's membership totalled some 193 states (UN 2011).
- **Aims and activities.** The activities of the UN are guided by its initial aims (Figure 11) and they have expanded along with the number and diversity of the political, economic, social and cultural issues that have forced their way on to the global agenda since 1945.

We the people of the United Nations determined

- to save succeeding generations from the scourge of war, which twice in our lifetime has brought untold sorrow to mankind, and

- to reaffirm faith in fundamental human rights, in the dignity and worth of the human person, in the equal rights of men and women and of nations large and small, and

- to establish conditions under which justice and respect for the obligations arising from treaties and other sources of international law can be maintained, and

- to promote social progress and better standards of life in larger freedom …

Have resolved to combine our efforts to accomplish these aims.

Figure 11   Preamble to the Charter of the United Nations

Source: (UN 2005)

Take a look at the structure of the UN (2006) and you can see its sheer presence on the world stage at all sorts of levels and in relation to all sorts of issues, including the United Nations Children's Fund, World Food Programme, Office on Drugs and Crime and its many specialized agencies. The UN certainly deals with 'hard' security issues through the Security Council but its approach to managing inter-state relations goes much wider and deeper than that.

Media coverage of the UN's role in trying to resolve international disputes (for example, the question of the existence of Weapons of Mass Destruction in Iraq in 2001–3) can skew our impression of what the UN does. Using its website, make a list of some of its best known economic, social and cultural programmes run by the UN and this will help you understand more about the breadth and scale of its activities.

THE EUROPEAN UNION

The EU as we know it today was formally brought into being by the Maastricht Treaty (1993). But the EU did not 'start' then. Maastricht (and subsequent revisions such as Amsterdam 1999 and the Lisbon Treaty 2008) extended and formalized processes of integration that had begun in the 1950s. It was this growth and development of institutions for European cooperation in the early post-war years that helped drive Liberal Institutionalism. We will briefly review these developments before summarizing what these two case studies tell us about this particular strand of Liberal thinking. Three key developments took place in terms of European cooperation in the 1950s:

1 **European Coal and Steel Community (ECSC)** – Based on the Schuman Plan of May 1950, in April 1951 six countries in western Europe (France, Germany, Italy, Belgium, the Netherlands and Luxembourg) announced that they were to pool their coal and steel resources and run those industries under a common management. Its aim was to end 'the frequent and bloody wars between neighbours, which culminated in the Second World War' (Europa undated). This was a version of the Wilsonian principle that states enmeshed economically are unlikely to fall out diplomatically and politically. Membership of an international organization changes

states' calculations about the relative pay-offs to be gleaned from engaging in conflictual and cooperative behaviour respectively.

2 **European Defence Community (EDC)** – In June 1950 France announced a further plan to place military forces from consenting states in Europe under a single command. The EDC had internal and external security dimensions. Internally it sought to ensure security in Europe by containing German forces within European as opposed to national military structures. Externally it sought to help defend Europe against possible attack from the Soviet Union by promoting military rearmament in leading European nation-states. The EDC collapsed in 1954 when the French parliament failed to ratify the treaty. Prime amongst many concerns was the loss of French sovereignty or decision-making authority over its military forces (Ruane 2000). This shows that, ultimately, international organizations can only be as effective (indeed, can only come into existence) as states wish them to be.

3 **European Economic Community (EEC)** – Undeterred by the failure of the EDC, the six countries that developed the ECSC extended integration to many other sectors of their economies in 1957 with the Treaty of Rome, which aimed to enhance the free movement of people, goods and services across borders. As with the ECSC, the EEC used financial means to secure a political end: lasting peace and prosperity through economic cooperation. The EEC was renamed the EU in 1993 after the ratification of the Maastricht Treaty.

Liberal Institutionalism grew directly out of the efforts by states to cooperate by coming together in international organizations such as the UN and the EU. The latter provided particularly fertile ground for theoretical innovation and has come to be associated with two writers in particular:

- **David Mitrany.** Worked on the **functionalist integration theory** after the First World War. 'Functionalism is concerned with the ways of creating … a working peace system. It involves a diagnosis of the problems of disorder in international society, and a prescription for ways of shaping a better world' (Groom and Taylor 1975: 1). Mitrany argued (1933) that state authority in the modern era had been called into question as people began to find solutions to shared security, economic and political concerns across state borders, rather than working within the confines of those borders. Such efforts would increase as individuals saw the benefits of collective endeavours and this interdependence would then lead to peace and further integration across state borders through what has become known as the 'spillover' effect of integration.

Functionalists assume (Groom and Taylor 1975: 3–4):

- Economic development promotes shared and recognizable values.
- There is a need to develop mechanisms for the delivery of individual welfare across state borders.
- That states are not necessarily the best way of organizing society.

- **Ernst B. Haas.** Developed Mitrany's ideas via neo-functionalist integration theory after the Second World War. In *The Uniting of Europe* (2003, first published in 1958) and *Beyond the Nation-State* (1964), Haas argued that Mitrany had gone too far in theorizing integration at the global level. Integration at the regional level, however, could provide the kind of results Mitrany had predicted via spillover from lower levels of integration (economic/ social) to higher levels (political). Such 'spillover' came from two forces. One is functional, as cooperation in one lower level issue led to cooperation in a related area. The other is political, as the creation of supranational organizations such as the UN and EU propelled integration forward into newer, possibly more politically sensitive areas such as defence and security (the EDC might have gone too far in the 1950s but look at the development of the European Security and Defence Policy since the 1990s).

CONTEMPORARY LIBERAL IRT

Work on functionalism by Mitrany and Haas set about applying Liberal assumptions to the post-1945 world of international relations. Their ideas and associated work in the realm of interdependence, international institutions and international governance (most famously Moravcsik 1998) draw on centuries-old Liberal ideas about human nature, the organization of states, the causes of wars and how to manage inter-state relations in an apparently conflict-ridden international system. So what, in sum, are the main assumptions of Liberal IRT and how does it make sense of contemporary international affairs?

A concentration on organizations, institutions and Democratic Peace Theory helps bring the story up to date.

ORGANIZATIONS AND INSTITUTIONS

Liberalism, at least until the 1970s, developed in recognition of the growth of international organizations (IOs). It assumed that states were the main actors in the international system and the locus for the key decisions affecting war and peace. It assumed that these states existed in the classic condition of systemic anarchy. Liberal IR theorists assumed that states were rational actors in the sense that leaders could more or less accurately calculate the pay-offs to the state coming from strategic choices open to them. It finally assumed (and here is the main departure from Realism) that the existence of IOs changed the nature of the calculations states made about war and peace. Organizations create opportunities for wider and deeper strategic interactions between states and they in turn inspire trust, build confidence and remove some of the element of fear that characterizes relations between states in a Realist war of all against all.

Kenneth Abbott and Duncan Snidal highlight three principal functions of international organizations (see also Keohane 1995: 291): on the one hand they centralize collective activities 'through a concrete and stable organizational structure and a supportive administrative apparatus'. For example the World Health Organization (WHO) smallpox campaign is more effective as a centralized effort than a series of individual state-led efforts 'because global scope avoids gaps in coverage' (Abbott and Snidal 1998: 4–5). Second, membership of IOs holds participants to account and avoids 'duplication and unproductive competition' and ensures that outputs are shared (Abbott and Snidal 1998: 14).

Finally, international organizations can, especially when they do act and/or are perceived to act independently from leading member state control, help manage inter-state conflicts and promote agreements in the realms of both 'hard' and 'soft' security. IOs provide information, stability over time and a degree of 'neutrality' in dealing with potentially divisive issues. In the WHO smallpox campaign its stable structure and the 'reputation-staking effect of membership' encourages wide participation, while free-riding problems can be mitigated using its own resources (Abbott and Snidal 1998: 14). Abbott and Snidal conclude as follows: 'Rational states will use or create a formal IO when the value of these functions outweighs the costs, notably the resulting limits on unilateral action' (1998: 5).

John Duffield (2007) has observed a considerable jump from the early Liberal focus on organizations-as-rules to today's Liberal focus on institutions-as-norms. Abbott and Snidal also explain that (1998: 8), 'the role of IOs is best understood through a synthesis of rationalist (including realist) and constructivist approaches', such that the gains from cooperation feature alongside a consideration of the habits and norms of working in a collective as motivations for state action.

Why is this expansion of meaning important? Well, the first thing to say is that this change in approach to the games states play globally has been seen in the development of regimes and Neoliberal IRT (considered in Chapter 2.3) as well as in some Constructivist and English School thought (Chapters 2.4 and 2.5), so you will read more about it later in the book (and see, for instance, James 1993: 271). Robert Keohane might be considered a pretty traditional theorist of IR, but even he wrestles with understandings of institutions that show the synergies between 'social scientific' and more 'reflectivist' approaches to explaining cooperation in international politics (Keohane 1995: especially 285–92).

International organizations, Duffield argues, kept the focus on the 'game-playing' element of state-on-state interactions, with material costs and benefits accruing to states the driving force of their decision-making. By giving them better information, some rules and laws to abide by, and a better working knowledge of other states' intentions, membership of an organization helps a state better measure the pay-off that making move X on the world stage might offer up in terms of reaching its economic, security or diplomatic objective Y. This long-held rationalist conception of institutions-as-organizations is of 'consciously constructed frameworks established by agents seeking to promote or protect their interests' (Duffield 2007: 5). States are still selfish utility-maximizers but they choose to limit their more assertive or revanchist tendencies because they better perceive the incentives that a more pragmatic, diplomatic approach can bring them over the long term.

Duffield goes on to draw a distinction between the earlier (organizational) understanding of formalized international cooperation and the more recent (institutional) setting. In the work on institutions, material gains still matter to states; they want to survive as states; they do not want to be attacked; and they seek to maximize their opportunities for economic growth. However, underpinning the material is the **ideational** connection between them, fostered in large part by the growth of transnational actors which can bring new issues and norms of behaviour to play, especially if they successfully act as 'norm entrepreneurs' which lobby for the promotion of new values and issues to be taken seriously by states.

Table 2 Organizations and institutions

	Organizations	Institutions
Membership	States	States plus transnational actors
Actorliness	Sovereign	Negotiated/pooled sovereignty
Nature of relations	Regulative (rules and laws)	Constitutive (… plus norms and practices)
Behaviour	Constrained and ordered	Constraint by choice

States in the Liberal view not only alter their behaviour because they are forced to through hard-nosed and sometimes reluctant membership of international organizations, but because they come to share values and other ways of 'being' in the world that imply their destinies are more and more tightly bound up with the fate of each other. The similarities yet also the subtle differences between organizations on the one hand and institutions on the other are summarized in Table 2 above.

John Ruggie's definition of institutions is telling: 'persistent and connected sets of rules, formal and informal, that prescribe behavioural roles, constrain activity and shape expectations' (quoted in Onuf 2002: 226). In an institutional setting states act not just because they have to (because they are 'ordered' to by being signed up to agreements) but because they want to. Institutions are thus something broader and deeper than organizations, where identities as well as interests are in play: 'rules working together "through human agents"' (Onuf 2002: 218). Institutions, Duffield concludes (2007: 2), are: 'relatively stable sets of related constitutive, regulative, and procedural norms and rules that pertain to the international system, the actors in the system (including states as well as non-state entities), and their activities'.

So, the EU might have started life as an international organization but might now credibly be called an institution by virtue of its intention to create a 'zone of peace' across the continent of Europe and to lobby for the promotion of human rights and economic development around the globe. EU member states sign up to procedures and rules which shape their conduct (rules and laws or European Commission 'directives') and share in the promotion of the 'acquis Communautaire' – the Community 'way' of doing things. This has evolved as a norm over time, and as something which applicant member states have to accept when joining the club. The national law changes they make in line with the 'acquis' make them signatories to the Community method in spirit and practice. The EU has transcended state-on-state war (the founding rationale for its organizational dynamic) and is now busying itself with many other activities, with Brussels home to a lively range of lobbyists, pressure groups, and so on. An emphasis on 'stronger' Liberalism in the form of institutions perhaps better explains more about contemporary international relations than the 'weaker' organizational understanding.

Thinking about Liberal IRT through institutional lenses changes the way we view international relations because: first, it lays emphasis on the cooperative as well as the conflictual elements of world politics; second, it decentres the idea of states as utility-maximizers out to protect their own interests by putting the spotlight on wider networks of actors in international politics; and third, it highlights the complexity of defining sovereignty in an era of complex interdependence. In English School and Constructivist theories which we cover below, institutions have a yet more sociological content to them (see Buzan 2004: 167–204).

International organizations are said to differ from international institutions in a variety of important ways. Keep lists in your notes of how scholars approach the two settings for state-on-state interactions. Where are the two said to be similar and dissimilar, and do different theoretical traditions treat them differently?

DEMOCRATIC PEACE THEORY

The Wilsonian worldview, that global history could vindicate the liberal democratic project, never left IR circles, even if it was rather overtaken by Realist pessimism in the formative years of the Cold War. Liberal IR scholars routinely investigated whether there was something in the *character* of liberal states that predisposed them to conduct their international relations in a more pacific fashion than their illiberal counterparts (see for instance Babst 1964; Doyle 1983, 1986).

The end of the Cold War did not, therefore, instigate but surely helped popularize the interpretation that the 'victors' in the Cold War, the US and its Western allies, had triumphed over an ideologically bankrupt and politically repressive Communist Soviet empire in part because of the character of Liberal democracy (Owen 2011: 162). Confidence was high that the Liberal vision could come to be shared the world over, enabled by technologies of globalization and backed by the spread of progressive norms within multilateral IOs and institutions. Democratic Peace Theory, as it came to be known, emerged as a robust research programme in the post-Cold War years. In this section we will briefly review the core tenets and metatheoretical persuasions of the theory before surveying some of the main criticisms that have been levelled against it.

AN OPTIMISTIC INTERPRETATION AND A POSITIVIST RESEARCH PROGRAMME

Democratic Peace Theory (DPT) is, in a nutshell, 'the claim that democracies rarely fight one another because they share common norms of live-and-let-live and domestic institutions that constrain the recourse to war' (Rosato 2003: 585). As DPT has developed, the headline claim that democracies tend not to fight each other has been 'deepened to include the claim that "pairs of democracies are much less likely than other pairs of states to fight or to threaten each other in militarized disputes less violent than war"' (Russett and Oneal quoted in Macmillan 2003: 234).

Look at the language DP theorists use. It is important to note that they do not deal in definitive statements (democracies *do not* fight one another) but in probabilistic statements (they *rarely* do so, or *tend* to do so less often). As Bruce Russett explains it (1995: 172): 'democracies are more likely to settle mutual conflicts of interest … short of the threat or use of any military force'. However, the nuances of their arguments sometimes get lost in the translation to public debate and practitioner discourse, as in the simplified assertion that two countries with a Macdonald's in them have never been to war. That said, many proponents of DPT have unashamedly looked to positivist, mostly large-*n* (number) quantitative studies using statistical methods to advance the 'scientific' cause of IR, opening interesting debates between rational actor and more normatively inclined approaches within DPT (Geis 2011: 166). In Jack Levy's words, the 'absence of war comes as close as anything we have to an empirical law in international relations' (Levy quoted in Hobson 2011b: 1905) – and this is what the subject is all about, right?

Why do Democratic Peace Theorists argue that democratic states rarely fight one another? A variety of factors are brought into play including the propositions that:

- The *'moral constraint' hypothesis* (Friedman 2008): Democracies view other democratic states as more legitimate than non-democracies; fighting them is thus considered illegitimate.
- Publics – and states – are assumed to be *rational actors*: 'People want peace because they do not want to suffer the miseries and material

losses of war, in contradistinction to them not wanting to impose miseries and losses on others' (Friedman 2008: 552).

- Democracies are also more responsive to lobby and interest groups, particularly economic interest groups which publicize the economic costs of war.
- This supports the *'pacific-foreign-policymaking-public' hypothesis* (Friedman 2008). Democracies express the essentially pacifist tendencies of the populace and because democratic states are more responsive to popular opinion the chances of the resort to force with other democracies are lower.
- The *'extension' hypothesis* (Friedman 2008): Good norms of internal behaviour become translated into good (pacific) norms of external action, building trust and cooperative tendencies.
- The *'zone of peace' hypothesis*: Wars still occur against 'outsiders' existing on the fringes of the zone of peace between states. Democracies more often resort to war with non-democracies because 'the bond of moral solidarity that constrains power politics in inter-democracy relations is simply a priori absent in democracy-non-democracy relations' (Friedman 2008: 550).

At heart, then, DPT uses a 'domestic analogy' to explain international relations. R.B.J. Walker (1995: 312) explains that a domestic analogy is 'the transfer of the philosophical and theoretical premises derived from the analysis of political community within states to the analysis of relations between states'. It suggests that the greater propensity for non-democracies to resort to force to solve issues at home impels them to follow those same (intolerant) norms of conflict in their dealings with other states. Democracies, by contrast, 'expect to be able to resolve their domestic disputes through peaceful means and with respect for the existence and rights of opponents' (Macmillan 2003: 237). Democratic tolerance at home breeds greater respect and tolerance for other states abroad.

The virtues of the DPT research programme are acknowledged by supporters and critics alike (for example, Smith 2011: 152). From the theoretical perspective that most interests us here, after years of being on the backfoot in the battle of ideas in IR, DPT emerged to counter the Realist contention that states are condemned to exist in a state of security competition because of the anarchic structure of the international system. If 'zones of peace' can be observed between states sharing political structures, then Liberals could claim that state character, rather than the systemic structure, is a more persuasive explanatory factor in states' foreign policy decision-making (Rosato 2003: 585). At a stroke, Waltzian Neorealism (which we cover in Chapter 2.3) would be fatally weakened, if not destroyed altogether.

KEY CRITICISMS AND QUESTIONS

Theories of IR can be criticized on a number of grounds and those levelled at DPT show the various ways in which theoretical debates are conducted by scholars in the discipline as theories get tested and refined over time.

1 **Empirical criticisms: how do we conceptualize 'democracy' and measure 'the history of war'?** Sebastian Rosato contends that the way Democratic Peace theorists have carved up the global history of wars and conflicts can be contested. This is an ontological criticism because it comes down to definitions of 'democracy' and 'war', which affect the 'world' theorists see and how they process it methodologically using statistical packages to carve up the 'facts' of history. First, says Rosato (2003: 591), during the Cold War American interventions were most often against democratic states such as Guatemala, Brazil and Chile. These governments were replaced by dictatorial regimes. Second, in each case the clash of interests between the US and the target government was not especially severe, bolstering the Realist hypothesis that security interests overrode respect for democratic norms of international action. Third, American economic interests often overrode support for democracy during the Cold War. Meanwhile, DPT overlooks colonial wars which sought to re-impose autocratic governments favouring the imperial power (Rosato 2003: 589). The global history of conflict is not quite as easy to access as DPT seems to assume. David Spiro adds that the DPT finding is actually insignificant in the bigger scheme of things: 'Both wars and democracies are rare, and that is why there are not many wars between democracies' (Spiro 1995: 177). There is insufficient evidence to prove a causal link between the character of a state and its propensity to engage in threatening or war-like behaviour.

2 **Metatheoretical criticisms.** These unpick the positivist underpinnings of the DPT research programme, which assumes a Democratic Peace 'out there'. As we saw in the previous part of the book, writers of a normative persuasion (for instance constructivist and postmodern theorists) say that the distinction between 'observer' and 'observed' is blurred. Thus writes Hobson (2011b: 1907): 'The Democratic Peace does not simply exist "out there",

it only comes into existence through the categories used to identify and define it'. As agents respond to the publication of these
supposedly objective empirical findings they shape their behaviour
accordingly and 'their new behaviour is liable to alter or falsify the
empirical observation which had been valid to that point'. No
theory, DPT included, can stand apart from the world. This links to
the normative, policy-focused criticisms.

3 **Normative criticisms.** In providing intellectual justification for
the controversial US-led invasion of Iraq in 2003, scholars
propounding DPT have been held to be, if not directly blameworthy,
then morally responsible to some degree for over-stating the case
for democracy promotion in the post-Cold War era; 'it did play a
role: one of a confluence of factors that brought about the mista-
ken choice to invade' (Hobson 2011a: 173). In overselling their
claims or not bothering to hedge their claims with sufficient cau-
tion, writers such as Piki Ish-Shalom are quite adamant that DPT
theorists helped market and legitimize the 'effort to democratize
Iraq, supposedly servicing America's strategic interest of achieving
a Middle East secured and stabilized as a zone of peace' (Ish-
Shalom 2011: 180).

These investigations into the ontology, epistemology and methods of
research into DPT illustrate in one relatively self-contained sub-field of
the discipline how theoretical work in academic International Relations generally progresses. It also highlights the huge overlap between
theory and practice and the influences of the one upon the other.

We are left with a series of questions that DPT has been wrestling
with since faith in the 'victory' of the West was shaken after 9/11,
the onset of the War on Terror and the invasions of Afghanistan and
Iraq (from Hobson 2011b: 1918): what is the point of a zone of liberal peace if wars are still occurring on its fringes (ethics)? How do
democracies weigh up the benefits of peace against the costs of war
with non-democracies? Should democracy be considered the main
way of spreading peace or is state sovereignty to be respected (an
echo of the pluralist–solidarist debate from English School theory;
see Chapter 2.4, p. 141)? Work by writers such as Gowa (2011) suggests that DPT may yet have theoretical and policy mileage in it,
even if the high Wilsonian optimism of the early post-Cold War
years has ebbed away.

QUESTIONS TO PONDER

'Why did the First World War provide such an impetus to the development of Liberal IR theory?'

There are a couple of promising approaches you might take when faced with this question. One is to use the literatures on the origins of the discipline which we explored in Chapter 1.4 to trace the overlap between the worlds of academia and practice, which came together in 1919 to produce the discipline of IR we know today. From here you would study the early agenda of the discipline as being normatively concerned with the promotion of peace, perhaps using a figure such as Woodrow Wilson as an exemplar of this early Liberal thinking. A second approach might be to focus on the Liberal agenda and key themes in Liberal IRT in the inter-war years. This is a reverse of the first approach because you begin with the theory and work back to the impact of war, rather than the other way round.

> When answering questions containing references to momentous events like the First World War it is tempting to 'pad' the essay out with lots of details about the event in question, especially if you have studied the history of the Great War before. In this example, the question does not ask for a history of the First World War, so only include as much as you need to make your point. You will get all your marks for demonstrating knowledge about Liberalism as opposed to the detail of the unfolding of the conflict.

However you answer this question you might also want to include elements of the Liberal agenda which predated the war, helping you to a sophisticated argument that the war accentuated aspects of Liberal thought but did not provide their 'origins' in any simple sense.

'Does the existence of the EU bear out the accuracy of Liberal IRT?'

This question invites you to consider the relationship between the theory and practice of IR so far as the formation of international organizations goes. As with the previous question you will have to strike a balance between the detail you include on the history and development of the EU and the room you set aside for developing your response to the question. If you are ever in doubt about how much background material to put in an essay, a useful rule of thumb is: if in doubt, leave out. Your tutor will not want a history of the EU and all its treaties from 1957 to the present day. He/she will knock marks off if this forms the bulk of your essay, and will be much kinder if your essay is balanced in favour of critical analysis of the question.

Your answer will very much depend on your 'reading' of IR since 1945. Has the growth in the number and influence of international bodies like the EU (and the UN for that matter) stopped states from going to war, once and for all? Or have they only helped reduce the likelihood, without changing basic features of the international states system? Whatever you choose to argue, make sure you set your main case out in the introduction and follow it through logically in the rest of the essay, leading towards a conclusion (see Part III of this book on good essay writing). The shift within Liberalism from organizations to institutions is a feature you might draw upon to give critical depth to your answer. The question talks about 'Liberal IRT', but as the Duffield article demonstrates there are many varieties of contemporary Liberalism which overlap with other theories such as Constructivism and the English School. 'Stronger' Liberalism (institutions) versus 'weaker' Liberalism (organizations) could be an organizing frame for your argument here.

NB, it is easier to answer this question when you know about Realist IRT which we cover in Chapter 2.2. Realists criticize Liberals for placing too much emphasis on the power of international organizations to alter fundamental state interests, flowing from concerns about their security and survival. In an essay you would probably want to mention this element of the dispute between the two traditions as a way of developing your own argument and giving critical depth to your answer.

REFERENCES TO MORE INFORMATION

General PowerPoint overview:
Rey Ty (2008) 'Liberalism in International Relations', www.youtube.com/watch?v=5RfRCo-Qwls&feature=fvwrel (accessed 10 July 2012).

Inter-war Liberalism:
Angell, N. (1909) *The Great Illusion*. London: Weidenfeld and Nicolson.

Argues against the then popular view that war was profitable for states by showing how, in fact, it undermined prosperity by disrupting or destroying commercial and political ties between states.

Woolf, L. (1933) *The Intelligent Man's Way to Prevent War*. London: Gollancz. Encapsulates the essence of inter-war Liberalism. Note its gendered title (see Chapter 2.8 in this book).

Curry, W.B. (1939) *The Case for Federal Union*. Harmondsworth: Penguin.

Ashworth, L. (2006) 'Where are the Idealists in Interwar International Relations?', *Review of International Studies*, 32(3): 291–308.
Argues lucidly against the conventional tendency in IR to identify the idealist tradition in IR between the two World Wars. For more historical context see also:
Sylvest, C. (2005) 'Continuity and Change in British Liberal Internationalism, c.1900–1930', *Review of International Studies*, 31(2): 263–83.

Caedel, M. (2011) 'The founding Text of International Relations? Norman Angell's Seminal Yet Flawed, *The Great Illusion* (1909–1938)', *Review of International Studies*, 37(4): 1671–93.

Overviews of the League of Nations, the UN and the EU:
Kennedy, P. (2007) *The Parliament of Man: The United Nations and the Quest for World Government*. London: Allen Lane.
Knock, T.J. (1995) *To End All Wars: Woodrow Wilson and the Quest for a New World Order*. Princeton, NJ: Princeton University Press.
Ostrower, G.B. (1997) *The League of Nations*: From 1919 to 1929. Garden City Park, NY: Avery Publishing Group.
Pinder, J. and Usherwood, S. (2007) *The European Union*: A Very Short Introduction. Oxford: Oxford University Press.
Bache, I. and George, S. (2006) *Politics in the European Union*, 2nd edn. Oxford: Oxford University Press.
See Part I on theories of integration and Part II on the history of the organization.

Hill, C. and Smith, M. (eds) (2005) *The International Relations of the European Union*. Oxford: Oxford University Press.

On Functionalism and Neofunctionalism:
Ghébali, V. (1975) 'The League of Nations and Functionalism', in A.J.R. Groom and P. Taylor, Functionalism: *Theory and Practice in International Relations*. London: University of London Press, pp. 141–61.

Haas, E.B. and Whiting, A.S. (1975) *Dynamics of International Relations*. Westport, CT: Greenwood Press.

Makes the case for the Liberal approach to IR; see especially Chapters 1–3.

Rosamond, B. (2000) *Theories of European Integration*. Basingstoke: Macmillan.
Overview of integration theories, including functionalism and neo-functionalism.

To get a flavour of the general themes in IR that exercise Liberals:
Franceschet, A. (2001) 'Sovereignty and Freedom: Immanuel Kant's Liberal Internationalist "Legacy"', *Review of International Studies*, 27(2): 209–28.

McGrew, A. (2002) 'Liberal Internationalism: Between Realism and Cosmopolitanism', in D. Held and A. McGrew (eds) *Governing Globalization: Power, Authority and Global Governance*. Cambridge: Polity, pp. 267–89.
Maps the Liberal tradition from the 1800s and unpicks its different strands.

Bertelsen, J. (ed.) (1977) *Nonstate Nations in International Politics: Comparative Systems Analysis*. New York and London: Praeger.
A fascinating collection of essays on what are called in the book 'Nonstate Nations': entities that operate as if they were nation-states but which are not confined to territorial borders, for example, the Palestinian Arabs, the Zionist Movement and the Basques. This serves to undermine the state-centricity of Realist IRT and therefore offers much food for thought.

Risse-Kappen, T. (1995) *Bringing Transnational Relations Back In: Non-State Actors, Domestic Structures and International Institutions*. Cambridge: Cambridge University Press.
Uses case studies in economics, multinational corporations, security-building, and social and environmental movements to show that we cannot explain state behaviour without taking the cross-border activities of these non-state actors into account.

Axford, B., Browning, G.K., Huggins, R. and Rosamond, B. (2006) *Politics: An Introduction*, 2nd edn. London: Routledge.
Chapter 15 by Axford gives you a succinct overview of the processes and impacts of globalization, as well as a short section on backlashes against it, which will help you begin thinking about Marxist IRT (Chapter 2.6 in this book).

On Democratic Peace Theory and its critics:
Brown, M. et al. (eds) (1997) *Debating the Democratic Peace*. Cambridge, MA: MIT Press.
Doyle, M.W. (2012) *Liberal Peace: Selected Essays*. London: Routledge.
Fearon, J.D. (1994) 'Domestic Political Audiences and the Escalation of International Disputes', *American Political Science Review*, 88(3): 577–92.

Ikenberry, J.G., Knock, T.J., Slaughter, A.M. and Smith, T. (2009) *The Crisis in American Foreign Policy: Wilsonianism in the 21st Century*. Princeton, NJ: Princeton University Press.

Maoz, Z. and Russett, B. (1993) 'Normative and Structural Causes of the Democratic Peace, 1946–86', *American Political Science Review*, 87(3): 624–38.

2.2 REALISM

Key Terms

- Anarchy
- State
- Power
- Interest
- Human nature
- Security dilemma

Liberal IR theorists are optimistic about the potential for some sort of order to emerge between states existing in a condition of international anarchy. For Liberals, the potential for conflict between states is diminished, but not ruled out altogether, by involving themselves in processes of cooperation undertaken in international organizations and institutions such as the UN and the EU. These act as forums for communication, trust and confidence-building, open diplomacy and the peaceful resolution of disputes, with rules and laws put in place to constrain and order state behaviour.

Early Liberal theory depicted states as selfish utility-maximizers, but membership of organizations changed the perceived pay-offs to them from engaging in cooperative endeavours. More recent Liberal theory (crossing over into Neoliberal theory and Constructivism) has stressed the constitutive elements of institutions which incorporate state and non-state actors in a deeper and more meaningful game at the international level. In particular, institutions work on a social level to alter not just interests but identities and values, building something akin to an English School 'society' of states (see Chapter 2.4 below) that encourages peaceable norms of behaviour without the coercive dimension implied by the interest-driven 'organization' element. For Liberals, international anarchy is a real and pressing condition, but it does not necessarily lead to states continually knocking against each other like balls on a snooker table.

Realists take a quite different approach; they 'are pessimistic about the prospects for international cooperation; they believe that competition between the major powers in the international system is the normal state of affairs' (Glaser 1994/95: 50). They begin at the same place – explaining

Figure 12 Same startpoint, different endpoints

state behaviour in a condition of international anarchy. But the basic units of analysis and the central problem to be explained are the only things the two sets of theorists share. From here the two traditions diverge dramatically over the consequences for international relations. Where Liberals see cooperation as the likely outcome, Realists see the perpetual threat of conflict and war because states are trapped in a cycle of fear caused by lack of trust and competition to dominate the system (Figure 12).

Realism is the theory we most associate with the study of international affairs because it deals so manifestly with the hard security concerns that directly affect the potential for human and state survival on the global stage. As Randall Schweller (2011) has put it, 'Realism is a theory essentially about power and security. States relentlessly seek power and security because they exist in a self-help system'.

Why do the two theories share the same beginning but end up with two almost polar opposite views of IR? Exploring the basic tenets of Realist IRT will help us discover why.

REALISTS ON HUMAN NATURE

In our survey of the Liberal tradition we saw that the essential goodness of human beings was the touchstone of much Liberal thought. In order to understand state-on-state relations Liberals extrapolate up from this essential goodness at the lowest level of international affairs to the level of the international system. They use the domestic analogy to explain international relations, with individual human agents in a national society replaced by state agents living in a condition of anarchy. Liberals argue that people do not want to fight each other unnecessarily, and if their opinions can be voiced democratically to their governments, cooperation can and will occur at the international level through the medium of international organizations and institutions. But what if human beings are not peace-loving? What if they are aggressive, constantly expressing a lust for power and a will to dominate? What stops them if they wish to do harm to others? It is on this other side of the coin that Realist theory works its considerable magic over the discipline.

HOBBES AND THE STATE OF NATURE

An excellent way to get to grips with the basics of Realist thought is to see how the English political and legal philosopher Thomas Hobbes (1588–1679) viewed the dynamics of political life. His 1651 work *Leviathan* contains an analysis of human nature which has become central to Realist IRT. Hobbes tried to think through what the world would be like in a 'state of nature' – a world in which men and women live together but before the 'invention' of sovereign states.

In such a world humans revert to animalistic behaviour because this is a world in which no one is safe from the potentially harmful behaviour of others. Trust on all sides is lacking; fear of the outside is pervasive. As Jackson and Sørensen put it (2007: 65) 'life is constantly at risk, and nobody can be confident about his or her security and survival for any reasonable length of time. People are living in constant fear of each other'. In a state of nature there is nothing to regulate people's behaviour; no consequences for uncivilized behaviour towards others. This Hobbesian world of self-interested individuals looking to protect their safety and security produces a 'state of war' in which, as he famously puts it, life is 'solitary, poor, nasty, brutish, and short' (Hobbes 2007: Part I, Book 13). It is the 'dog eat dog' approach to societal relations.

Realism and human nature in *Shutter Island*

Based on the novel by Denis Lehane (2003) the 2010 film *Shutter Island* tells the story of Teddy Daniels (Leonardo diCaprio), a confused individual seeking, but more often than not in conflict with, memories of his past. The story unfolds in and around Ashecliffe Hospital for the Criminally Insane, overseen by the sinister Dr Lester Sheehan (Ben Kingsley). The location for the movie is the eponymous Shutter Island, reminiscent of the isolated

Alcatraz prison off the coast of San Francisco, only reachable by boat. The film is about separation, madness, pain, control, escape, and the blurring of fiction and reality. In that regard it is much like the average lecture in IRT. Ashecliffe, apparently, is where bad things happen to people who have done bad things in their lives. The movie is full of fear, suspense, edginess and the constant threat of violence.

About two-thirds of the way through Teddy goes exploring the island trying to uncover more information to piece together what is going on. He bumps into the warden who gives him a lift back to the main hospital. On the way the warden discusses his view of human nature. Violence, he remarks, is 'God's gift … God loves violence'. Teddy (standing in for the Liberal, optimistic approach to IRT) says he does not understand this position. 'Why else would there be so much of it?' asks the Warden. 'It's in us. It comes out of us. It is what we do more naturally than we breathe. We wage war. We burn sacrifices. We pillage and tear at the flesh of our brothers. We fill great fields with our stinking dead. And why? To show Him that we have learnt from His example.' With Teddy shocked into contemplative silence, the warden rams the message home. 'He gave us lust and fury and greed and our filthy hearts. So that we could wage war in His honor. There is no moral order as pure as this storm we've just seen. There is no moral order at all. There is only this – can my violence conquer yours?' (Lehane 2003: 244–5).

Lehane's warden should have been a Realist IR theorist. He is a pessimist, sees the worst in humans as the timeless product of Original Sin, and treats states as flawed entities clashing with each other out of greed, selfishness and a lust for power, control and domination.

HOBBES AND THE INTERNATIONAL STATE OF NATURE

The Hobbesian world is not a nice one. Unfortunately, he argued, things do not get much better when people come together to try and get around the problems of living in this state of nature. In order to overcome their fear of each other, one approach is to create states in which men and women agree not to harm each other. These states are ruled by sovereign governments which have the 'absolute authority and credible power to protect them from both internal disorders and foreign enemies and threats' (Jackson and Sørensen 2007: 65). However, when different groups of men and women constitute themselves into distinct states to overcome their fear of each other, we then have the creation of a state of nature *between* all these different states. Where before it was people living in fear for their own livelihoods and security, it is now states experiencing this same fear. This is the classic Realist **security**

dilemma: the enhancement of security at the domestic level (within states) goes hand in hand with the creation of insecurity at the international level. The agent or unit of analysis has altered from humans to states, treated as singular entities with given interests, but the central problematic has not changed. Anarchy within states is replaced by anarchy at the international level.

Hobbes gave IR theorists two key concepts: self-help and the security dilemma. As you go through your course keep a record of how each theorist you study uses (or not) these concepts. What do they mean by them, and why are they more important in some theories than others?

Why is it different at the international level? Why can states not come together to resolve their mutual security issues as men and women can? The main difference is in the parties to the contract. Whereas individuals are happy to give up some of their independence to a state government in return for a resolution of their personal security dilemmas, 'sovereign states are not willing to give up their independence for the sake of any global security guarantee' (Jackson and Sørensen 2007: 66).

Why is this? Because the international state of nature is not perceived to be as threatening to states as the original state of nature is perceived to be to men and women living in it. States are better placed to provide for their security than are the individuals in a state of nature because they are less vulnerable. Jackson and Sørensen point out, for example (2007: 66), that unlike men and women states do not have to sleep, they can be permanently on the alert and have more means with which to fend off potential attackers. The rise of the security state is testament to the material means states have at their disposal to safeguard them against potential threats and challenges.

Hobbesian or classical Realism attributes human characteristics to states: it is **reductionist**. How realistic do you think it is to explain state behaviour in the same way we explain human behaviour? What do the two have in common – or is the state of nature the guiding influence on the behaviour of both?

REALISTS ON POWER

If you are a human living in the original state of nature, or a state existing in the international state of nature, it is obviously useful to have 'power' of some kind to help you out. Possession of 'power' will either help protect you from the aggression of other humans/states, or you can use your power to enable you to extract what you want from other humans/states. Power can coerce others; it can compel them to act in ways they might not otherwise; and power can deter others from attacking you. Possess power, possess more security. But how much security is enough?

'Power' is another of those IR terms that crops up in many theories. Keep track of all the different ways in which it is understood by theorists. How many different definitions can you find and why is it such a popular word in IR?

Where does the interest in power come from and how does it feature in Realist IRT? We can find out how by looking at how three Realist writers, one classical and three modern, use power to inform their explanations of IR.

THE 'TIMELESS WISDOM' OF THUCYDIDES

The enduring anarchic character of international politics accounts for the striking sameness in the quality of international life through the millennia, a statement that will meet with wide assent. (Waltz 2010)

Thucydides was a fifth-century Athenian general who wrote *History of the Peloponnesian War*, documenting the conflict between Athens and Sparta in 431–404 BC (Thucydides 2004). This work of history has inspired many a Realist to take a 'tragic view of life and politics' spanning a period of over 2,500 years (Lebow 2007: 54). Claiming a timeless wisdom for Thucydides' work gives Realists a real propaganda coup when it comes to attracting support for their explanations of international affairs because they can portray them as being applicable far beyond 'any condition or attribute of the modern world … but … as a central feature of prior epochs as well' (Sterling-Folker 2006e: 15; see also Little 2005: 46). Alongside Thucydides we find (Niccolò) Machiavelli, Hobbes, (Benedict De) Spinoza and (Jean-Jacques) Rousseau marshalled together in the 'classical' Realist canon (Forde 1996). James Der Derian remarks that in the 'eternal return of the ghost' of the classical writers such as Thucydides, writers like Robert Gilpin (1984) can claim 'transhistorical power' for their actually historically situated and context-bound readings of the global past (Der Derian 1995: 383).

As Stanley Hoffman has observed (1995: 239–40): 'Much of the study of power in international affairs has been remarkably Athenian'. Thucydides tells the story of an age of a few 'great powers' and many lesser powers, an inequality that was 'considered to be inevitable and natural' (Jackson and Sørensen 2007: 62; for an overview of Thucydides and his work see Nye and Welch 2011: 16–21). Thucydides' harsh dictum was that in order to survive and prosper states had to adapt to the reality they found themselves in. They needed to make pragmatic assessments of their relative size and capabilities and conduct themselves accordingly to stay safe – from here you can trace a line to Hobbes' international state of nature. Thucydides opened the way for a discussion of morality and justice in the conduct of foreign policy that later Realists such as Hans Morgenthau would build upon.

Most treatments of Thucydides concentrate on the passage from the 'Melian dialogue' of 416 BC where he highlights how power relations played out between the powerful Athenians and the weaker Melians: 'the strong do what they can and the weak suffer what they must' (quoted in Mearsheimer 2001: 163). Yet it is not simply what Thucydides said but his whole approach to writing his history that should be of interest to you in terms of understanding the Realist tradition in IRT. Gregory Crane makes this point by writing that 'Thucydides' *History* exhibits four characteristics common to many "realist" schools of thought – not only political, but literary, artistic, and scientific' (Crane 1998: Chapter 2). Realism, like all IR theories you will cover, is much more than a list of foreign policy maxims. It is a way of seeing the world and of writing about it, so studying Thucydides can be doubly instructive. Let us take each of Crane's observations in turn.

1 **Procedural Realism.** Thucydides 'insisted upon a high level of observational accuracy', involving 'careful observation and precise reporting'. He castigated previous historians (such as Herodotus on the Persian wars) for inaccuracies and located himself firmly in what we know as the positivist tradition of assuming

a world external from him which he could experience and report on objectively. Thucydides did not just not rely on the merits of his account to speak for themselves, he knocked down rival approaches. IR theorists enjoy doing this too.

Scientific Realism. Follows from procedural realism. Thucydides was well aware of the methodological problems he encountered in trying to report the evolution of the Peloponnesian War, but was nonetheless convinced such a task was possible. He wrote of examining 'the facts themselves' to get at the truth of this long conflict.

Ideological Realism. In setting his account against less faithful and slipshod histories, Thucydides could claim that only he had 'a monopoly on truth'. He placed his work directly in opposition to 'idealism', which he took to mean 'the pursuit of an attractive, but ultimately ill-founded, vision of the world'. By stressing his emotional detachment, Thucydides could claim a special authority for his work that he denied to fanciful histories not rooted in observed facts and faithfully reported. Unlike those imagined histories, Thucydides dealt with the 'real world'.

Paradigmatic Realism. Using a word popularized by the philosopher of science, Thomas Kuhn, Crane suggests we should see Thucydides' self-proclaimed advances towards objective history as a shift in **paradigm** (see also Holsti 1985). Thucydides set down a new method for history and set more demanding benchmarks by which histories should be judged. But in doing so things got lost, some methods fell into abeyance, facts were overlooked. For example, Thucydides privileged military and political history; he ignored the role of women in Greek society and the conduct of the war. Thucydides' new paradigm claimed objectivity, completeness and impartiality, but like all paradigms of scientific inquiry we find that we perhaps see what we want to see. Can social scientific inquiry ever be impartial?

REALISM IN THE INTER-WAR YEARS

Echoes of both the style and substance of Thucydides' *History* are to be found in Realist IRT. Three writers spanning three-quarters of a century illustrate this: E.H. Carr, Hans Morgenthau and John J. Mearsheimer.

E.H. CARR

Carr's reflections on international relations were held in high regard because he was a mover and shaker in both the political and academic worlds. He worked as a diplomat in the British Foreign Office between 1916 and 1936. As we have seen already (see Chapter 1.4) these were tragic decades encompassing the First World War and its volatile aftermath, as well as being IR's formative years as a distinct discipline of academic study. Carr's attitudes to international relations were strongly influenced by both sets of events. In 1936, Carr resigned from the Foreign Office to take up a Chair (Professorship) in International Relations at what was then Aberystwyth University. While a student at Cambridge University it might well be noteworthy that Carr had studied Herodotus' account of the Persian Wars and was clearly acquainted with the work of Thucydides (Carr 2001b: xi, 81 and 104).

A 'sustained critique of the way in which utopian thought had dominated international relations in the inter-war years' (Hollis and Smith 1991: 21). This is how Martin Hollis and Steve Smith correctly summarize the crux of E.H. Carr's *The Twenty Years' Crisis* (2001a), which was first published in 1939. What did Carr mean by 'utopian thought', and why did he attack it? Carr was dissatisfied with the key tenets of Liberal thought we identified in Chapter 2.1. He branded it 'utopian' in order to contrast it with an approach he deemed more 'realistic' – Realism. According to what Carr took to be utopian thought, human progress is achieved by essential human goodness being allowed to flourish in democratic states. These democratic processes are replicated and enhanced at the international level through international organizations where disputes can be resolved peaceably through dialogue between states. Taking the distinction we drew between international organizations and international institutions in Chapter 2.1, Carr focused more on the former than the latter, criticizing organizations for trying to control state behaviour through rules and laws.

For Carr, however, *willing* world peace was not the same as *achieving* world peace. Practical products of Liberal thought, such as the League of Nations, did not take into account realities that had to be dealt with in the world of foreign policy-making such as power, cunning and the use of force. Thus, Carr argued that Liberals had got everything the wrong way round. Instead of developing a theory (of human nature and IR) and trying to mould reality to fit the theory, they should be looking at the reality and building theory to explain it. Utopian thinking, he believed, had 'delayed the advent of social science' (Hoffman 1995: 215).

On your IR course you are more than likely to find Carr presented as a founding father of the classical Realist tradition in the UK and US, so it is well worth looking at the 2001 version of *The Twenty Years' Crisis*. This contains an excellent introduction by Michael Cox that interrogates the view that Carr was a Realist thinker.

CARR'S CONTEXT: A REALIST REALITY

The reality of the inter-war years in Carr's eyes was that international anarchy led inexorably to war and conflict in the international system. That his book was first published on the eve of the Second World War (1939–45) must have helped convince his audiences in the political and academic worlds that international reality in 1919–39 was a Realist rather than a Liberal reality. He was certainly on to something.

Two issues in particular helped persuade Carr of this conclusion. First, the collapse of the League of Nations undermined Liberalism's explanation of international political relations. The outbreak of the Second World War confirmed what many had feared for many years previously, that the League, established in accordance with Wilsonian principles in 1919, did not have the diplomatic, political or military clout to prevent inter-state wars. The rise and actions of the Axis powers, Germany, Italy and Japan, further showed Carr the truth of the Thucydidean principle that 'might is right' – the powerful do what they want, the weak do what they can.

Second, the Great Depression in the US, and the global recession it produced, undermined Liberalism's claim that free trade would promote harmonious international economic relations between states. Economic statistics from this period offer a glimpse of the scale of the depression: US unemployment rose from 3 per cent in 1929 to over 25 per cent in 1933 (Darby, cited in Schenk 1997–2006). Over the same four-year period, US Gross National Product halved from well over $100 billion per quarter to just over $50 billion per quarter (Moore, cited in Schenk 1997–2006). In Carr's view, inter-war international economic disorder on this scale showed the frailty of the assumption that letting the free market do its work would promote global economic harmony, as the Liberals suggested. What was called for was new economic thinking, and this meant interventionist policies to promote full employment, equality and social justice. Carr was helped to this view by the success of the Russian five-year economic plans from 1929, which contrasted sharply with the downturn in the capitalist world over the same period.

From Carr to Cameron: the Realist tradition into the twenty-first century

It is argued that Realism has taken a firm hold in (especially but not exclusively) Western foreign policy establishments since its popularization in the inter-war and post-war years. By this we mean that for one reason or another (the transmission mechanisms are surely too complex to nail down precisely) core Realist tenets about international security and global order have become the dominant lens through which policy-makers interpret and act upon the actions of other states in the system. Foreign policy speeches are quite rich sources of evidence on which theory is doing best, practice-wise, at any given time.

In opposition, Conservative leader David Cameron, now British Prime Minister, and William Hague, now British Foreign Secretary, developed an understanding of British foreign policy they called 'liberal Conservatism'. They spelt out its implications in a series of speeches, both men sticking to a tightly worded script. In the two quotations that follow the underlined words show Liberal themes, the italics show themes the English School might privilege, and the bold font indicates Realist themes.

David Cameron: 'I am a liberal Conservative, rather than a neo-conservative. Liberal – because I support the aim of spreading freedom and democracy, and support *humanitarian intervention*. **Conservative** – because I recognise the **complexities of human nature**, and am **sceptical of grand schemes to remake the world**' (Cameron 2006).

William Hague: 'David Cameron and I have spoken in recent years of our approach to foreign affairs being based on 'Liberal **Conservatism**' in that we believe in freedom, human rights and democracy and want to see more of these things in other nations. But **Conservative**, because we believe strongly in the **continued relevance of the nation state** and are **sceptical of grand utopian schemes to re-make the world**' (Hague 2009).

This rough and ready piece of text analysis shows the place of Realism in contemporary foreign policy thought in the UK. The government has come to the conclusion that foreign policy must have a 'conscience', see for example the Libya intervention of 2011. However, crusading neo-conservativism is not for Cameron or Hague. In Carr-esque fashion they believe the world will not be re-made easily or quickly; we have to work pragmatically with what we have (human nature and nation-states) and be cautious about what we can achieve. Their foreign policy outlook has Liberal-English School leanings but ultimately entails a critique of utopianism and takes British foreign policy towards a Realist understanding of international affairs. Realist IRT has proved remarkably durable both in terms of language and practice.

REALISM AFTER THE SECOND WORLD WAR: MORGENTHAU

As Robert Jervis has remarked, 'the experience of Hitler was a greater sponsor of Realism than any written text could be' (Jervis 1994). Although Carr went a long way to expounding the core principles of the Realist tradition it was left to Hans Morgenthau to develop them in a rigorous 'scientific' fashion. Morgenthau was a German émigré to the US who arrived there two years before the outbreak of the Second World War, having spent his early career teaching public law in Geneva and Madrid. His major IR-related books were written while he worked as a political scientist in various US universities (*Encyclopedia of World Biography* 2005–6). His *Politics Among Nations*, first published in 1948, responded directly to Carr's call for IR to be studied 'scientifically' and he developed IR's appreciation of power and used this to inform his six principles of political realism. Hoffman (1995: 216–18) credits Morgenthau with being the true founder of the discipline of IR in the US, because he used his work to instruct US policy-makers dealing with their new-found global power after the Second World War.

Morgenthau (1985) suggested that a nation's power stems from many interconnected elements. First, its geography could be important; for example the size and position of the US or Britain's separation from the Continent of Europe by the English Channel. Second, its natural resources such as food and raw materials could be key, with self-sufficiency the ideal state because it diminishes the reliance on other nations for the basic means of survival. Third, nations require the industrial capacity to get the best out of the available natural resources. Fourth, they need military preparedness to support the preferred foreign policy orientation of the nation.

Fifth, not size but the ability and preparedness of the population to apply the material implements of national power is crucial. Sixth, he stipulates the presence of 'national character'. Seventh, 'national morale' or the determination with which a nation supports the foreign policy of the government in peace and war is deemed to be important. Eighth, and 'the most important factor', is the quality of a nation's diplomacy. Ninth, the quality of government in allocating resources and sustaining support for its policies at home is a further vital element.

The conduct of both domestic and international politics can be understood, Morgenthau argues (1985: 4–17), if we appreciate that:

1 **Politics has its roots in human nature.** As Jack Donnelly observes (1996: 86), 'Human nature is the starting point for realism. And the core of human nature, for realists, lies in the

egoistic passions, which incline men and women to evil'. This nature is essentially as Hobbes described it and it has not changed over thousands of years (Morgenthau elaborates in his third principle). If we take this as one of several 'objective laws' of politics, we 'must also believe in the possibility of developing a rational theory that reflects ... these objective laws'. This possibility exists because we also assume that we can untangle 'truth' (deduced rationally from evidence) from 'opinion' (subjective judgement divorced from facts).

2 **Foreign policy-makers 'think and act in terms of interest defined as power'.** In international politics, power political considerations are everything, whereas ethics, morals, economics and religion are all subservient. They might be used to 'dress up' foreign policies to make them palatable for public consumption, but these policies should and will be all about preserving the national interest (is that what Cameron and Hague were doing in their speeches analysed above?). Morgenthau's assumption 'infuses rational order into the subject matter of politics, and thus makes the theoretical understanding of politics possible'. We can only measure the quality of foreign policy decisions in terms of the extent to which they enhance a state's security; in other words, with regard to the extent to which they are 'rational' decisions.

3 **(i) Humans are basically self-interested, as are states.** Relations between humans and states play out via politics at the domestic and international levels respectively, and this is where their different interests are liable to collide. **(ii) A state's definition and use of power depend on the cultural and political context within which it is exercised.** Put broadly, power 'covers all social relationships which serve that end, from physical violence to the most subtle psychological ties by which one mind controls another'. Transforming the contemporary world means working with these enduring realities of international political life: interest and power.

4 **We can only judge the morality of a leader's actions on the basis of a careful examination of the choices open to him or her at a particular point in time.** There is no universal moral code by which we can judge such actions. 'The ethics of international relations is a political or situational ethics' (Jackson and Sørensen 2007: 70).

5 **No nation has the right to claim its moral code as the world's moral code, or to impose its ideology on others.** Such folly 'is liable to engender the distortion in judgment which, in the blindness of crusading frenzy, destroys nations and civilizations'. In fact, one test of morality is the extent to which we respect the decisions of others to live and act differently from ourselves. Here we see the Realist basis for criticizing campaigning neo-conservative approaches to foreign policy, for example the Iraq invasion of 2003.

6 **Restatement of the autonomy of the political sphere with examples of how it works in practice.** 'The economist asks: "How does this policy affect the wealth of society, or a segment of it?" The lawyer asks: "Is this policy in accord with the rules of law?" The moralist asks: "Is this policy in accord with moral principles?" And the political realist asks: "How does this policy affect the power of the nation?" International politics is not for the faint of heart but we cannot wish human nature away.'

JOHN J. MEARSHEIMER

The title of Mearsheimer's most famous book, *The Tragedy of Great Power Politics* (2001), sets him firmly in the Thucydidean camp. Mearsheimer is an **offensive realist** (not literally) as opposed to a **defensive realist**. Defensive realists such as Waltz, whose Neorealism we encounter in the next chapter, maintain that states are mainly interested in survival and above all they seek security. There is a competition for power because it is the best means to survive in a condition of anarchy. However, such competition as there is does not flow from the search for power for its own sake (Mearsheimer 2001: 19). As Charles Glaser has suggested (1994/95), Realists can be optimists too! Out of a strongly Realist self-help system can come the impulsion to cooperate.

Offensive realists are those like Morgenthau who root the conduct of international politics in the aggressive impulses of human nature. In this image international relations are the product of fallen humans (states) seeking self aggrandizement and lusting after power and domination on the world stage. It is a world of would-be Hitlers and Mussolinis, so well captured by the Shutter Island warden in his speech studied earlier in the chapter. Violence is not something done to others out of self-defence; there is almost a sense of enjoyment about it, a grotesque revelry in bloodshed. Offensive realists believe the security dilemma will never truly give rise to a status quo because states are potentially revisionist by virtue of exhibiting the same characteristics as human beings.

Like Carr and Morgenthau, Mearsheimer has written a wide-ranging text which is difficult to summarize in a few lines. However, his explication of the five 'bedrock assumptions' on which he theorizes offensive realism serve as a useful way of summarizing the general thrust of Realist IRT (from Mearsheimer 2001: 30–32):

1 **The international system is anarchic.** This ordering principle means that states have no overarching authority above them, telling them what to do.

2 **Great powers inherently possess some military capability which they can use to hurt and even destroy each other**. Nuclear weapons are potentially the most devastating way in which this can be achieved, but they are certainly not the only way of causing harm on a large scale and definitely have not been the most frequently used. 'After all', writes Mearsheimer rather depressingly, 'for every neck, there are two hands to choke it'.

3 **States can never be certain about other states' intentions.** States do not always have hostile intentions, but even supposedly benign states might be masking ulterior motives, and intentions can change quickly. The possession of any offensive capability (including human beings, as Mearsheimer states in assumption 2) offers the potential for conflict at any moment in time, day or night.

4 **Survival is the main goal for great powers.** They want to maintain their territorial integrity and the autonomy of their domestic political order. Security is their most important objective.

5 **Great powers are rational actors.** They are aware of their external environment 'and they think strategically about how to survive in it'. They think about how their behaviour affects the behaviour of other states in an endless game of power politics.

From these assumptions, Mearsheimer goes on to build a theory of offensive realism based on patterns of behaviour that cause states to act aggressively to one another: fear, self-help and power maximization. The rest of the book is a historically based series of case studies of great power rivalry and expansion over recent centuries, allowing Mearsheimer to highlight the recurring patterns in international relations over long periods of time. In his account, the relative peace of the 1990s are something of an anomaly. Growing instability and violence in the twenty-first century has returned the international system to its 'normal' or Realist condition. His final recommendation is policy driven: 'It would be a grave mistake, however, for the United States to turn its back on realist principles that have served it well since its founding' (Mearsheimer 2001: 402).

SUMMARY ON LIBERAL AND REALIST IRT

This chapter and Chapter 2.1 have provided a necessarily brief overview of the Realist and Liberal traditions in IR. It is up to you to generate a deeper appreciation of these traditions by reading around them as widely as you can. Let us recap some of the key elements by way of summary: first, Realists and Liberals share key assumptions about IR; second, they draw on different sources of evidence for their arguments; third, where Realists see conflict, insecurity and the perpetual threat of war between states, Liberals emphasize the possibilities for peace brought about by cooperation and international institutions; fourth, both theories make claims about how accurate/reliable they are based on appeals to history and tradition; finally, neither theory is monolithic – they have different 'wings' to them, for example the debate between organizationalists and institutionalists in Liberalism and that between offensive and defensive Realists. In the next chapter we will see how both theories have been updated in the form of Neoliberalism and Neorealism.

Realists tend to have a more pessimistic view of IR than Liberals. How would you describe your own view of IR: more optimistic or pessimistic? On what do you base this view?

QUESTIONS TO PONDER

'How relevant is Thucydides to the contemporary study of international relations?'

A good place to begin is to set out the claims on behalf of Thucydides made by IR scholars – Realist scholars in particular. One way to do this is to make a note of all the writers who show direct knowledge of his work (for example, Carr, Morgenthau and Mearsheimer), and they can form the basis of one side of the argument, that Thucydides *is* relevant.

Equally, however, there will be writers who disagree. They proceed by questioning the utility of understanding contemporary international politics by looking at political relations between Greek city-states thousands of years ago, and attacking some of the Thucydidean/Realist assumptions about human nature, security, power, morality and the lust for violence. Here you can use Realism's traditional opponent, Liberalism, to make the case that it is not only Thucydides but the entire tradition inspired by him that misconstrues the nature of contemporary IR. You could profitably bring in 'Realist optimists' such as Glaser to add critical depth to the view that this is a simple contrast between Realist pessimists and optimistic Liberals.

David A. Welch has written an article entitled 'Why IR Theorists Should Stop Reading Thucydides' (2003). When you come across provocative articles like this, you should certainly read them – they provide you with a whole set of tools for challenging established theoretical positions.

Remember throughout the essay to make a central argument about 'relevance'. It is quite hard to set benchmarks, so one approach when planning your answer might be to give Thucydides a very simple score out of 10. If you think he's a 9/10: why? If you think he's a 2/10: why? Presumably if you are a Realist, your score will be higher than if you agree more with other IR theories.

'What role does morality play in Realist IR theory?'

This question invites you to consider the core assumptions and arguments about IR put forward by Realist theorists, and to gauge the place they give morality in the conduct of international politics. To begin with you will have to specify what you mean by 'Realist', so explain which theorist or set of theorists you take to be representative of the tradition. In this chapter we have explored a few seminal writers but there are dozens to choose from.

You next need to highlight where morality features in, say, the works of three writers you take to be representative of the tradition. You could see how these writers approach questions of morality in the international sphere in a number of ways. For instance, explore their views on private and public morality and consider how for writers such as Morgenthau there is no universal moral code – morality is to be judged in the context of particular decisions at particular times. Power is more of a concern to Realist writers, that and safeguarding the national interest.

You might also think laterally by comparing how the 'average' Realist writer treats morality compared to the 'average' Liberal writer, emerging with the conclusion that morality plays less of a role in this theoretical tradition than in others – or perhaps it is more accurate to say a more ambiguous role. The speeches by Cameron and Hague, explored above, highlight the confusing place ethics hold in much contemporary Western foreign policy thinking. To a degree, Realist thought itself struggles to quieten a concern with normative concerns – what 'ought' to be done can implicitly appear within supposedly impartial descriptions of what 'is' done. This kind of additional material might provide you with a case study to develop if you can track the overlooked ethical components of Realist thought (in Morgenthau for example).

REFERENCES TO MORE INFORMATION

For coverage of the general themes and issues pertinent to the Realist tradition:

Gilpin, R.G. (1984) 'The Richness of the Tradition of Political Realism', *International Organization*, 38(2): 287–304.

Jervis, R. (1978) 'Cooperation under the Security Dilemma', *World Politics*, 30(2): 167–214.
   Explication of the defensive Realist approach. These are Realists operating at the most optimistic end of the spectrum of Realist theory.

Williamson, D. (2003) *War and Peace: International Relations, 1919–39*, 2nd edn. London: Hodder and Stoughton.

Herz, J.H. (1959) *International Relations in the Nuclear Age*. New York: Columbia University Press.
   Shows the link between Realist thinking and events 'on the ground' during the formative years of the Cold War.

Hirst, P. (2001) *War and Power in the 21st Century*. Cambridge: Polity.
   See Chapter 2 on the international system since 1648 and Chapter 4 debating possible futures for the international system.

Mearsheimer, J.J. (2003) 'Conversations with History: John J. Mearsheimer', 8 April, http://conversations.berkeley.edu/content/john-mearsheimer and on Youtube, www.youtube.com/watch?v=AKFamUu6dGw. Discusses the Realist tradition and US foreign policy and role in the world.

James, A. (1989) 'The Realism of Realism: The State and the Study of International Relations', *Review of International Studies*, 15(3): 222–6.

On Thucydides and his legacy:
Chittick, W.O. and Freyberginan, A. (2000) '"Chiefly for Fear, Next for Honour, and Lastly for Profit": An Analysis of Foreign Policy Motivation in the Peloponnesian War', *Review of International Studies*, 27(1): 69–90.

Bagby, L.M.J. (1994) 'The Use and Abuse of Thucydides in International Relations', *International Organization*, 48(1): 131–53.
Argues that Realists deploy Thucydides rather simplistically and offers alternative readings that are more useful, especially to foreign policy practitioners.

Monten, J. (2006) 'Thucydides and Modern Realism', *International Studies Quarterly*, 50(1): 3–26.
A further reassessment of Thucydides' Realist credentials.

Critical work on the Realist canon:
Beitz, C.R. (1979) *Political Theory and International Relations*. Princeton, NJ: Princeton University Press.
Elaborates the theory of cosmopolitanism through a critique of the state-centricity of Realism, especially its assumption that states exist in a Hobbesian self-help environment. Useful if you want to critique Realist theory.

Cozette, M. (2008) 'Reclaiming the Critical Dimension of Realism: Hans J. Morgenthau on the Ethics of Scholarship', *Review of International Studies*, 34(1): 5–27.
Reassesses Morgenthau's credentials as a critical thinker about IR through a close reading of his work on truth, power and the ethics of scholarship.

Similar in intention to:
Bain, W. (2000) 'Deconfusing Morgenthau: Moral Inquiry and Classical Realism Reconsidered', *Review of International Studies*, 26(3): 445–64.

Guzzini, S. (1998) *Realism in International Relations and International Political Economy: The Continuing Story of a Death Foretold*. London: Routledge.
Considers the theory, practices and crises in Realist thought as well as the Neorealist response to these crises in the theory (see the next chapter in this book).

Gilpin, R. (2002) 'A Realist Perspective on International Governance', in D. Held and A. McGrew (eds) *Governing Globalization: Power, Authority and Global Governance*. Cambridge: Polity, pp. 237–48.

Waltz, K.N. (2008) *Realism and International Politics*. New York: Routledge. A collection of Waltz's essays from across his career. Part I on theory includes responses to critics and is particularly useful.

2.3 NEOREALISM AND NEOLIBERALISM

Key Terms

- Anarchy
- State
- System
- Balance of power
- Rationality
- Regimes
- Political Economy

The debate between the Neorealists and the Neoliberals emerged in the 1970s and developed over the next two decades into the major theoretical controversy within IR. Each body of writing is strongly rooted in the 'classical' variants of Realism and Liberalism discussed in the previous two chapters, taking nascent ideas from these traditions in new directions. With the emergence of the Neo-Neo debate, as it is sometimes called, we see how theoretical innovations in the field of IR continue to take a good deal of inspiration from changes in the international political, strategic and economic context. We begin this chapter by considering Kenneth Waltz's brand of Neorealism and move on to the Neoliberal reaction which took a variety of forms, but which is largely associated with work on cooperation occurring in regimes and institutions.

NEOREALISM

In the previous chapter we pulled out key Realist assumptions, arguments and approaches by looking at the work of E.H. Carr, Hans Morgenthau and John Mearsheimer. We saw that in the early Realism which emerged through the inter-war years and took hold of the discipline especially tightly after the Second World War, inter-state war and conflict was explained at two levels:

- **Level 1: Human nature.** Inspired by Hobbesian ideas about human insecurity in a state of nature, writers such as Morgenthau argued that if we understand the failings in human nature and the condition of insecurity in which we live, we understand most of the dynamics of international politics. Fear and mistrust of other agents 'out there' is exaggerated by a lust for power which can be another potential cause of conflict.
- **Level 2: State interests in a condition of anarchy.** By transposing Hobbes' state of nature onto the realm of the international we can explain international relations with reference to the quest for security on the part of self-interested and perpetually insecure states. Waltz developed Realist thinking on 'defensive' realism, arguing that states generally want to survive and seek to enhance their security to the degree necessary to achieve this. Mearsheimer's 'offensive' realism argues that states are as flawed as individual humans in a state of nature. Their ongoing quest for power and domination over the system causes instability, even when a notional balance of power is in operation.

One of Waltz's key works, *Man, the State and War* (1959), echoed Morgenthau and Carr's treatment of international relations as a never-ending series of conflicts among states trapped in a condition of anarchy, and was pitched largely at the levels of analysis outlined above. Twenty years later, Waltz went a stage further, publishing his *Theory of International Politics*, in which he sought to explain the causes of wars more systematically than Realists had previously managed. 'It is not possible', he wrote, 'to understand world politics simply by looking inside of states' (Waltz 2010: 65). He suggested that for a viable theory of international relations to exist we need to focus on a third, higher, level. 'The repeated failure of attempts to explain international outcomes analytically – that is, through examination of interacting units [levels 1 and 2] – *strongly signals the need for a systems approach*' (Waltz 2010: 68, my emphasis). We do not explain international politics with reference to its principal actors but with regard to observable phenomena at the system level. Investigating this new level 3 helps us account for the remarkably stable and predictable interactions between quite differently organized states over long periods of time, particularly their propensity to engage in war.

We build level 3 theory by:

1 Conceiving international politics as a bounded realm, distinct from what goes on within states.

2 Discovering law-like regularities in international politics.

3 Explaining these observed regularities.

4 Identifying the units in the system.

5 Specifying the comparative weight of systemic and sub-systemic causes of continuity (and change) in the system.

6 Showing how forces and effects change from one system to another.

Explaining IR via the behaviour of states took us some way towards a genuine theory, Waltz argued, but there was a crucial dimension missing. He observed that the Capitalist US and the Communist USSR both sought out military power and influence and competed for strategic advantage, for example, by conducting 'proxy' wars in Latin America. The question that exercised him was *why* the similar behaviour when the ideologies of each state were so different? If international anarchy exists, yet we cannot explain state behaviour using either of the two levels previously identified by Realist writers, then we need to search for an additional factor. Waltz argued that this factor was the international system itself, which compels states to preserve their security by constantly building up their power. Waltz's structural realism is captured in his concept of the **balance of power**, which structures systemic level interactions between units in any given period and is 'defined by the arrangement of the system's parts and by the principle of that arrangement' (Waltz 2010: 80).

THE BALANCE OF POWER AND STABILITY THEORY

'If there is any distinctively political theory of international politics, balance-of-power theory is it' wrote Waltz (2010: 117). Waltz assumed that: states are essentially unitary, rational actors; that they give priority to ensuring their own security; and that they exist in an international realm characterized by anarchy (Glaser 1994/95: 54). He said that to explain international relations the idea of the *system* is all important, defining a system as a set of interacting units exhibiting behavioural regularities and having an identity over time. In other words, a system and the changes in that system are both observable elements of international relations. In terms of states, balance of power theory assumes that they act rationally to, at minimum, seek self-preservation and, at maximum, universal domination in a self-help system. They do this in two main ways. On the one hand they use 'internal efforts'; they build up economic capability and military prowess, and 'develop clever strategies'. On the other hand they use 'external strategies' such as alliance building and attempting to weaken opposing alliances (Waltz 2010: 118).

The system is where we need to focus our attention because its units – individual states – all do the same things in that system, regardless of where they are located, their prevailing ideology, culture, and so on. They only differ in terms of their relative capabilities, and as these capabilities change so the system changes. 'In other words, international change occurs when great powers rise and fall and the balance of power shifts accordingly. A typical means of such change is great power war' (Jackson and Sørensen 2007: 76).

Waltz goes on to define two types of system:

- a **bipolar system** is one in which there are two major powers such as the US and the USSR between 1945 and 1989.
- a **multipolar system** is akin to the international states system that preceded and followed the Cold War, where many powers co-exist.

What kind of international system prevails today? Do Waltz's categories have it covered or is it something altogether different? How many 'great powers' are there in the world today? On how to measure 'great power' status see Waltz (2010) and Morris (2011).

In Waltz's view (2010: 161) 'few are better than many', and bipolar systems are more stable than multipolar systems, albeit not *that* stable if the powers are great powers (Waltz 2010: 163); yet in theory at least 'with only two great powers, both can be expected to act to maintain the system' (Waltz 2010: 204), because it is in their respective interests to keep the status quo as it is. In a multipolar system there is less incentive for states to act in this way, both because the potential for control is far less, and because the potential outcome of their actions is far less, certain. Rationally calculating the outcome of state actions is easier in bipolar systems, and successfully imposing one or other great power's will on other actors in the system is easier too.

So what, in sum, are the continuities and changes between Realism and Neorealism?

- **Continuity** – Waltz assumes states are the key actors, that there is a condition of anarchy and that international relations are shaped by power politics. He contrasts the ordering principles of hierarchy which pertains at the domestic level with that of anarchy at the international level: 'National politics is the realm of authority, of administration, and of law. International politics is the realm of power, of struggle, and of accommodation' (Waltz 2010: 113).
- **Continuity** – Waltz assumes states are trapped in an international state of nature, leading them to focus on security and survival in a self-help system.
- **Change** – Waltz does not root his explanation of international relations in Hobbesian theories of human nature, *à la* Morgenthau, although the echoes of levels 1 and 2 are rarely far from the surface of *Theory of International Politics*, for instance: 'States, like people, are insecure in proportion to the extent of their freedom. If freedom is wanted, insecurity must be accepted' (Waltz 2010: 112).
- **Change** – Waltz's structured account gives far less room for state leaders to employ cunning and skilful diplomacy, although his maxim that they 'develop clever strategies' could be interpreted as a nod to this tradition. The human facets of state-to-state interactions were qualities that Thucydides highlighted in his *History*, and which Morgenthau said could provide benchmarks for judging leaders' foreign policy decisions.
- **Change** – Waltz critiqued previous (Realist) theories of IR for paying insufficient attention to the systemic level. 'Blurring the distinction between the different levels of a system has, I believe, been the major impediment to the development of theories about international politics' (Waltz 2010: 78). Neorealism is more like a 'proper' theory because it theorizes at the systems level as well as the unit level.

To summarize, we can use the words of Hoffman: 'The Waltzian synthesis is referred to as neorealism, to indicate both its intellectual affinity with the classical realism of Morgenthau ... and its elements of originality and distinctiveness' (Keohane 1986: 15–16).

Books such as Keohane's *Neorealism and its Critics* are a great source of information. Not only do they explain the nuts and bolts of each theory, they also include chapters by critics of the theory (and sometimes responses to the critics). It is like buying two books for the price of one.

NEOLIBERALISM

Just as Neorealism accepts the basic premises of Realism and pulls them in new directions, so Neoliberalism has the same relationship with inter-war and early post-war Liberal IRT considered in Chapter 2.1. Neo-liberal IRT is an attempt to explain developments in the global political economy that gathered pace after 1945, with renewed attention 'upon the central role of institutions and organizations in international politics' (Martin 2007: 110).

Particularly influential in this tradition has been the work of Robert Keohane (1982), Keohane and Nye (1977) and Stephen Krasner (1983). Their ideas developed around the theme of relative stability in patterns of international economic cooperation despite the uneven distribution of international economic power around the globe (Martin 2007: 111). Such cooperation was all the more remarkable given the volatile nature of international relations in the 1970s brought about by such factors as:

Economics:

- The collapse of the **Bretton Woods economic system** in 1971.
- A quadrupling in the price of crude oil brought about by steep price hikes by the Organization of the Petroleum Exporting Countries (OPEC) in 1973 and 1979. This was comparable in impact to the global financial crisis, banking collapse and sovereign debt crisis, especially in the Eurozone, that has massively heightened attention to the politics of international economic relations since 2008.

Politics:

- The Yom Kippur War in the Middle East, 1973.
- The Vietnam War between North Vietnam and American-supported South Vietnam, 1959–75.
- The Soviet invasion of Afghanistan, 1979–88.
- Ongoing talks between the US and USSR over nuclear arms limitations.
- The general perception of a decline in US hegemony and the rise of powers such as Japan and blocs such as the EU (see Kratochwil and Ruggie 1986: 759).

The advance Keohane and Nye made on conventional Liberalism was to introduce the concept of **international regimes** to the vocabulary of IRT. 'International regimes have been defined as social institutions around which actor expectations converge in a given area of international relations' (Ruggie 1998a: 63). They are 'governing arrangements constructed by states to coordinate their expectations and organize aspects of international behaviour in various issue-areas. *They thus comprise a normative element, state practice, and organizational roles'* (Kratochwil and Ruggie 1986: 759, my emphasis). Regime theory assumes that: states are the main actors in world politics 'and that they use IOs to create social orderings appropriate to their pursuit of shared goals' (Abbott and Snidal 1998: 6).

The idea of looking at regimes is that cooperation takes place in international organizations such as the EU but also in forums like the **General Agreement on Tariffs and Trade (GATT)**, which was so influential on the early regimes literature (Kratochwil and Ruggie 1986: 769). Regimes were not international organizations with all the formalized rules and procedures implied by that term, but more basic international economic agreements that helped shape and regulate state behaviour. Cooperation in regimes implies complex interdependence between states which share systemic-level power and influence with other non-state and para-state actors possessing the capacity to influence state calculations about when to and when not to cooperate with each other.

Regimes are comprised of four elements: principles ('beliefs of fact, causation, and rectitude'); norms ('standards of behavior defined in terms of rights and obligations'); rules ('specific prescriptions and proscriptions for action'); and decision-making procedures ('prevailing practices for making and implementing collective choice') (Kratochwil and Ruggie 1986: 796, quoting Krasner).

Neoliberal thinking as applied to regimes is therefore founded on several main assumptions (see Lamy 2008: 132; Martin 2007: 111–12):

1 **States are the main actors** in the international system but not the only actors. 'With a disaggregated approach to authority structures, we can more meaningfully trace a middle position in which the nation-state is viewed as having declined in importance even as it still continues to be important' (Rosenau 1976: 14).

2 **States are rational actors**, weighing up the potential costs and benefits of different courses of action and choosing that course most likely to give them the highest net pay-off. 'International cooperation does not necessarily depend on altruism, idealism, personal honor, common purposes, internalized norms, or a shared belief in a set of values embedded in a culture' (Keohane 1995: 281).

3 States operate in a condition of **international anarchy** …

4 **... but cooperation is not impossible in an anarchic system** because states will 'shift loyalty and resources to institutions if these are seen as mutually beneficial and if they provide states with increasing opportunities to secure their international interests' (Lamy 2008: 132).

5 **The scope and depth of integration between states** is increasing at both the regional and global levels.

6 **'Absolute' gains are more important to states than 'relative' gains.** 'Genuine cooperation improves the rewards of both players' (Keohane 1995: 281). This is counter to the Neorealist perspective of Waltz: 'When faced with the possibility of cooperating for mutual gain, states that feel insecure must ask how the gain will be divided. They are compelled to ask not "Will both of us gain?" but "Who will gain more?"' (Waltz 2010: 105).

Absolute versus relative gains

Neorealist and Neoliberal theories differ sharply on how states interpret the potential gains to be made from cooperating in an international setting. By 'gains' we mean 'benefits that accrue to participants that cooperate' (Jackson and Sørensen 2007: 118).

Neoliberals argue that international regimes (incorporating but going beyond organizations and institutions) not only facilitate cooperation but help states make more rational choices about the outcomes of their cooperation, because states involved in these institutions are both less likely and less able to cheat by reneging on commitments. So, for example, State A whose economy currently grows at an average of 1 per cent per year will cooperate with other states in an international economic organization if it predicts that by doing so it will increase its growth rate to 5 per cent per year.

Neorealists argue it is more about the relative place of states within the international system. States will be wary of cooperating if they fear other states may benefit more than they do from participating in a cooperative venture. If we take our example from above, Neorealists would propose that if another State B with a current growth rate of 1 per cent predicted growth of 8 per cent per year by joining that international organization, then State A will be inhibited about cooperating because in *relative* terms it will be worse off inside the organization than outside it. It is the comparison/prediction element and the fear of lagging behind in relative 'power' terms that is key

(Continued)

TAKING IT FURTHER

(Continued)

for Neorealists. 'A state worries about a division of possible gains that may favor others more than itself. That is the first way in which the structure of international politics limits the cooperation of states' (Waltz 2010: 106).

CRITIQUING THE NEO-NEO AGENDA

To return to the 'problem of the subject' identified in Chapter 1.1, there was very little problem for the writers explored in Chapters 2.1 and 2.2 in defining the subject matter of IR. It was all about the nature and level of state interactions in an anarchic system. As Holsti observed, 'States and the system of states – the essential actors and their behaviour, the units of analysis – remained the centerpieces of the study of international politics from the seventeenth century until the 1970s' (Holsti 1985: 23). Realists and Neorealists were much more pessimistic about the extent to which states could transcend the self-help system and give order to their interactions than their Liberal and Neoliberal counterparts. But while they disagreed in terms of outcomes, they shared a lot in terms of assumptions and procedures for investigating international relations.

Neorealism, in particular, spawned some trenchant criticisms for its theoretical impoverishment and moral bankruptcy, not to mention its logical contradictions (most famously, Ashley 1986), and these helped feed wider dissatisfaction about the 'state of the art' in IRT during the 1990s. Writing in 1995 Steve Smith had the following to say about the Neo-Neo debate which erupted in IR in the 1980s: 'The debate is a Western, even North Atlantic one. It hardly begins to deal with the concerns of the vast majority of humanity, and very effectively silences those who do not fit into this US view of what international political is all about' (Smith 1995: 24).

In 2001, Chris Brown echoed Smith's concerns about the narrowing IR agenda at that time. He pointed out that Neoliberal scholars such as Robert Keohane essentially accepted all the basic assumptions of Neorealism, merely interpreting differently the extent of the possibilities for cooperation in an anarchic international environment. He summarized the dispute between the two as follows: the problem for Neoliberals is in maintaining cooperation, whereas for Neorealists the problem is getting cooperation going in the first place (Brown 2001: 49–50).

The upshot for Smith and Brown was that the two sets of 'neo' theories represented a dangerous narrowing of IR's disciplinary agenda. They shared many of the same contentious assumptions about the main actors on the world stage, they assumed that states were unitary, rational actors; and the task of each theory was to explain the extent to which states might or might not cooperate in international organizations and institutions, usually set up within the 'Western' world after 1945. A further assumption was that these facets of international relations could be measured scientifically and therefore accurately.

The critiques levelled at the Neo-Neo debate highlight the fact that there were other things going on in the discipline from the 1980s – new ways of defining and studying the problematic subject matter of IR. In the following chapters we consider a whole array of other theories that tend to be ignored, damagingly, when the spotlight gets put on Realism and Liberal thought. We begin with English School theory.

QUESTIONS TO PONDER

'What are the similarities and dissimilarities between Neoliberal and Neorealist theories of IR?'

It is tempting with questions such as this to fall into the trap of explaining one theory and then the other without addressing the core of the question – to compare and contrast them. Clearly you will have to demonstrate a robust working knowledge of the basis of each theory, but how much detail you include in this regard involves a judgement call on your part. Too much description will crowd out the space for analysis of the elements of overlap as well as the clear water between them. So one approach is to describe, first, Neoliberal theory, second, Neorealist theory and, third, weigh up where they overlap and where they differ. A possible problem here is that by leading off with a description of each theory, you leave yourself less time (in an exam) and space (in a coursework essay) to demonstrate to the marker that you can identify the similarities and differences between the two.

A second approach is to structure the essay in two parts: first, deal with the similarities and, second, the differences. This takes more planning, organization and knowledge of the respective traditions, but it will pay dividends because you will be getting to the heart of the matter right away. The very best answers will explain the similarities and dissimilarities and then go on to make some judgement about whether the one set outnumbers the other set. They may also take into account the metatheoretical critiques of the Neo-Neo debate by critics such as Richard Ashley, Steve Smith and Chris Brown, who argue that, compared to the theories that 'hit' the discipline through the later 1980s and 1990s, these two theories share many unfavourable qualities in common.

'Do you think Waltzian Neorealism successfully created a "proper" theory of IR?'

Your answer to this question will need to address three issues. The first is to identify what Waltzian Neorealism is. You can do this via a simple explanation of the key themes of his *Theory of International Politics*, focusing on such concepts as the international system, the balance of power and his structural account of state interactions in a condition of anarchy. Even if you don't read this early offering from Waltz, you should demonstrate familiarity with something relevant he has written on Neorealism, perhaps in a journal article. Textbooks will take you some of the way, but displaying knowledge of original Waltz would get you the most credit by far.

Having demonstrated that you understand Waltz's theory you then have the slightly more difficult task of explaining Waltz's claims about this being a 'proper' theory of IR. Why does he say this? On what grounds? It all comes down to his aim of generating a science of politics, and you can quote from his 1979 study and later work to support you here, particularly his work on the system level and balance of power theory.

In light of all this, you then have to judge whether Waltz is right to present his theory as a 'proper' theory. What does 'proper' imply in the context of the question and how do we judge when a theory is 'proper' or not? The best answers will use this element of the question to investigate metatheoretical debates about the nature of theory and whether we can study IR as scientifically as Waltz suggests.

REFERENCES TO MORE INFORMATION

Neoliberalism:
Keohane, R.O. (1984) *After Hegemony*. Princeton, NJ: Princeton University Press.

Keohane, R.O. and Nye, J.S. (1977) *Power and Interdependence: World Politics in Transition*. Boston: Little Brown and Co.

Clark, I. (1999) *Globalization and International Relations Theory*. Oxford: Oxford University Press.
Shows how globalization unsettles existing IR theoretical categories and helps us rethink both the concept of globalization and the framework of the discipline.

Mitrany, D. (1975) 'A Political Theory for the New Society', in A.J.R. Groom and P. Taylor (eds) *Functionalism: Theory and Practice in International Relations*. London: University of London Press, pp. 25–37.
See also the chapters in this collection by Nina Healthcote (Neofunctionalism), Michael Hodges and John Burton.

Nye, J.S. (1975) 'Transnational and Transgovernmental Relations', in G.L. Goodwin and A. Linklater (eds) *New Dimensions of World Politics*. London: Croom Helm, pp. 36–53.
Examines the actors in IR overlooked by state-centric theories and makes the case for integration theory and interdependence. See also the chapter by Richard Rosecrance.

Neorealism:
Berridge, G.R. (1997) *International Politics: States, Power and Conflict since 1945*, 3rd edn. New York: Prentice Hall.
On pp. 166–83 Berridge explores the Neorealist concept of the 'balance of power' and illustrates how it has featured in the international system. This chapter ends with a good list of further reading.

Kreisler, H. (2003) 'Theory and International Politics: Conversation with Kenneth N. Waltz', Institute of International Studies, University of Berkeley, http://globetrotter.berkeley.edu/people3/Waltz/waltz-con0.html
Waltz talks about his educational influences, about being a political theorist and about the Neorealist vision of international politics. You can read the interview transcript, watch it as a webcast or listen as a podcast.

Mearsheimer, J.J. (1990) 'Back to the Future: Instability in Europe after the Cold War', *International Security*, 15(1): 5–56.
Tries to update Waltz's Neorealist balance of power thesis to predict trends in international relations after the end of the Cold War.

James, P. (1993) 'Neorealism as Research Enterprise: Toward Elaborated Structural Realism', *International Political Science Review*, 14(2): 123–48.
Linklater, A. (1995) 'Neo-Realism: Theory and Practice', in K. Booth and S. Smith (eds) *International Relations Theory Today*. Cambridge: Polity Press, pp. 241–61.

Ashley, R.K. (1986) 'The Poverty of Neorealism', in R.O. Keohane (ed.) *Neorealism and its Critics*. New York: Columbia University Press, pp. 1–26.

Review of International Studies (2004) 'Forum on the State as Person', 30(2): 255–316.

2.4 THE ENGLISH SCHOOL

Key Terms

- System
- Society
- State
- Order

- Rules
- Justice
- Pluralism
- Solidarism

English School thinking ... provides social structural benchmarks for the evaluation of significant change in international orders; sets out a taxonomy that enables comparisons to be made across time and space; and provides some predictions and explanations of outcome. (Buzan 2004: 25)

> You can open essays or exam answers with relevant quotes like this to focus your reader's attention on the central issue(s) you will raise in your work. They can be used to say that essentially your argument agrees or disagrees with the author in the context of the question set.

In this chapter and the next we analyse two IR theories that are alike in some ways but very different in others: the English School and Social Constructivism. I have classified them as 'mid-range' in the sense that they sit between the positivist, science-like theories of Realism, Liberalism, Neorealism and Neoliberalism, and the more critical, **post-positivist** inclined theories such as Critical Theory, feminism, Postcolonialism and Green theory (for a useful overview of this distinction see Griffiths 2011: 11–12). Hence, when thinking about the 'place' they occupy in the broader canon of IR theories, you might see the English School and Social Constructivism as raising the profile of themes and issues which had previously been ignored or overlooked by earlier theorists; in so doing, they opened the door for a more radical reassessment of what IR theory was and how to 'do' it.

INTRODUCTION TO THE ENGLISH SCHOOL

This theory is slightly oddly named in that it was formed by scholars of varying nationalities – 'the English School was never very English and is even less so today' (Dunne 2007: 128) – and because it does not offer a 'theory' clothed in the language of natural science that a Neorealist, for example, might find congenial. Rather, the English School gathers together a methodologically eclectic range of scholars. They put forward an empirically grounded 'interpretation' of world history which identifies the progressivist elements in international relations often, but not always, construed as a 'society' (Suganami 2005: 42).

English School theorists have affinities with several of the theories you might cover on an IRT unit, notably Realism, Liberalism and Constructivism, with some taking a recognizably 'genealogical' approach to international affairs that calls to mind more critically inclined post-modernist theories (Reus-Smit 2002: 494). One might reasonably argue that the English School advances a broadly Liberal agenda whilst remaining cognizant of Realist international realities such as the international states system. English school theorists deploy a wide variety of methods and look for inspiration to history, philosophy and international law as much as to 'political science' in its positivist guise. As canonical writers such as Hedley Bull have demonstrated, English School writers veer – sometimes in the same book or article – between Liberal optimism and Realist pessimism (Wheeler and Dunne 1996).

Given that the English School ranges so widely in methodological and empirical terms, there is some disagreement about which writers best 'represent' the tradition as it developed through the 1950s and beyond. Significantly, it has been more popular outside US academic circles than inside, causing something of a disconnect between the US and 'the rest' over questions of ontology, epistemology and methodology. In the 1990s especially, 'the English School was rejuvenated as a major "non-American" research programme' (Reus-Smit 2005: 82). Debates about English School theory, perhaps better than any other, compel attention to the 'problem of the subject' in IR. Amongst its early proponents, Martin Wight, Hedley Bull, R.J. Vincent and Adam Watson are all central figures in the canon and are worth seeking out; Charles Manning is a rather overlooked figure but Tanja Aalberts (2010) makes the case for including him as a seminal thinker working at the boundary where the English School today meets Constructivism.

Barry Buzan, Richard Little, Tim Dunne, Nicholas Wheeler, Alex Bellamy and Richard Jackson are amongst those who have developed English School theory in recent years, particularly as far as work on humanitarian intervention is concerned. Looking across this diverse oeuvre it can be argued that despite some differences 'the identity of the English School reveals itself … as a historically constituted and evolving cluster of scholars with a number of plausible and inter-related stories to tell about [their similarities and differences]' (see Suganami 2005: 29). They speak to increasingly pressing concerns in IR, such as sovereignty, intervention across state borders, and the institutions of global governance.

Like all theories of IR the English School is contested from within and without whilst retaining a certain consistency of approach that does allow it to retain a separate identity from other 'movements' in the discipline.

> The English School is quite difficult to 'capture' theoretically speaking. This makes it all the more important to define what you mean by it when writing or talking about 'the English School'.

One way to appreciate the somewhat precarious positioning of the English School in IRT is to turn to one of its leading historians and practitioners who judges that the English School avoids 'either/or' theorizing; it is a 'synthesis of different theories and concepts' combining 'theory *and* history, morality *and* power, **agency** *and* structure' (Dunne 2007: 128, original italics). Limited chapter space unfortunately precludes an in-depth examination of all the major English School theorists. However, we will explore the English School approach to IR first by considering how Hedley Bull positioned it within prevailing IRT and then by unpacking its major concepts: state, system, society and order. We will end by surveying the intra-theory debate between **pluralists** and **solidarists** to illustrate the different 'wings' of the theory as they have developed in the post-Cold War era.

BULL: *THE ANARCHICAL SOCIETY*

The title of Hedley Bull's foundational English School text from 1977 (Bull 2002) gives us clues about where he was trying to take IRT. His reference to the concept of anarchy shows that Bull was accenting a central theme of Realist and Liberal theories – states exist in an environment where there is no orderer, no chief to regulate their behaviour at the international level. As we have seen, early Realists held that without an orderer, the potential for conflict between self-interested states was ever-present because they were trapped in an irresolvable security dilemma. Neorealists such as Kenneth Waltz built their theories around the concept of the balance of power, arguing that the causes of conflict lay not so much with the actions of the units (states) but at the level of the system itself.

Liberal and Neoliberal theorists took the same assumption about the existence of anarchy but drew different conclusions. They argued that conflict did not have to be, and was not empirically, a permanent or necessary feature of international relations. Early Liberals eulogized the spread of democracy and good governance, while Liberal theory after the Second World War concentrated on the growth of international organizations/institutions and showed how these could help mitigate the negative effects of anarchy.

It is probably fair to suggest that Bull's work was Realist in inspiration and Liberal in aspiration. It was Realist in inspiration because he wanted to open up dialogue about the implications of accepting the two founding assumptions of IR theory: that sovereign states are the main actors and that they exist in a condition of anarchy. As Richard Little has argued, 'Bull's conception of the international system corresponds almost exactly with the one formulated by Waltz. In other words, both theorists acknowledge the importance of anarchy for understanding international relations and they argue that in such a system every state takes into account what every other state is doing (Little 2005: 48).

But from this Realist starting point he brought distinctively Liberal-inspired ideas about the nature of IR to the fore. We can see this by looking at his central case that 'a group of states, conscious of certain common interests and common values, forms a society in the sense that they conceive themselves to be bound by a set of rules in their relations with one another, and share in the working of common institutions' (Bull 2002: 13). A glance at some of the key terms in this statement reveals Bull's Liberal agenda:

- Common interests
- Common values
- Society
- Rules
- Share
- Institutions

The main distinction between Bull and Liberal/Neoliberal theorists was his effort to theorize the term 'society' into existence. His belief was that 'order is part of the historical record of international relations; … modern states have formed, and continue to form, not only a system of states but also an international society' (Bull 2002: 22–3). Or as Alex Bellamy puts it, English School writers share the Constructivist belief that 'states form an international society shaped by ideas, values, identities, and norms that are – to a greater or lesser extent – common to all' (Bellamy 2005: 2). The systemic stability that Neorealists take to be produced by a settled balance of power, is for Bull something more intrinsic: 'stability and order are not a product of the anarchic international system, but the product of the common interests, institutions, rules, and values that characterize an international society' (Little 2005: 48).

Bellamy's book *International Society and its Critics* is another of the 'two-for-one' style books you should find useful. It helps you both understand and critique English School theory through direct engagement with its major exponents.

They might only be two short words, but Bull's notions of 'society' and 'order' were crucial to the development of English School thought. Let us now see how and why Bull worked so heavily with them, and how they informed his reading of IR.

FROM SYSTEM TO SOCIETY

Bull built his theory around four key words: state, system, society and order. He uses these in specific ways to advance his argument that international relations are more ordered than Realists and Neorealists assume, and more like a society than Liberals and Neoliberals assume.

STATE

Bull defined 'state' similarly to Realists, Liberals and Neo-Neo theorists. A state, he argued, has three attributes:

- sovereignty over a group of people;
- a defined territory;
- a government.

Bull was not satisfied with theories such as Neorealism which explained state behaviour at the level of the international system. Bull put more emphasis on the agency of states; that is on the 'diplomats and leaders who think and act on behalf of the state and its institutions' (Dunne 2007: 132). With this move Bull helped to expand the study of IR to take in Constructivist thought which opens up the 'black box' of the state. When IR is viewed as a conglomerate of social relations we can appreciate that what people and organizations *within* states believe are held to matter at the level of the international system because they influence state foreign and defence policies. Bull suggested that the flow of influence was not, as Waltz had it, mostly top down (from system to states) but involved more complex interactions in which state behaviour could also work upwards to affect the international system (we return to Constructivist theory in the next chapter).

An interesting way to think through the differences between a 'system' and a 'society' is to play a simple word association game. Think of the first word or image that jumps into your head when you think of the word 'system'. Do the same for the word 'society'. Ask three friends to do the same. You should notice some interesting patterns in the responses that help you understand what Bull was trying to get at by envisioning international relations in social rather than systemic terms.

SYSTEM

Bull's understanding of the international system was essentially Waltzian. The word 'system' implies functional cooperation without any sense of the shared purposes or interests that we find in an international society (see below). Bull argues that two or more states form a system when they 'have sufficient contact between them, and have sufficient impact on one another's decisions, to cause them to behave – at least in some measure – as parts of a whole' (2002: 9). Systemic interaction between states is thus fairly limited and comes down to state perceptions of their 'technical interest in manipulation and control as opposed to the practical interest in promoting diplomatic agreement and understanding' (Linklater 1995: 256).

Unlike Waltz, however, Bull put the concept of a system to different empirical and theoretical uses by asking what the change from one system to another tells us about the possible existence of an international society over time. English School theorists have conventionally looked to history for evidence of what has characterized state systems in the past, notably 'the

Western, the Greco-Roman, and the Chinese of the Warring States' (Watson 1990: 100). This helps the English School achieve perspective and context by getting beyond a Euro-centric or Cold-War-heavy definition of the term. In turn, Watson suggests that we can carve up these different types of system along a spectrum of 'control' ranging across 'independence, hegemony, dominion and empire' (Watson 1990: 104–6). English School theory can therefore help us clarify what we mean by a system and to theorize change over time, between one type of system and another.

SOCIETY

The term 'international system' was deployed by IR theorists to explain the structured nature of state interactions. The word 'system' has natural science-like associations which helps us explain how things are ordered and how different parts or units in the system interact with each other to comprise a whole. Think about planets in the solar system or the component parts of a computer system, it is a 'remarkable inanimate connotation, hinting, at least, at the functional and utilitarian' (James 1993: 282).

Bull did not believe international relations could be classified in this rather abstract, cold way, with the units performing functions unthinkingly as part of a larger entity. After all, the relations between states and nations are conducted by, and reliant upon, the actions of the individuals within them – system misses the human element. An international society for Bull is more than a system but less than a civilization, in the sense that we might talk about the Greek or Roman civilizations in previous centuries, or Western civilization today.

A society might be something that comes about for more pragmatic reasons, less organically, we might say, than a civilization. But it is certainly a stage further on in terms of understanding the depth and scale of inter-state transactions than Realists would have us believe. 'International society', writes Justin Morris (2005: 206), 'does not, anymore than does domestic society, require unanimous acceptance of its underpinning values and goals, but it does necessitate a sufficiently broad consensus among its membership to ensure that its existence can be preserved against the acts of recalcitrant states'.

In its solidarist form (see below) international society 'is none other than mankind, encumbered and thwarted by an archaic fiction of an international society composed of sovereign states' (Wight 1987: 223) – a paradox of IR's own making. Societies emerge around agreed laws and rules that shape the conduct of states and connote what the term 'system' is unable to: 'an associational relationship which lacks some kind of formal or holistic coherence' (James 1993: 284 and 279).

Christian Reus-Smit (2005) has even raised the prospect that the English School is incapable of proffering valuable interventions on the nature of contemporary international society and that it should be left to the more holistic approach of the Constructivists. Writers such as Richard Little do not go that far, but have posed searching questions about Bull's system/society construct by probing the following questions: first, how do we identify a society (global or regional?) and can apparently cohesive, values-based societies, such as 'European' and 'Chinese' co-exist? Second, what separates a system from a society? Third, what are the boundaries between systems and societies? Fourth, how and why do the notional 'boundaries' of international society alter over time? Finally, what is the relationship between a society and an Empire? This links to the Marxist perspective we cover in Chapter 2.6 (Little 2005).

Do you believe there can ever truly be a 'world' society, even in the age of Facebook, Twitter and technological globalization? Or will the English School's 'international society' be about as deep as it gets? Do several 'regional' societies co-exist in the modern world?

Adam Watson's work attempts to engage with these questions by tracing the evolution of international society from ancient times (the 'ancient states system') through 'European international society' and 'global international society', showing the historical lineage of what might appear to be 'new' or unrecognizable developments in the international system today (Watson 2001). The detail of these interrogations is interesting and insightful but a bit beyond what we can hope to cover in this overview.

The point to take away is that English School IRT has blended together elements of earlier IR theories. Hard-headed Realist calculations about national interest combine with Liberal institutionalism to create a theory in which the anarchical international system creates the impetus for groups of states to work together to achieve common goals. 'World society' is something deeper still and we return to that in our exploration of the pluralist–solidarist debate below.

ORDER

How is order in international relations generated and maintained? For Bull, **diplomacy** and a respect for international law (as agreed in international institutions) are the foundations of international order and the prerequisite for the promotion of justice. This order, moreover, could be developed and maintained even among states with diverse, even *opposed* political, economic and social traditions.

Take the period of the Cold War, 1945–89, when two rival power-blocs, one led by the Soviet Union, the other by the US, competed for economic/ political/cultural hegemony over the international system. Even then, the threat of 'hot war' between the main protagonists was somewhat mitigated by their participation in common organizations such as the UN. This helped reduce inflamed tensions between the blocs via regular communication and decision-taking on events of global political, economic and strategic significance. (Although it could be argued that this view largely depends on the 'theatre' we look at, and that it ignores the 'proxy' wars that were fought out in continents such as South America.)

TAKING IT FURTHER

When states engage in wars or, more likely today, humanitarian interventions, these interventions are, in theory at least, rule-bound exercises. It is not a case of 'anything goes' in times of conflict. Most states are signed up to the UN Hague Convention on the Law and Customs of War, and the Geneva Convention which concentrates on 'the rights of individuals, combatants and noncombatants, during war'. It includes Conventions on genocide and torture and the treatment of prisoners of war (UN 1997). Even in times of 'hot' conflict, then, states order their interactions to such a degree that something as apparently chaotic and violent as war demonstrates their shared commitment to sticking by the rules for the good of international society as a whole.

Perhaps this is why, today, the treatment of prisoners of war receives so much attention and why the abuse of Iraqi prisoners of war, such as in Abu Ghraib detention camp during the coalition invasion from March 2003, was so widely vilified. Not only did the mistreatment lead to a dwindling of support for an already controversial use of force, but the US military personnel involved were seen to be abusing the basic human rights of the Iraqi prisoners. Added to the alleged extraordinary rendition and torture of suspected terrorists (Phythian 2011: 201–2), the Abu Ghraib detainees were said to be held in contravention of the laws of armed conflict, undermining both the official rules and the unofficial norms underpinning the international society in which we live.

SOLIDARISM AND PLURALISM

... the disagreement between the two positions is to some extent an empirical one about how far, in the contemporary circumstances, it is possible to pursue higher goals such as the international protection of human rights without undermining the more basic goal of international order. (Suganami 2005: 39)

Since the end of the Cold War, key states such as the US, UK, Canada and Australia, and international organizations such as the UN, EU and NATO have engaged in increasingly intense discussions about whether and how to intervene in the affairs of another state for humanitarian or other security purposes. These debates have arisen because of the rise in the number of acute humanitarian emergencies and inter-ethnic violence accompanying the fragmentation of states such as the former Yugoslavia into smaller, territorially bounded nation-states. Bosnia, Kosovo, Sierra Leone, East Timor and Libya have all shaped post-Cold War thought and practice on intervention, just as Iraq, Afghanistan and the War on Terror more generally have posed dilemmas about the way states produce order in the contemporary international system.

The practice of intervention poses a challenge for politicians and IR theorists because it strikes to the heart of one of the legal and ethical touchstones of the international state system: sovereignty. An intervention, by definition, violates both the sovereignty and the territorial integrity of states, and is therefore subject to heated dispute around difficult sets of questions: Should internal state matters remain internal state matters in a globalized world? When is a state in such disarray that external intervention is desirable? What is a 'grave humanitarian' crisis and how does it relate to genocide and humanitarian atrocities? Who decides when it is ethical to undertake an intervention? What types of intervention are ethical and effective? Do the supposedly ethical ends of an intervention justify the means? Which states or organizations are responsible for picking up the pieces after the 'intervention' phase?

English School theory has been well placed to consider these questions because it is attentive to the cross-cutting elements of 'international society' and 'world society' (Williams 2005), as well as the normative concerns emanating from the tension between human justice and international order. Questions of human rights and intervention 'pose the conflict between order and justice at their starkest' (Wheeler and Dunne 1996: 92). The rise of modern humanitarianism 'reveals how commitments to the improvement of social arrangements transcend national frameworks' (Linklater 2010: 170–1).

This is encapsulated in the intra-theory debate between the pluralists and the solidarists which has 'further underlined the different enterprises that realism and the English School are engaged in' (Dunne 2005: 74). As Reus-Smit explains (2002: 490), 'scholars of the English School have consistently explored the potential for moral action in a world of sovereign states, fuelling a debate between pluralists and solidarists'. Bull's early approach to solidarism was on the potential for solidarity among states in an international society 'with respect to the enforcement of the law' (quoted in Wheeler and Dunne 1996: 95). This rather minimalist, legalistic appreciation has given way to stronger forms in recent years. For example, solidarists such as Nicholas Wheeler believe it to be 'the responsibility of the richer and more powerful states to take care of intolerable miseries experienced in less successful states' (Suganami 2005: 39), and that as long as interventions are the exception rather than the rule, order in the international system can be maintained. Solidarists are thus associated with the cosmopolitan tradition in English School theory and with 'world society' approaches.

> The nub of the disagreement between solidarists and pluralists is ontological and concerns the location of moral responsibility in a sovereign states system. Solidarists believe humankind forms a unified moral community despite being artificially divided into states; pluralists see sovereign states as responsible for their own citizens' welfare (Suganami 2005: 40).

By contrast, pluralists such as Richard Jackson are more Realist inclined and associated with the 'international society' strand of English School thought. They have countered that interventions are 'likely to undermine international order, and even that humanitarian intervention is a form of paternalism which is morally objectionable'. Pluralists do not rule out 'pacification, reconstruction, or development' of any country but stress that they should only be undertaken with the consent of the host government (Suganami 2005: 39).

The violation of what Constructivists might see as a deeply entrenched 'norm' of international society is at best destabilizing and at worst downright unethical, especially when imposed by the powerful on the weak as a new interventionist norm. 'The conservative needs of order should be placed above the pursuit of justice should that pursuit conflict with the core tenets of international society' (Williams 2005: 23).

Solidarism and pluralism in action: from the Blair Doctrine to R2P

Developments in IRT often reflect the practice of international relations as undertaken by states, international organizations and other actors in the international system, particularly when these are novel or unexpected (see for example the impact the end of the Cold War, and, just over a decade later, the terrorist attacks of 9/11 have had on our thinking about order, helped

(Continued)

TAKING IT FURTHER

(Continued)

and security in the twenty-first century). The solidarist–pluralist divide within English School theory closely parallels a debate on 'intervention' and the 'responsibility to protect' in the era of global interdependence. Tony Blair's 1999 Chicago speech, delivered during the Kosovo intervention, helped transform thinking on intervention and sovereignty, partly by making a robust case for 'just war' theory at a profound moment of uncertainty in the international system. Talking of the 'unspeakable' things happening in Kosovo, 'ethnic cleansing, systematic rape, mass murder', Blair intoned that 'We cannot let the evil of ethnic cleansing stand', in Europe or on its borders. Why not? 'We are all internationalists now whether we like it or not … We cannot turn our backs on conflicts and the violation of human rights within other countries if we want to be secure' (Blair 1999).

Global interdependence, said Blair, brought the notion of a world society closer than ever before, meaning that we had to rethink the legitimacy of cleaving to outdated notions such as sovereignty if we are to safeguard basic human values of security, dignity and welfare (see also Blair 2001; for a reassessment of Blair's Chicago speech see Daddow 2009). It could be argued that Blair was putting a weak but nonetheless noticeably *solidarist* case for intervention, albeit one in which nation-states remained the pre-eminent actors on the global stage.

Blair's clarion call came at a time of introspection from other members of the international community (especially in 'the West') on how best to deal with the ethical concerns to which Blair had drawn attention. In 2001 the International Commission on Intervention and State Sovereignty (ICISS) published its report on how to respond to atrocities which, as then UN Secretary General Kofi Annan said, 'affect every precept of our common humanity' (quoted in Evans 2004). The Responsibility to Protect (R2P), as it became known, challenged the Blair doctrine in three main ways (Evans 2004). First, it shifted the focus of attention from those planning to intervene to the needs of those requiring support (the subjectivity of the Blair 'conditions' for intervention are well covered in Ralph (2011)). Second, R2P acknowledged that it is the responsibility of individual states not to engage in mass killing or other atrocities within their borders, and that intervention would only be considered if the state in question proved unable or unwilling to uphold its duties. Third, R2P incorporated the associated responsibilities to 'prevent' and 'rebuild', so is more comprehensive than the Blair doctrine. Prevention, in particular, was the emphasis in R2P. By reasserting the essential inviolability of state sovereignty except in what would be exceptional circumstances, R2P would seem to have put the *pluralist* case for the responsibility of states before and after the breach of sovereignty entailed by intervention.

Looking at where the Blair doctrine landed Britain, the US and their coalition of the willing in Iraq, could it be argued that the pluralists and proponents of R2P have a point?

QUESTIONS TO PONDER

'Why did Hedley Bull posit the existence of an "international society"? Was he correct to do so?'

This question invites you to explain Bull's reasoning and then tell the reader what you make of it, so an essay in two parts would be logical. Clearly it is sensible to concentrate mainly on Bull, but if you want to illustrate the English School's position with reference to other writers in the tradition, then that would be fine. Make sure to keep Bull's ideas to the forefront though.

In the first part you have to explain the steps Bull took to move IRT from considering systems, power and interests towards the idea that these relations constitute a society. As such, you are being asked to summarize the key facets of Bull's thought, as they echo previous IRT (for example Waltz) and depart from it. You can legitimately narrow your essay to focus on one seminal text (*Anarchical Society*), or you could pick ideas from across his oeuvre. The first option is probably the easier to sustain because it is a relatively self-contained work; you might tell the reader that Bull developed his ideas over time, but that for the purposes of answering this particular question you are sticking to his first major foray into the subject. You could summarize *The Anarchical Society* chapter by chapter, but in order to remain within the recommended word limit for your essay you will surely be better off to take a thematic approach, using foundational quotes to illustrate your reading of Bull's work. The essential issue is to define what you think Bull meant by 'international society'.

In the second part you have to give your opinions on Bull's ideas about the existence, and conceptualization, of an 'international society'. You should demonstrate a familiarity with criticisms levelled at the concept (for example James 1993) and the follow-on questions asked of it (for example, Little's, explored above). These include: first, the vagueness of the distinction between 'system', on the one hand, and 'society', on the other; just when does the one become the other? Second, does 'international' in fact mean 'European', undermining the applicability of the theory to anything beyond the notional and rather limited borders of 'Europe' or 'the West'? Third, did Bull's theory overlook the elements of a human 'world society' of values that exist among human beings as opposed to states; was he too state-centric? Have technological innovations over recent years challenged or supported early English

School thought or 'states' as key elements of society? Realist theorists critique Bull for being insufficiently Realist; Liberals critique him for being too Realist, so you could couch your evaluation in these terms. What do you make of their attacks? You could answer this by considering what Bull would have said to his Realist and Liberal critics.

'How does English School theory differ from Realist and Liberal theories? Which theory do you find most convincing and why?'

Whereas the last question concentrated on just one theory, this answer requires a good working knowledge of three. That you have to cover so much ground makes your response harder to structure, so good planning and organization are vital. In an exam your time management will have to be rigorous so that you effectively address both parts of the question.

Let us deal with the first half of the question. On the surface it might appear that the best way to approach it is to take each theory in turn, explaining their central tenets and then comparing and contrasting in a section at the end. The flaw in this approach is that it may be impossible to cram in all the information you need. Say you only have 2,500 words for your essay – how are you going to summarize three theories and then evaluate them in this limited space? And bearing in mind this is an English-School-oriented question, it is worth showing your tutor you actually know a lot more about that theory than the other two! It may, then, be better to centre your analysis on English School theory, moving into the other two theories as and when necessary. You could, for instance, consider the use Bull and others make of Realist-inspired words like 'system' and 'interest' and Liberal words like 'institutions' and 'society'.

The best answers might engage with the Constructivist leanings of the English School, as well as referencing its solidarist (Liberal) and pluralist (Realist) writings. This approach is harder to manage because it assumes a strong knowledge base, but it certainly should pay dividends in terms of demonstrating your ability to meet higher order learning objectives for the course.

In the second part you have to pick your favourite theory (assuming you have one). The examiner will be looking for you to justify your choice with reference to either or both of two benchmarks. First, the coherence of the theory as *a theory*. Are its assumptions valid? Is it epistemologically grounded? Does it fit the 'facts' of international relations as understood by the theorist responsible? Second, you might consider the applicability of the theory today by asking: has it stood the test of time? Does it explain important facets of contemporary international relations? Making use of the pluralist/solidarist debate would help you show the development of the English School in the 1990s as a broad church for appreciating the historical dynamics of contemporary discussions about intervention and state sovereignty.

REFERENCES TO MORE INFORMATION

Bull, H. and Watson, A. (eds) (1985) *The Expansion of International Society*. Oxford: Oxford University Press.
  Analysis of the growth and development of European and, increasingly, global 'society' from the sixteenth century onwards.

Butterfield, H. and Wight, M. (eds) (1966) *Diplomatic Investigations*. London: George Allen and Unwin.
  See especially Hedley Bull's chapter on the Grotian approach to international society.

Manning, C.A.W. (1962) *The Nature of International Society*. London: London School of Economics.
  Unfortunately very difficult to get hold of!

Robson, B.A. (ed.) (1998) *International Society and the Development of International Relations*. London: Cassell.
  A collection of essays by leading English School writers assessing where they think the concept of 'international society' has taken IR.

Brown, C. (2002) *Sovereignty, Rights and International Justice*. Cambridge: Polity Press.

Buzan, B. (2001) 'The English School: An Under-Exploited Resource in IR', *Review of International Studies*, 24(3): 471–88.
  A forceful statement of the case that IR theorists neglect the English School at their peril.

Epp, R. (1998) 'The English School on the Frontiers of International Relations, *Review of International Studies*, 24 (special issue): 47–63.

Dunne, T. (1998) *Inventing International Society: A History of the English School*. Basingstoke: Macmillan.

Wight, M. (1991) *International Theory: The Three Traditions*. Leicester: Leicester University Press.
  A posthumously published collection of Wight's lectures at the LSE in the 1950s.

Suganami, H. (2000) 'C.A.W. Manning and the Study of International Relations', *Review of International Studies*, 27(1): 91–107.

Buzan, B. (2005) *From International to World Society? English School Theory and the Social Construction of Globalisation*. Cambridge: Cambridge University Press.
Chapters 1 and 2 are good on the weaknesses of English School theory and Chapter 6 on the institutions that constitute 'international society'.

Little, R. (2000) 'The English School's Contribution to the Study of International Relations', *European Journal of International Relations*, 6(3): 495–522.

Groom, A.J.R. (1975) 'Functionalism and World Society', in A.J.R. Groom and P. Taylor (eds) *Functionalism: Theory and Practice in International Relations*. London: University of London Press, pp. 93–111.
Shows the overlap between English School and Liberal thought.

Gong, G.W. (1984) *The Standard of 'Civilization' in International Relations*. Oxford: Clarendon Press.
A wealth of information on the changing faces of 'international society' through the ages by appreciating non-Western societies in China and Japan. Also useful as a precursor to Postcolonialism (Chapter 2.10 in this book).

Hoffman, S. (2000) *World Disorders: Troubled Peace in the Post-Cold War Era*. Lanham, MD: Rowman and Littlefield Publishers Ltd.
Chapter 2 covers Hedley Bull; Chapter 4 is on world order beyond Realist and Liberal perspectives.

Review of International Studies (2001) 'Forum on the English School', 27(3): 465–513.
A series of six short articles. See also the same journal's (2002) five-article section on the English School, 28(4).

Reus-Smit, C. (1997) 'The Constitutional Structure of International Society and the Nature of Fundamental Institutions', *Review of International Studies*, 51(4), 555–89.

Hjorth, R. (2011) 'Equality in the Theory of International Society: Kelsen, Rawls and the English School', *Review of International Studies*, 37(5): 2585–2602.

Buzan, B. (undated) 'English School of International Relations', University of Leeds, www.leeds.ac.uk/polis/englishschool/
Contains links to conference papers, reading lists and contact lists for people working on the English School.

Zhang, Y. (2003) 'The "English School" in China: A Travelogue of Ideas and their Diffusion', *European Journal of International Relations*, 9(1): 87–114.

On solidarism and pluralism:
Wheeler, N.J. (1992) 'Pluralist or Solidarist Conceptions of International Society: Bull and Vincent on Humanitarian Intervention', *Millennium: Journal of International Studies*, 21(3): 29–34.
Wheeler, N.J. (2000) *Saving Strangers; Humanitarian Intervention in International Society*. Oxford: Oxford University Press.
Jackson, R. (2000) *The Global Covenant: Human Conduct in a World of States*. Oxford: Oxford University Press.
Linklater, A. (2009) 'Human Interconnectedness', *International Relations*, 23(3): 481–97.
Weinert, M.S. (2011) 'Reframing the Pluralist–Solidarist Debate', *Millennium: Journal of International Studies*, 40(1): 21–41.

2.5 SOCIAL CONSTRUCTIVISM

Key Terms

- Anarchy
- State
- Security dilemma
- Identity

- Interest
- Norm
- Norm entrepreneurship

In giving form to the world, the mind makes the world real – *in our heads*. And yet the world *appears* to exist, more or less as we sense it, outside the mind. (Onuf 2009: 194; original emphasis)

At the time of writing this book I have a nephew who is seven years old and a niece who is five years old. Being the dutiful and generous uncle that I am, I have spent considerable money and time over the past few years purchasing Christmas and birthday presents for them. Last Christmas I wanted to buy them each a t-shirt for the summer, so off I went to Mothercare to choose their gifts. I emerged with a mainly blue t-shirt for Joe and a mainly pink one for Freja. My choice was made in part because of my preconceptions about what colours we associate with boys and girls, while in part it reflected the nature of the dominant colours in the boys' and girls' clothing sections in the shop. The girls' section contained lighter tones and more pinks and yellows, whereas the tones for boys' clothes were darker, with blues, blacks and browns more apparent.

As they have grown up I have had great fun choosing toys for them as well as clothes. There are many toys that both will enjoy playing with, such as jigsaw puzzles and board games. But there are toys I would give Joe but probably not consider giving Freja, such as Action Men and footballs. By the same token Freja might prefer dolls, dressing-up clothes and glitter make-up. For their sticker books Joe prefers gladiators, Freja fairy princesses. You can probably see where this is heading. The choice of gifts for my niece and nephew is shaped both by my own reading of what they might want, but more, no doubt, by my expectations of what they would want, given *societal expectations* about what young boys and girls wear, and what toys young boys and girls play with.

> What appear to be natural, taken-as-read realities about the social world are in fact not natural or forever given to us, they are made by us.

This slightly simplified (and gendered – see Chapter 2.8) example works as a way in to thinking about the intersubjective nature of social reality: social facts are not given to us but made by us. Take the examples John Ruggie offers up: money, property rights, sovereignty, marriage, football and Valentine's Day (Ruggie 1998b: 856). Or from Stefano Guzzini and Anne Leander (2006: 79): 'If we watch a red light as a social scientist, we are not interested in the residual matter of electric circuits but, for instance, in the norms which the interpretation of this sign mobilizes'. I could have purchased my niece and nephew completely different coloured t-shirts from blue and pink had they not been the 'accepted' male and female colours of choice. Replace blue with red and pink with black as the dominant colours and my own preference might have been red for Joe and black for Freja, not blue and pink. This change would have been down to a combination of my own expectations about what colours boys and girls wear, but also a function of material reality; had these been the dominant colours, Mothercare would presumably have stocked more red and black clothes as opposed to blue and pink.

The point is a simple one: things could have been different; identities are intersubjectively constituted as well as being in a constant state of negotiation, although some (such as gender colours) can be more resistant to change than others. For that reason, these socially constructed norms and practices can be unmade or transformed, and this is the crux of constructivist work, to stress that identities and interests are not magically given to us, they are made by us in our interaction with the world 'out there'.

In IR, the Constructivist agenda aims to 'interrogate defining concepts of the discipline and unravel alleged naturalness of concepts' (Aalberts 2010: 253). Or as Ruggie explains:

> The constructivist project has sought to open up the relatively narrow theoretical confines of the field – by pushing them back to problematize the interests and identities of actors; deeper to incorporate the intersubjective bases of social action and social order; and into the dimensions of space and time to establish the 'duality' of structure, in [Anthony] Giddens's terms, at once constraining social action but also being (re)created and, therefore, potentially transformed by it. (Ruggie 1998b: 862)

This chapter will consider this wide-ranging approach to IR in three parts. The first will provide some context and a survey of a few core disciplinary understandings of Social Constructivism. The second part will outline the thought of a leading 'thin' Constructivist, Alexander Wendt. The third part will look at 'thick' Constructivism using work on norms and the norm life cycle as a deeper way of explaining the emergence and changes to state identities and interests over time.

CONTEXT

Social Constructivism has formed part of a wider intellectual movement within the social sciences and was simultaneously a response to key trends within IR from the later 1980s. Where Neorealists and Neoliberals took a ready-made microeconomic theory to inform their appreciation of the games rational states play in the international system, Social Constructivists have looked for inspiration to sociologists such as Emile Durkheim and Max Weber to inform their understanding of processes of socialization and the creation of intersubjective understandings of world politics that take on the character of 'the real'. Put another way, 'constructivism concerns the issue of human consciousness in international life' (Ruggie 1998b: 857 and 878). For a constructivist, it is not the existence of a world independent of our thought that is at stake, but whether we can have unmediated access to it' (Guzzini and Leander 2006: 79).

Social Constructivism in IRT is not a neat, self-contained entity or singularly identifiable 'theory'. It is a movement housing a diverse array of methodological perspectives and epistemological commitments. 'Constructivism is not a theory of international politics', more a 'sensibility' (Wendt 1999: 7). 'Constructivism is a different kind of theory from realism, liberalism or marxism and operates at a different level of abstraction. Constructivism is not a substantive theory of politics. It is a social theory about the nature of social life and social change' (Finnemore and Sikkink 2001: 393). Constructivism can be used to unpick theoretical constructs in IR such as the notion of the 'national interest' or the balance of power' (for example Kratochwil 1982), as well as the discipline's modes of knowledge production and vital reference points more generally. In its 'thinner' guise it retains strong connections to the state-centric approach of the Neorealists. In its 'thicker' manifestation it shares strong affinities with English School Liberal/Neoliberal theories, as well as some weaker postmodernist approaches to identity in IR.

The multiple categorizations of this theory over recent years say something about the complexity of hammering out a one-size-fits-all definition, in particular as one approaches the 'thicker' end of Constructivism (for different ways of carving up constructivist work see Lupovici 2009: 198; Reus-Smit 2002: 493; Ruggie 1998b: 880–82).

'Constructivism' in the singular does a disservice to the variety of Constructivist work in IRT. Knowing its various 'wings' will help you establish a definitional benchmark from which to work in assessed submissions and oral presentations. What do *you* understand by this term?

Social Constructivism is therefore quite hard to place, because in terms of its ontological and epistemological orientation it undergirds work that goes on in those 'neater' theoretical traditions, yet in another way it has enough of a distinctive 'feel' to it to mark it apart.

THE NORMATIVE TURN

... the steps through which some fundamental normative prescriptions lead to conclusions about what should be done. (Suganami 2005: 34)

In this book we have already discussed the social science debate between positivist and normative theorists. Positivists believe that the social world can be studied using methods drawn from the natural sciences; that facts can be disentangled from values; that regularities in the social world can be discovered in the same way that a natural scientist can discover regularities in the natural world; and that we judge truth claims on the basis of an appeal to our value-free facts (for more on the philosophy behind positivism see Giddens (1974)).

Normative theorists question each and every positivist assumption and in so doing provide serious grounds for us to investigate both the epistemological status of positivist theory (its claims to produce accurate, testable and objective knowledge) and the methodological underpinnings of positivist research (its naturalist approach). Smith and Owens point out (2008: 178) that in the study of IR, normative theory, sometimes referred to as **reflectivist** theory, only began to challenge the disciplinary dominance of positivism from the late 1980s.

First of all, normative theorists disagreed that the study of the world should (could, even) be all about the way things were. They pointed out that this was a small 'c' conservative position which entrenched rather than challenged existing power arrangements. Second, normative theorists raised the question of the values inherent in all theory – even theory which claims to tell us simply the way things are. Believing that one can do this is to adopt a normative position because you are masking the fact that in telling 'the way things are' you are in fact telling *your version* of the way things are. It might not be my version, and it almost certainly won't be the same as Victoria Beckham's, Rupert Murdoch's or Sarah Palin's versions.

Normative theorists doubt the existence of a single vantage point from which we can either 'view' the reality of the social world or tell it in terms that are anything other than partial, skewed and relative to our own theories and preconceptions about the world and its workings.

THE NORMATIVE TURN IN IR

Normative theorists in IR raised awareness of their concerns about positivist research by challenging some of the assumptions about how to 'do' IR theory which appeared in the most popular works in the field until the 1980s. For the purposes of your course in IR you might see Social Constructivism and the normative theories we cover in the next few chapters as a reaction against Realism, Liberalism and their Neo-Neo off-shoots.

Constructivist writers work from the premise that IR is a far more complex field than these theorists have led us to believe (Onuf 1998). They point up the linguistic and communicative bases of our apprehension of the world, working the compelling idea that:

> hardly anyone – even among the most ardent constructivists or pragmatists – doubts that the 'world' exists independent from our minds. The question is rather whether we can recognise it in a pure and direct fashion, i.e., without any 'description', or whether what we recognise is always already organised and formed by certain categorical and theoretical elements. (Kratochwil 2000: 91)

A variety of factors have led to dissatisfaction with the prevailing theoretical consensus in IRT and the perceived need for new questions to be asked and new answers to be found (following Smith and Owens 2008: 176):

- **The sudden demise of Neorealism.** First of all, the end of the Cold War in 1989 severely undermined the Neorealist argument that the bipolar international system that had prevailed since the end of the Second World War would be an enduring feature of international politics. 'Mainstream IR theory simply had difficulty explaining the end of the Cold War, or systemic change more generally' (Wendt 1999: 4). Suddenly, theorists wedded to explaining the 'facts' of the world as they saw them had to account for myriad 'facts' in the Soviet Union and its satellite states that were neither predicted nor well explained by prevailing Neorealist thought. As James Rosenau explains (2003: 10): 'One would be hard pressed to find a textbook on International Relations (IR) of the 1980s that had a single paragraph, let alone a single sentence, in which allowance was made for the possibility of the Cold War and the Soviet Union coming to an end'. Renewed uncertainty about causation and the motivators of change in the international system animated Constructivists to ask: 'are structures *real* – really "out there" in the world?' (Onuf 2009: 184). Were Neorealists correct to impute so much causative influence to them in their explanations of international relations?
- **Globalization.** We could write a whole book on this phenomenon and still not explore each and every aspect of it! Take the term here to mean increasing political, economic, technological and cultural interconnectedness between peoples and states around the world. Until the 1980s IRT was state-centric and not adept at explaining the rise and influence of such non-state activity; by definition, such activity falls outside the scope of any theory which takes the state as the main unit of analysis. By the end of the 1980s, therefore, it was felt that many significant aspects of international activity were not being explained by core IR theories. In particular the creation of state identities and their impact on the external behaviour of states were felt to be under-theorized.
- **Ignoring other issues.** Globalization has not only increased the degree of interconnectedness between individuals, organizations and states around the world, it has intensified those connections and thereby increased our awareness of all sorts of issues and problems in the global arena. In Thomas Friedman's words, contemporary globalization goes 'farther, faster, cheaper and deeper' (quoted in Nye and Welch 2011: 258). IR theory by the 1980s was seen to be ignoring major cross-border politico-social movements such as the women's movement, human rights, environmentalism, global inequality, oppression, exploitation and ethnicity as both source of identity and cause of conflict in the post-Cold War era. Social Constructivism, like other normative theories provided a way of plugging these and another gap in IR's knowledge base: that associated with the impact of *perception* on state behaviour.

> Normative theories such as Social Constructivism, feminism and Green theory have emerged in recent years to fill gaps scholars feel 'traditional' IR theorists left open. What does this tell you about the relationship between theory and practice in the field of IR?

'THIN' SOCIAL CONSTRUCTIVISM

In 1992, Alexander Wendt published an article in the leading US academic journal *International Organization* called 'Anarchy is What States Make of It: The Social Construction of Power Politics' (Wendt 1992), a prelude to his book *Social Theory of International Politics* (1999). It helped raise the profile of what has become known as Social Constructivist theory of IR, adding to earlier works in this tradition, including (Kratochwil 1989) and (Onuf 1989). On your course you are likely to find Wendt listed as *the* essential reading on this theory, so here we will concentrate on his 1992 article.

Wendt admits that 'there are many forms of constructivism' and that by the standards of other approaches in the field his is a 'moderate one' (Wendt 1999: 1). I have therefore called Wendtian Constructivism 'thin' to denote that it does not so much seek to overturn Neorealist approaches to the study of IR as to add the issue of 'identities' into the mix (for a critique of Wendt's under-theorization of 'identity see Zehfuss 2006). 'Thin' Constructivism could equally be called 'Realist' Constructivism because as Wendt himself argues, while his theory competes with Waltz's argument in some ways, 'it supports it in others', and he primarily tries 'to explain the latter's cultural conditions of possibility' (Wendt 1999: 15).

Wendt's 1992 article develops the Social Constructivist position by ranging over the theory and practice of IR; so how to summarize? All references below are to Wendt (1992):

Commitment to rationalism on the part of Neoliberals and Neorealists.

Rational choice is a social theory which treats 'the identities and interests of agents as exogenously given' (i.e. given to them rather than being created by them). Rational choice theory explains processes and institutions as impacting on behaviour instead of identities and interests (pp. 391–2). Wendt wants to give the constitution of identities and interests more of a say in the explanation for state behaviour and the outcomes that result from the interaction between states in the international arena.

Other theorists can help us bring identities and interests into the IR arena.

Cognitivists, feminists, poststructuralists, among others, all privilege identity and interest formation in their theories. These 'reflectivists' are also known as 'constructivists' and it is to these groups of scholars that Wendt turns for his ideas (p. 393).

Neorealists such as Waltz give too much explanatory weight to systemic factors.

They erroneously suggest that states operate in a self-help system which is mysteriously given to them 'by anarchic structure exogenously to process' (p. 394); it is as if states have no say over how they think and act. For Wendt, this structured view of IR is too **deterministic**.

Self-help and power politics are, for Wendt, not fixed, unchanging certainties.

They 'do not follow either logically or causally from anarchy' (p. 394); they 'are institutions, not essential features of anarchy' (p. 395). If states exist in a self-help world, it is because of processes they themselves have brought into existence. *'Anarchy is what states make of it'* (p. 395, italics in original).

The distribution of power is significant, but its effects are unpredictable.

State calculations are based on more than their assessment of the absolute or relative capabilities of other states. Leaders are also concerned with perceptions of their own and other states' identities and possible future behaviour: on 'conceptions of self and other'. These identity perceptions are not given but dynamic, context-specific and relational to the actions of those other states (p. 397). Put another way, the international system is more fluid than systemic theories would have us believe because states ultimately have a good deal of say over what goes on in the international arena.

Reifying anarchy prompts us to overlook uncertainties in international relations.

To **reify** an abstract entity is to treat it as if it had human or living existence. Wendt believes that IR scholars such as Waltz erroneously did this too readily with the abstract (non-existent) concept of anarchy. 'Actors do not have a "portfolio" of interests that they carry around independent of social context; instead, they define their interests in the process of defining situations' (p. 398). Interests and identities are not given to states but are constructed by those states on the basis of learning from past experiences, the experience of present actions and expectations about the future.

Underspecified nature of Waltz's definition of structure.

Self-help is just one kind of institution among several. Wendt identifies three types of security systems: 'competitive' (Realist version), 'individualistic' (Neoliberal version) and 'cooperative' (Liberal version) (p. 400; developed in Wendt (1999: Chapter 6), where they are labelled the Hobbesian, Lockean and Kantian versions respectively). If several types of security system have come and gone over the centuries, then how do we predict what type of system we might live in in the future? It is all dependent on what states do now and in the future – nothing is predetermined. For Wendt, Waltz cannot help us here because his definition of structure overlooks states' identities and interests.

Case studies.

Wendt invites us to imagine what it was like to live in the original 'state of nature', a time when one state ('ego') first encounters another ('alter') (pp. 404–5). He elaborates by asking how we would react to being contacted by members of an alien civilization. Our response, he argues, would be highly context dependent and shaped by our 'reading' of their various gestures (words/actions) towards us (p. 405). Again, nothing about our response is determined in advance of this first encounter (pp. 404–7).

Theories of state behaviour to the 1980s ignored the question of **authorship***.*

An elaboration of the perils of reifying anarchy – Wendt argues that Neorealists reified anarchy 'in the sense of treating it as something separate from the practices by which it is produced and sustained' (p. 410). Anarchy is taken to be something given to us, as existing out there, not produced by human beings and the states they govern. Wendt's view is quite the reverse: that anarchy is authored by states and therefore a social construct – 'what states have made of themselves' (p. 410). Things could be very different. States do not have to operate in a condition of anarchy.

Institutional transformations of power politics.

The title of Part II of Wendt's article in which he examines sovereignty, cooperation and critical strategic thought. He highlights the theoretical routes by which states might escape the supposedly all-conquering, all-structuring Hobbesian state of nature, and identifies how such escapes have been put into practice in global politics since 1945 (pp. 410–21).

Variety of possibilities for systemic transformations.

Using the example of Soviet President Mikhail Gorbachev's 'New Thinking', Wendt illustrates the capacity for state leaders to engage in critical, self-reflective learning, which in turn helps them change the nature of the world political 'game' they play. Action at the domestic and international level is needed to transform embedded attitudes, institutional practices and perceptions of identity of 'self' and 'other' (pp. 419–22).

Wendt's use of the experience of Gorbachev's Soviet Union shows the context-specific nature of our theories about IR. Gorbachev's actions led to the end of the Cold War and the demise of the bipolar international system, so academics started searching around for new explanations to replace theories such as Neorealism, which suddenly appeared empirically flawed, out of date, and unable to account for change in IR.

International Relations theories are intimately connected to social theories.

In conclusion, Wendt restates his position and adds a few important caveats. His opening remark is that IR theories are not divorced from wider debates about the nature of academic knowledge and what we can ever 'know' about the world. These social theories 'structure the questions we ask about world politics and our approaches to answering those questions' (p. 422).

Sovereign states will remain preeminent.

Having spent an entire article trashing many assumptions and explanations put forward by Neo-Neo writers, Wendt then takes a step back from some of the potentially more radical aspects of his thought. It is as if he does not want to go too near the 'postmodern' position (see Chapter 2.9 in this book). Any of the possible transformations he talks about will, he says, have to be brought about and mediated by sovereign states. Ultimate responsibility for the nature of international relations will rest with them (p. 424).

Making a bridge between rationalism and reflectivism?

Wendt's article has been heralded as the cornerstone of Social Constructivist thinking in IR. However, his parting remark that 'I am a statist and a Realist' (p. 424) has been used by critics to undermine his claim to have built a real and lasting bridge between the two traditions.

'THICK' SOCIAL CONSTRUCTIVISM

Wendt's work is important because it emphasizes the need for an IR theory of change and makes a conscious effort to theorize identity issues in IR. For some writers, however, Wendt did not go far enough in either direction. We can call these 'thick' Constructivists who approach their research not through Neorealist lenses, as Wendt did, but with an eye on other sources of identity creation and how they become manifest in the conduct of global politics.

We could equally call these 'Liberal' Constructivists because they bring non-state actors into the equation and show how they can be as crucial as states at developing and spreading norms around the international system. These norms can come to influence state behaviour by moulding leaders' perceptions of how their state is seen on the world stage, and by affecting the balance of values and interests that come into play in determining foreign policy decisions (for a good example of this work in action see Epstein (2008) on the rise of anti-whaling discourses since 1945).

NORM ENTREPRENEURSHIP

In a 1998 article, Martha Finnemore and Kathryn Sikkink used Neoliberal regime theory as a point of departure to generate some propositions about norms – their origins, how they exercise influence – and to specify the conditions under which they can be influential in world politics (Finnemore and Sikkink 1998: 888). In effect they were asking how norms can be brought in to explain the workings of regulative (formally drawn up) and constitutive (informal, habitual) institutions, with reference to processes of socialization. 'Used carefully … norm language can help to steer scholars toward looking inside social institutions and considering the components of social institutions as well as the way these elements are renegotiated into new arrangements over time to create new patterns of politics' (Finnemore and Sikkink 1998: 891).

Take the example of the EU. Neoliberal work on functionalism saw it as a technocratic project which recalibrated state perceptions of the benefits to be gleaned from tighter cooperation through integration. Read through Constructivist lenses, however, functionalist theory looks slightly different – it is all about socialization and the build-up of 'habits of trust'. As trust builds (even between states which had been at war not much more than a decade earlier) it becomes 'internalized and internalized trust would, in turn, change affect among the participants. Changed affect meant changed identity and changed norms as empathy with others shifted' (Finnemore and Sikkink 1998: 905). We can explain the EU with reference to changes in the calculations states make about the gains to be made from cooperation. But we can tell an equally compelling story about the social processes involved, whereby states come to think and act 'European' because they have become conditioned to do so by regular formal and informal interaction with other states building the European 'project'. This is where norms come in to IRT.

THE NORM LIFE CYCLE

Using the case studies of the women's rights movement and human rights norms, Finnemore and Sikkink went on in their article to develop a 'norm life cycle' to explain the origins, acceptance and spread of norms around the international system (all the below from Finnemore and Sikkink 1998: 896–909 unless otherwise stated):

- The first phase is 'norm emergence', which requires two elements. One, 'norm entrepreneurs' (these can be individuals, groups, societies, lobbyists, international organizations or agencies thereof, or states themselves). Two, an organizational platform on which to build consensus around a proposed new norm. This could entail the creation of new platforms or the reorientation of existing platforms. Norm entrepreneurs 'create' issues by inventing language that names, interprets and dramatizes them. 'In order to develop, transmit, and promote norms, a force must be dedicated to changing the meaning ascribed to certain material practices within the relevant community'. Norm entrepreneurs achieve social change by: signalling commitment to change; creating coalitions; making defiance of norms seem more costly ('shaming') and making compliance with new norms seem more beneficial (Wexler 2003: 565; see also Finnemore and Sikkink 2001: 400–1).

- The second phase is 'norm cascade', which follows the creation of a tipping point. At this juncture one of two things will have happened at the level of the international system. Either a critical mass of states has chosen to adopt the new norm (one third of the states in the system), and/or a sufficient number of 'critical' states with the capacity to influence the decisions of other states has accepted the new norm. 'Critical states' could be defined either by their leadership position within the system or their 'moral stature'. Either way, their adoption of the norm enhances the prospect of the norm being validated and legitimated for onward adoption by other states.

  The norm cascade is a dynamic process of 'international socialization intended to induce norm breakers to become norm followers'. States might want to adopt a new norm to be seen to be belonging to the international community, or conversely to not want to be seen as 'rogue' states; they might act out of 'peer pressure', to gain 'esteem' from other states, or because membership of international organizations and institutions encourages them to take the new norm seriously despite their previous inclination to reject or challenge the change in policy and outlook it implies.

- The third phase is 'norm internalization': 'norms may become so widely accepted that they are internalized by actors and achieve a "taken-for-granted" quality that makes conformance with the norm almost automatic'. In this phase, norm contestation has been replaced by norm acceptance (see the anti-slavery norm in contemporary IR for example), with what was an emergent norm at the beginning is now a dominant or hegemonic norm. 'Once norms are internalized, one abides by them not out of fear of the pending sanctions associated with them, but out of some inner conviction' (Ullmann-Margalit 1977: 172).

Failed norm entrepreneurship

Most of the work on norm entrepreneurship studies why and how they succeed in terms of being accepted and internalized. What about rubbish norm entrepreneurs?! Sometimes consideration of an exception can help test and refine a theory (see for example Bailey 2008).

In my book on New Labour and the European Union (Daddow 2011: 66–76) I applied the norm life cycle model to the case of the Blair and Brown governments' attempt to 'sell' the idea of the EU to the British people. My method was discourse analysis, quite popular among Constructivist researchers. New Labour leaders perceived that the 'norm' (the dominant, instinctive, habitual appreciation) in Britain–EU relations was for the British to be spoken about (and to play the role of) the organization's 'awkward' or 'reluctant partner'. They wanted to develop and legitimate a 'pro-European' norm that could overthrow the pervasive discontent with the EU that put Britain at the lowest end of opinion polls on support for the EU across the 27 member states. Blair was the lead 'entrepreneur' and he used organizational platforms such as the Britain in Europe group as well as many set piece speeches on the subject to get his message across. Unfortunately, the powerful Chancellor of the Exchequer, Gordon Brown, was working somewhat at odds with his Prime Minister, taking some highly sceptical positions on opinion-forming elements of British European policy such as the single currency. There was no real coordinated 'entrepreneurship' in the first place because both men feared a strong backlash from a vocal and influential Eurosceptic press, especially newspapers in the Rupert Murdoch stable such as the *Sun* and *The Times*. This finding went some way to supporting Finnemore and Sikkink's assertion that norm entrepreneurs sometimes need to risk their reputations and show strong-willed leadership to advance their cause: fear of failure can inhibit norm entrepreneurship.

New Labour never managed to reach a tipping point to cause a norm cascade, although it was possible to ascertain what that tipping point might have entailed. Extrapolating from the Finnemore and Sikkink model, a tipping point would have been reached in one of two ways: first, when a reasonable majority of the polled population expressed support for continued membership of the EU; or, perhaps, a majority of any size voted to join contentious sectoral initiatives such as the single currency; and second, when a number of 'critical' (Murdoch-owned in this case) newspapers switched from Euroscepticism to a supportive line on the EU, or at least showed more balance in the coverage over a period of time (on the 'Murdoch effect' in this policy realm see Daddow (2012)). Arguably, achieving the first task was always conditional on achieving the second. In the course of the New Labour years, Euroscepticism in the press did not diminish; if anything it increased, as did the general Euroscepticism of the British people. As a result, New Labour's much vaunted push for Europe never resulted in the establishment of a new norm. There were some decisive yet all too fleeting moves made to create and sell a new norm.

This domestic or intra-state case study tested the norm life cycle model and found that it travelled nicely to explain the social, cultural and psychological underpinnings of political decisions. New Labour possessed one image of British identity and role in the world, the press and public quite another. Blair and Brown tried – so they claimed – to be developing a new approach to British foreign policy, but they in fact fell prey to structural constraints (such as media ownership and ideology) only partly amenable to influence. Research into failed norms can help us unpack the interplay of interests and identities that shape state behaviour, as well as helping us get to grips with the 'fear' that holds states back from creative and/or cooperative ventures on the world stage.

QUESTIONS TO PONDER

'Critically evaluate Wendt's judgement that "anarchy is what states make of it"'

Answering this question successfully relies on two things: first, a solid understanding of Wendt's 1992 article; second, knowledge of some of the key critiques levelled at this piece. Lower marks will go to students who show some familiarity with Wendt's position but who do not bother critiquing his theory. The average student will spend a good deal of time exploring the nature of Wendt's argument and then skip through a critique or two fairly briefly at the end of the essay. To achieve marks at the higher end of the spectrum you should demonstrate an incisive understanding of Wendt's central themes and then make sure you devote at least as much time to exploring the critiques. The term 'critically evaluate' implies you are not just setting out those critiques but weighing up their merits (just as those writers weigh up the strength of Wendt's article). To this end, you might in your reading for this theory look for articles (for example, Wendt 2000) where writers including Wendt himself respond to the criticisms levelled at him. Using his own words is a good way of showing you have read around the subject and will reinforce your understanding of Wendt's position, as well as how he has modified it over time.

'How does a focus on norms help us explain state behaviour in the international system?'

Your emphasis in this essay can be on the use of norms by 'thick' Social Constructivist scholars. You can begin by assessing what you mean by a 'norm', how they have been theorized as part of the wider Constructivist project on identity and change in the international system, and you could get a lot of mileage from Finnemore and Sikkink's norm life cycle. It is probably worth pointing out that Social Constructivists did not 'invent' norms but they developed Neoliberal work on regime theory to divert our attention to the social basis of international action. In the introduction to the answer you will need to be clear about what you think a study of norms can contribute. Whatever you argue be sure to structure the answer around advancing that case robustly and from an informed position rooted in a knowledge of the relevant theoretical literature. It sounds easy; it isn't!

Having demonstrated that you are familiar with the concept of norms and how they have been put to work in Constructivist case studies, it is worth stepping back and comparing and contrasting the key moves 'thick' Constructivists have made with regard to 'thin' Constructivists such as Wendt and, ideally, Neorealists and their structuralist approach to explaining IR. There is a line to be drawn between Waltz, Wendt and Finnemore and Sikkink in the sense that Waltz basically ignored identity as a cause of state action; Wendt took it seriously but did not fundamentally challenge core tenets of Neorealism; whereas Finnemore and Sikkink challenge the state-centricity of both. In the debates and dialogue between them we see the 'old' debate between Realists and Liberals playing out in a different form, alongside the development of new priorities within IR that have moulded the discipline into the twenty-first century in some decisive ways.

REFERENCES TO MORE INFORMATION

General overview including Matrix analogy:
Gallemore, C. (2011) 'Theory in Action: Constructivism', 10 June. Available at: http://www.youtube.com/watch?v=kYU9UfkV_XI&feature=relmfu (accessed 10 July 2012).

Constructivism in IRT:
Checkel, J.T. (1998) 'The Constructivist Turn in International Relations Theory', *World Politics*, 50(2): 324–48.
Biersteker, T.J. and Weber, C. (eds) (1996) *State Sovereignty as a Social Construct*. Cambridge: Cambridge University Press.
Gergen, K.J. (2003) *An Invitation to Social Construction*. London: Sage.
Adler, E. (1997) 'Seizing the Middle Ground: Constructivism in World Politics', *European Journal of International Relations*, 3(3): 319–63.
Hopf, T. (1998) 'The Promise of Constructivism in International Relations Theory', *International Security*, 23(1): 171–200.

Weldes, J. (1996) 'Constructing National Interests', *European Journal of International Relations*, 2(3): 275–318.
Theorizes the concept of 'national interest' using Wendt's brand of Constructivism and uses a case study from US foreign policy during the 1960s Cuban Missile Crisis to illustrate the applicability of this approach to IR.

Gaskarth, J. (2006) 'Discourses and Ethics: The Social Construction of British Foreign Policy', *Foreign Policy Analysis*, 2(4): 325–41.

Like Weldes, uses a case study to illustrate the applicability of Constructivism to the study of IR.

Katzenstein, P.J. (ed.) (1996) *The Culture of National Security: Norms and Identity in World Politics*. New York: Columbia University Press.
See Chapters 2 (co-authored by Wendt among others), 12 and 13 where the big theoretical questions are addressed.

Jepperson, R.L., Wendt, A. and Katzenstein, P.J. (1996) 'Norms, Identity, and Culture in National Security', in P. Katzenstein (ed.) *The Culture of National Security: Norms and Identity in World Politics*, New York: Columbia University Press, 33–75.

Price, R.M. and Reus-Smit, C. (1998) 'Dangerous Liaisons: Critical International Theory and Constructivism', *European Journal of International Relations*, 4(3): 259–94.

Sterling-Folker, J. (2000) 'Competing Paradigms or Birds of a Feather? Constructivism and Neoliberal Institutionalism Compared', *International Studies Quarterly*, 44(1): 97–119.

Suganami, H. (2002) 'On Wendt's Philosophy: A Critique', *Review of International Studies*, 28(1): 23–37.

Zehfuss, M. (2002) *Constructivism in International Relations: The Politics of Reality*. Cambridge: Cambridge University Press.

Cederman, L. and Daase, C. (2006) 'Endogenizing Corporate Identities', in S. Guzzini and A. Leander (eds) *Constructivism and International Relations: Alexander Wendt and his Critics*. London: Routledge, pp. 118–39.

Smith, S. (2001) 'Foreign Policy is What States Make of It: Social Construction and International Relations Theory', in V. Kubálková (ed.) *Foreign Policy in a Constructed World*. Armonk, NY: M.E. Sharpe, pp. 38–55.

Fierke, K.M. and Jørgensen, K.E. (eds) (2001) *Constructing International Relations: The Next Generation*. Armonk, NY: M.E. Sharpe.

Prügl, E. (1998) 'Feminist Struggle as Social Construction: Changing the Gendered Rules of Home-based Work', in V. Kubálková, N. Onuf and P. Kowert (eds) *International Relations in a Constructed World*. Armonk, NY: M.E. Sharpe, pp. 123–46.
Introduces you to the constructedness of gender taken up in Chapter 2.8 of this book.

On norms and the norm life cycle:
Klotz, A. (1995) *Norms in International Relations: The Struggle Against Apartheid*. Ithaca, NY: Cornell University Press.
Keck, M.E. and Sikkink, K. (1998) *Activists Beyond Borders*. Ithaca, NY: Cornell University Press.

Cortell, A.P. and Davis Jr., J.W. (2000) 'Understanding the Domestic Impact of International Norms: A Research Agenda', *International Studies Review*, 2(1): 65–87.

Legro, J.W. (1997) 'Which Norms Matter? Revisiting the "Failure" of Internationalism', *International Organization*, 51(1): 31–63.

Klotz, A. (2002) 'Transnational Activism and Global Transformations: The Anti-Apartheid and Abolitionist Experiences', *European Journal of International Relations*, 8(1): 49–76.

Towns, A.E. (2012) 'Norms and Social Hierarchies: Understanding International Policy Diffusion "From Below"', *International Organization*, 66(2): 179–209.

Tarrow, S. (2003) *Power in Movement: Social Movements and Contentious Politics*, 2nd edn. Cambridge: Cambridge University Press.

Tarrow, S. (2007) *The New Transnational Activism*. Cambridge: Cambridge University Press.

Applied work on norms:

Goertz, G. and Diehl, P.F. (1992) 'Toward a Theory of International Norms: Some Conceptual and Measurement Issues', in *The Journal of Conflict Resolution*, 36(4): 634–64.
A state-centric, pre-Finnemore and Sikkink attempt to come to terms with norms using the case study of decolonization.

Krook, M.L. and True, J. (2012) 'Rethinking the Life Cycles of International Norms: The United Nations and the Global Promotion of Gender Equality, *European Journal of International Relations*, 18(1): 103–27.

Stevenson, H. (2011) 'India and International Norms of Climate Governance: A Constructivist Analysis of Normative Congruence Building', *Review of International Studies*, 37(3): 997–1019.

Skarbek, D. (2012) 'Prison Gangs, Norms and Organizations', *Journal of Economic Behavior and Organization*, 82(1): 96–109.

Bratberg, Ø. (2011) 'Ideas, Tradition and Norm Entrepreneurs: Retracing Guiding Principles of Foreign Policy in Blair and Chirac's Speeches on Iraq', *Review of International Studies*, 37(1): 327–48.

Wapner, P. (1996) *Environmental Activism and World Civic Culture*. Albany, NY: State University New York Press.

2.6 MARXISM

Key Terms

- Historical materialism
- Class
- Capitalism

- World System Theory
- Imperialism
- Inequality

The theories we have covered so far in this book form what you might call the 'core' of the discipline. Ask any man or woman on the street what they think makes the 'stuff' of international relations and their answers would probably include: power politics, diplomacy, war and conflict, alliance building, and the work of international organizations, including summits and treaties signed by states. The world they describe would probably resonate with many of the theorists whose work we studied in Chapters 2.1–2.4. Realists would identify with the war/conflict and alliance building elements; Liberals would identify with the emphasis on negotiations, treaties and multilateral action; while the ears of English School writers would prick up at hearing your interviewees mention laws, rules and the resulting order that develops out of them.

In the last chapter we saw Constructivist writers working on some of the themes left neglected by this conventional agenda. They have tried to bring the study of 'identity' to the mainstream study of IR, but simultaneously, in its Wendtian form at least, they underscored the place of states in our understanding of who 'makes' IR by using them as the main units of analysis. In effect, we found popular forms of Constructivism alleging a departure from IR's mainstream but not making as decisive a contribution as promised. Several other theoretical traditions have sought to make a more thoroughgoing break from the mainstream of IR. In this chapter and the next two we consider the best known of these: Marxism, Critical Theory and feminism.

MARX AND MARXISM

Neither Marx, Lenin nor Stalin made any systematic contribution to international theory.
(Wight 1995: 24)

Karl Marx's key works were written well before the discipline of IR was established and as a result there has been something of an awkward relationship between the 'core' of the discipline and Marxist and neo-Marxist agendas (documented in Holsti 1985: 61–80). The two main works you will probably have heard of were both published in the nineteenth century: *The Communist Manifesto*, co-authored with Friedrich Engels, appeared in 1848 (Marx and Engels 1998) and the three volumes of *Capital* appeared in 1867, 1885 and 1894 respectively (Marx 2008). In *Capital* Marx sought to explain the evolution of the capitalist system of economic production, and to diagnose its ills – his account of historical materialism. His normative goal was to bring about revolutionary change by highlighting what he considered to be the exploitation of the masses (what he called the 'proletariat') by a privileged few (the 'bourgeoisie').

To grasp the triangular relationship between Marx, the writers inspired by him and IR, it is helpful to bear in mind four features of this body of work:

1. **Capitalism is a 'system' in its own right.** We have seen the word 'system' used before by IR theorists. For example, Neorealists use system level explanations to account for inter-state relations in a condition of anarchy; Constructivists suggest that the international system is not something that exists 'out there', it is more 'in our heads'. Marx saw in capitalism a different type of system altogether, and in global capitalism in particular he saw forces structuring state interactions which Realists and Liberals totally ignored (Hobden and Wyn Jones 2008: 144). Within this system capabilities and interests are not defined in raw power terms, as in Realist and Neorealist theory, but in terms of whether you are a member of the bourgeoisie (owning the means of production and creaming off the profits) or a member of the proletariat (selling your labour but not receiving in terms of payment the full value for the labour you give). World System Theory used this terminology to explain IR in economic structuralist terms (see below).

2. **Economics as politics.** As Steve Hobden and Richard Wyn Jones explain (2008: 145–6), writers influenced by Marx hold

a 'materialist conception of history' whereby historical change reflects the 'economic development of society ... [and] economic development is effectively the motor of history'. Advances in technology change the nature of the productive process, and in turn this prompts changes in the means of production as producers try to get on board with new technology and make the most of their enhanced productive capacity. Marxist writers not only see economics and politics as intertwined, as the one *necessarily* affects the other, they go further in seeing economics 'as the driving force of world politics' (Sterling-Folker 2006c: 200). It is primarily developments in the economic realm that shape the social arrangements and configurations we observe in contemporary political life. For Marxist writers, economic relations determine the content and conduct of domestic and international political action.

Note how Marxist writers change our view of what makes the subject matter of IR: from politics and security in a condition of anarchy to economic relations in a global capitalist system.

Normative theory. Andrew Linklater cogently captures the essence of Marxist work: 'much of the influence of Marxism in IR is the result of its commitment to a critical or emancipatory project' (Linklater 2009a: 129). Marxist writers tend quite openly to blend elements of positivism with a normative agenda. In tracing the development of the capitalist system Marx was also thinking through how that system could be changed. He wanted to benefit the oppressed masses of workers whom he felt were not being paid sufficiently for the labour they sold to the owners of the factories where they worked. Marxist writers are generally quite comfortable about putting forward agendas for change – they write with a purpose.

Disciplinary development. Marxist ideas became popular in the discipline during the 1970s when even the domination over the system by the bipolar stand-off between 'East' and 'West' could not mask some highly divisive goings on at the systemic level. James Rosenau's 'International Studies in a Transnational World' (1976) provides an excellent illustration of the rather confused state of affairs at this time. 'Virtually each day's news seems filled with surprises, with a bewildering array of developments that do not seem to fit into any of the explanatory niches on which we have long relied' (1976: 2). Economic issues such as the Arab oil embargo were high on his list of systemically significant developments, as was the international monetary system which has 'teetered near collapse', challenging the power of governments to mobilize state resources and build alliances in the face of huge and unpredictable capital flows across national boundaries. The post-2008 global financial meltdown might in time come to be seen in exactly this light, as a stimulus to work in IRT that takes seriously the political consequences (for states and the 'system' of multilateral organizations) of the economic choices of, states, yes, but also influential non-state actors such as banks and mortgage lenders.

The crux is that Marx's economic focus is starkly at odds with the ideas and goals of mainstream IRT as I have presented its development after 1919. Conflict for Marxist writers is not the product of insecurity or other problems caused by an anarchic international arena; rather, it is the product of 'competition between capitalist classes of different states' (Jackson and Sørensen 2007: 187).

Security of a quite different kind is at work – economic security. Capitalism entails an endless search for new markets and resources. Capitalist firms can inadvertently draw states into conflict as they trawl the globe looking for new ways to expand their profit margins. Let us now have a look at the two main ways in which Marx's ideas have been used to explain international relations: World System Theory and imperialism.

WORLD SYSTEM THEORY

We saw in Chapter 2.3 how Neorealist writers such as Kenneth Waltz used the idea of an international system to explain the nature of the interactions between states. For Waltz, state behaviour in this system was shaped by the relative power each state possesses, power in this case being defined mainly by military capabilities. The system evolves from state choices about how best to survive in a condition of permanent insecurity and entails moves like alliance building, power-balancing, and so forth.

World System Theory (WST) developed around the work of Immanuel Wallerstein, particularly his three-volume *The Modern World System* (Wallerstein 1974, 1980, 1989). Wallerstein had a fresh take on the idea that state interactions are shaped by unseen systemic forces, the Marxist twist being that the system is not shaped by relative power but by the workings of the global capitalist economy. A state's behaviour in WST is shaped by the position it occupies in the global capitalist system, and it is this position that affects a state's 'capabilities, identities and interests' (Freyberg-Inan 2006: 225).

Remember Marx's idea that political life within states was defined by the fraught relations between the bourgeoisie (exploiters) and the proletariat (exploited masses) (Figure 13). In Marx's view, wealth creation in the capitalist system steadily trickles from the proletariat to the bourgeoisie. In Figure 13, the darker the shade the wealthier the class, so here we see wealth concentrated in the hands of very few capitalists. It is also noteworthy that capital tends to reside in the hands of few in society at the expense of many, hence the pyramidal structure.

Moving from the level of domestic society to the international level of the global capitalist system, states can be grouped into three categories which broadly map onto the class division Marx identified in the domestic arena (Figure 14). In WST the classic Marx model has been adapted so that 'bourgeoisie' equates to 'core' states and 'proletariat' with 'periphery' states. The difference, however, is the existence of a group of countries called the 'semi-periphery' which sits between the two others.

- **Core states** – These states are the most advanced in economic terms, meaning they incorporate 'mass market industries and sophisticated agriculture', ownership of which resides in the hands of an 'indigenous bourgeoisie' (Jackson and Sørensen 2007: 191). You might have heard these countries go by the name 'First World' – in economic terms they are 'the most prosperous and powerful' states in the international arena (Sterling-Folker 2006c: 202). The USA is the best example of a 'core' state today.

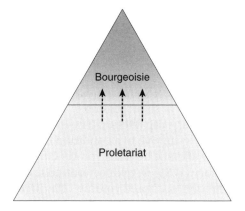

Figure 13   Marx's class system

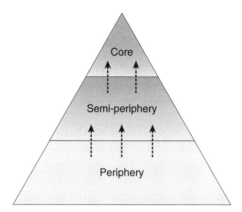

Figure 14   Marx's class system at the international level

It is important to note that the WST core-periphery model is dynamic: states can move between categories depending on changes to their political and economic structures over time.

- **Periphery states** – At the other end of the spectrum, we find states which export raw materials such as wood, grain and sugar to the core states (Jackson and Sørensen 2007: 191), and which sell unskilled labour to core producers (Sterling-Folker 2006c: 202). Core states manufacture goods using raw materials from the periphery and sell back the finished products to consumers in periphery states. The irony for periphery countries – popularly called the 'Third World' – is that they buy from core states goods made from the labour and materials they provided, but at marked up prices which are far in excess of what it would have cost to manufacture them indigenously, had they developed the capacity to do so. Poorer states in Africa and Latin America, such as Malawi, might today be considered periphery states.
- **Semi-periphery** – These states sit between the core and periphery combining economic, political and social attributes from them both (Sterling-Folker 2006c: 202). In the process of unequal exchange between periphery and core states, the semi-periphery states act out a crucial role as a buffer or 'shock absorber' (Jackson and Sørensen 2007: 191). Today, semi-periphery states might include Brazil and India.

Make a list of countries you think belong to each of the three categories set down in WST. What are the common features across your groupings and can you find statistics to support your positioning of each state?

In sum, WST provides us with a structuralist account of economic exploitation in the global arena. It helps us identify the position of various states within the system and theorizes the processes by which they have come to find themselves in that position.

WST offers a neat model of the workings of the global economic order often ignored or overlooked by even those theorists, such as Neoliberal institutionalists, who take seriously the economics of international relations. Marxist-inspired writers more often than not have a malign rather than benign view of ongoing developments in the international political economy, and this is well illustrated by the Marxist take on the phenomenon of 'globalization', as we shall see in the next section. Marxists are also pessimists about the state of contemporary IR!

TAKING IT FURTHER

The exploitation of child labour in periphery states

The term 'sweatshop' has come to mean a factory where unskilled labourers are paid a pittance for their labour, and where they are treated appallingly in terms of pay, hours and working conditions. We often associate the term with multinational corporations that have their headquarters in core states but which profit from the cheap resources and labour located in periphery states (see, for example, Fuller 2006). The UN's International Labour Organization (ILO) counts sweatshops amongst its research into 'forced labour', defined as the situation that exists when someone is trapped in a job by coercion or deception they cannot leave. In 2012 the ILO judged that there were 21 million people in forced labour today; over half of those were in the Asia-Pacific, with Africa and Latin-America also high on the list. Of these 21 million forced labourers, 18.7 million (90%) were in forced labour in the private economy. This figure broke down as follows: sexual exploitation accounted for 4.5 million, with 14.2 million in economic activities such as agriculture, construction, manufacturing or domestic work (sometimes slavery). The remaining 2.2 million were in state-imposed forced labour, for example in prisons, or in work imposed by the state military or rebel armed forces (International Labour Organization 1996–2012).

Writers in the Marxist tradition are inspired by these harrowing statistics and stories supplied by agencies monitoring forced, exploitative, unfair or cheap labour, to pen theory with purpose. They use such data to help advance our understanding of the subtle and sometimes not so subtle forms of coercion of the poor and weak by the wealthy and strong. The existence of sweatshops and 'invisible' global networks such as human trafficking challenge the state-centric approach to IR at the 'core' of the discipline. Meanwhile, indicators of economic inequality and the like would seem to provide support for the WST understanding of IR: they are empirically visible manifestations of the core exploiting the periphery. As Jackson and Sørensen explain: in the periphery, 'what little industrial activity exists is mostly under the external control of capitalists from other countries' (2007: 191).

GLOBALIZATION OR IMPERIALISM?

I could write a whole book trying to define the phenomenon of 'globalization' and we would still be no nearer a definitive account (on the perils and pitfalls of this undertaking see Scholte (2008)). In 2004 a new journal was launched, *Globalizations*, the pluralization in the title indicating how many definitions have developed around this signifier (Rosenau 2004). Globalization has many dimensions: political, economic, technological, social and cultural are just the main ones we tend to think of when we consider the ways in which the world is said to be shrinking under its effects.

The term 'global village' has been coined to describe the cumulative effects of globalization (McLuhan and Powers 1989). The apparent paradox of combining reference to the entire globe with something as small as a village helps highlight the idea that today, in the supposed era of globalization, we know much more about events going on around the world than we did previously. We are also more influenced by these events and there is a greater capacity for our actions and ideas to be carried around the globe. This is due to a lethal cocktail of: 24-hour news media; new technologies such as portable satellite systems and advanced communications such as mobile phones which bring us pictures from trouble spots the world over; and internet and social media which encourage instant reaction to breaking stories.

Already in July 2010 it was found that, with some 500 million members, if Facebook was a nation it would be the third largest in the world; if its rate of growth continued it would be as large as India by the end of 2012 (*Economist* 2010). In short, we experience more of the world more often and can travel around it faster than we used to, whether it be in the air or by surfing the net. It is rare, now, to go a whole day without hearing immediate Twitter reactions to political and other stories from one or other celebrity 'Twitterer', and these can in turn shape the news agenda on particular issues. In the good old days letters to *The Times* or *Washington Post* might have performed this function – much more slowly.

For some, globalization is an inevitability, a phenomenon that modern states have to adapt to and take advantage of, but also work *with* to solve cross-border problems such as environmental degradation, the credit crunch and pollution. As former British Prime Minister Tony Blair put it in a speech to the Foreign Policy Centre in March 2006, 'the defining characteristic of today's world is its interdependence'. But while economic globalization is now in its 'mature' phase, the politics of globalization are lagging behind. 'Globalisation is a fact … This is the age of the inter-connected. We all recognise this when it comes to economics, communication and culture. But the same applies to politics' (Blair 2006).

For Neoliberals such as Blair and US President Barack Obama, who subscribes to the same thesis, globalization exists, it is real, we can see and feel its effects and we can choose to embrace and work with them or ignore them. But we ignore them at our peril because they will affect us anyway; after all, we live in a 'global village' and are therefore always affected by goings-on elsewhere in our global neighbourhood. Look at the Asian financial crisis in the 1990s or the global financial crisis since 2008. The contagion spread around the markets with alarming speed, like a virus.

Globalization is one of those politics and IR buzzwords. In any essay or exam question where it features you will need to show knowledge of its essentially contested meaning, and establish how you will define it in what follows.

Marxist writers have a quite different view of globalization. Blair and Obama see it as an essentially benign force posing challenges, yes, but also offering the hope of solutions. For Marxist writers, globalization is not something that happens to us but something we have created. In a Constructivist take on things, a Marxist might argue that globalization is something that we in the West, or in WST terms, the 'core', have *authored*. Globalization in its economic guise has been driven by the spread of multinational corporations and cross-border financial transactions, all supported by an international financial and regulatory regime led by international organizations such as the International Monetary Fund (IMF) and the World Bank.

Alexander Anievas studies work by Marxists and Critical Theorists (see the next chapter) to make the point that they see globalization as having 'intensified the instances and possibilities of "transnational harm", rendering nation-states incapable of providing citizens with their basic needs of justice, social and physical security' (Anievas 2010: 151). Clearly, write Vijay Mishra and Bob Hodge, looked at from a post-colonial point of view, '"postmodern" globalization incorporates new forms of colonization ... which build on past practices, deployed by the usual suspects' (Mishra and Hodge 2005: 398). They might disagree on the solution, but they agree on the problem. Marxists are pessimists about globalization whereas Neoliberals are, broadly, optimistic about it. To illustrate this point, let us take a look at three examples of how a Marxist might respond to Blair's globalization thesis:

GLOBALIZATION IS NOT NEW

Hearing policy-makers talk of globalization, we might labour under the impression that there was a beginning to it – some year or event (never defined) that marked the beginning of the process. A Marxist would ask: can we pinpoint the 'start' of globalization? No, because as with the contemporary unfolding of any long-term process, locating its origins are problematic. This is key, because whereas policy-makers believing in globalization theory might want to present the era of globalization as 'new' or 'different' from previous eras, Marxists can place globalization in their longer story about the evolution of modern capitalism going back hundreds of years. Christopher Chase-Dunn, for instance, contends that what we are seeing today are 'continuations of trends that have long accompanied the expansion of capitalism'; the only difference is that we notice them more now (quoted in Hobden and Wyn Jones 2008: 220). Furthermore, since globalization has become 'part of the ideological armoury of elites within the contemporary world', and a driver of domestic and foreign policies in many states around the world, globalization is being used as the rationale for diminishing workers' rights as states seek to help their national businesses stay competitive (Hobden and Wyn Jones 2008: 221).

GLOBALIZATION IS A NEW FORM OF IMPERIALISM ('WESTERNIZATION' UNIVERSALIZED)

Noam Chomsky presents a damning indictment of the Neoliberal consensus on globalization by suggesting it is no more than a rhetorical smokescreen: 'it should be stressed that the economic doctrines preached by the powerful are intended for others, so they can be more efficiently robbed and exploited' (Chomsky 2007). Just as the British, French, Dutch and other European states conquered empires by force, a Marxist take on contemporary military interventions by leading Western powers would be that these are expressions of imperialist exploitation by a different name (an interpretation critiqued in Scholte 2008: 1476–8).

Postcolonial writers (on whom see Chapter 2.10) often join in the condemnation of the exploitative practices of globalization. Graham Huggan and Helen Tiffin, for example, argue that formerly colonized countries remain locked into 'European or Euro-American world views' under globalization. 'Just as colonies once provided the raw materials for European industrialization, post-independence states now frequently find themselves exploited by multinational companies, sometimes in league with corrupt post-independence politicians' (Huggan and Tiffin 2007: 2).

Western interventions notionally undertaken for humanitarian reasons, or to promote democracy, can be read in the same way. Work on the Kosovo intervention of 1999 (Cafruny 2006) and the contemporary War on Terror (Rupert 2007: 159–62) both point out that energy security (keeping open oil and gas pipelines and flows from these vital natural resources in Russia, Central Asia and the Middle East) surely played a part in the decision to intervene in these regions.

In fact, argues Alan Cafruny, the Kosovo intervention was partly predicated on a long established supposition by US and European policy-makers that they needed to diversify their sources of oil supply to counter the challenge from Middle Eastern exporters and 'ensure continued dominance of international oil markets' (2006: 217). Mark Rupert, meanwhile, suggests that the War on Terror has the longer-term goal of making the world safe for penetration by US businesses, a geo-political explanation with evidence reaching back decades into American foreign economic and political conduct (2007: 161–2).

Which account of these interventions do you believe? Do we have to choose? Can we combine elements of the Marxist take on them with elements of the policy-makers' justification to generate a multi-causal explanation?

INTERNATIONAL ORGANIZATIONS ENTRENCH INSTITUTIONALIZED INEQUALITIES BETWEEN STATES

Ngaire Woods well captures the Marxist take on international institutions such as the UN, the World Bank and the IMF, stating:

> Existing multilateral organizations are still hierarchically arranged. Their authority and effectiveness depend on the will and actions of their most powerful members and, as the most powerful states balance up the advantages of stronger and more effective institutions against possible losses in their own control and sovereignty, they repeatedly come down on the side of the latter. (1999: 9)

While ostensibly these bodies work to reduce poverty and enhance the integration of less developed states into the global economy, a Marxist views them quite differently: as covert agents helping to enmesh these states further into the exploitative structures of the capitalist system.

SUMMARY ON MARXISM

Contrary to the popular political idea that globalization exists and that it is a benign transformative force shaping the modern world, you can see that Marxists take a different view. They interpret economic, political and military interventions by core states in periphery states as starkly at odds with the high sounding moral rhetoric about preventing humanitarian disaster and advancing liberal democratic ideals about which we hear so much. The globalization thesis, in the Marxist view, is severely open to interpretation because it is a 'construct'.

QUESTIONS TO PONDER

'Do Marxist texts provide a valid theoretical intervention into IR when they are so obviously "positioned"?'

The fundamental issue raised by this question is one of theoretical validity which we discussed in Chapter 1.4. There are many ways to judge the quality of a theory: it needs to be reliable, to be evidentially sound, to be testable and subject to falsification, and perhaps to have predictive capabilities. One way to think through this question might therefore be to set out the basic Marxist position with reference to key exponents such as Wallerstein and others from your module reading list. The better answers will challenge the assumption that there is one coherent 'Marxist' tradition by making clear the variety of agendas pursued by writers influenced by Marx's ideas: some are more positivist and attempt to be more 'scientific' than others. Wide reading and preparation will alert you to the competing styles within this broad church.

The question is also alluding to the big debate within IR between positivists and normative theorists – the give-away is that the word 'positioned' is in quotes. Think about what it means to say a theory is 'positioned' – do you think a theory can ever be anything other than 'positioned'? However much we might aim to be scientific and objective – can we really be?

'"Men make their own history, but they do not make it as they please" (Marx). What is the significance of this quote for the study of IR?'

The first task here is to demonstrate that you understand where Marx wrote this and what he meant by it. You do not need to spell out his ideas on each and every aspect, but you should demonstrate a familiarity with key concepts such as structure and agency, and historical materialism. Thinking about the 'system' of IR for a Realist and a Marxist helps you unpack the essentials of Marxist thought.

From here you might go on to consider the issue of structure in greater detail. The structure/agency debate is a big one within IR and you could reference other writers who engage in it (especially Waltz versus the Constructivists), and then show what Marxist IR intended meant by concentrating on global economic structures. You could deploy WST to back your case and/or explore a case study in the application of Marxism to military interventions such as Kosovo (for example, from the Sterling-Folker book) to back your case about Marxists reading world political events through the lens of (usually sinister) economic forces. You could deploy the optimist-pessimist approach to understanding the Marxist take on globalization, set against many political speeches on it, especially in the 'core' Western states. It is then up to you to say how significant you think the Marxist emphasis on structures is.

We have not yet covered feminism in this book but note the gendered nature of the quote ('men' not 'women' or 'people'). The better student may well mention Marx's oversight here, and in the process demonstrate good knowledge of other IR theories.

REFERENCES TO MORE INFORMATION

Sens, A. (2012) 'Dependency Theory'. Available at: http://www.youtube.com/watch?v=JN6LIMY2ApQ&feature=related (accessed 11 July 2012).
A good overview with reference to World Systems Theory and Neo-Marxism.

Marx, K. (2008) *Capital: A New Abridgement*. Oxford: Oxford University Press.
Marx's works have been published and reprinted many times over and you can find books containing the full text and abridged versions. The first volume of *Capital* is probably the best known, so the above text is very useful as it contains almost all of Volume 1 and extracts from Volume 3.

Cox, R.W. (1987) *Production, Power and World Order: Social Forces in the Making of History*. New York: Columbia University Press.

Wallerstein, I. (2004) *World-Systems Analysis: An Introduction*. Durham, NC: Duke University Press.
An updated version of WST giving you the nuts and bolts of the theory and its application today. Will save you ploughing through the lengthy and densely written historical material in the original three volumes!

Axford, B. (1995) *The Global System: Economics, Politics and Culture*. Cambridge: Polity.
See Chapter 2 on Marxism, Imperialism and Wallerstein's World System Theory.

Burbach, R. (2001) *Globalization and Postmodern Politics*: *From Zapatistas to High-Tech Robber Barons*. London: Pluto Press.
Part I is especially recommended because it sets out neo-Marxist interpretations and responses to globalization.

Obama, B. (2008) Speech on globalization. Available at: http://www.youtube.com/watch?v=7owMXrLu2d8 (accessed 23 July 2012).
Callinicos, A. (2002) 'Marxism and Global Governance', in D. Held and A. McGrew (eds) *Governing Globalization: Power, Authority and Global Governance*. Cambridge: Polity, pp. 249–66.
Bieler, A. and Morton, A.D. (2010) 'Post-structuralism and the Randomisation of History', in C. Moore and C. Farrands (eds) *International Relations and Philosophy: Interpretive Dialogues*. London: Routledge, pp. 157–71.
Jenkins, R. (1970) *Exploitation: The World Power Structure and the Inequality of Nations*. London: MacGibbon and Kee.

Kubálková, V. and Cruickshank, A.A. (1980) *Marxism-Leninism and the Theory of International Relations*. London: Routledge.

Bush, R., Johnston, G. and Coates, D. (eds) (1987) *The World Order: Socialist Perspectives*. Cambridge: Polity.
See the chapter by Ankie Hoogvelt which gives empirical support to claims for the existence of a 'world capitalist system'. Hoogvelt has expanded and updated this thesis in:
Hoogvelt, A. (1997) *Globalisation and the Postcolonial World*. London: Macmillan.

Aronowitz, A. and Gauntney, H. (eds) (2003) *Implicating Empire: Globalization and Resistance in the 21st Century World Order*. New York: Center for the Study of Culture, Technology and Work, Graduate School and University Center of the City University New York.

Chang, H. (2003) 'Kicking Away the Ladder – Globalization and Economic Development in Historical Perspective', in J. Michie (ed.) *The Handbook of Globalization*. Cheltenham: Edward Elgar, pp. 385–94.

2.7 CRITICAL THEORY

Key Terms

- Communicative action
- Legitimacy
- Capitalism
- Hegemony

- Order
- History
- State
- Emancipation

Critical Theory (CT) is closely allied to, but seeks to go well beyond, the Marxist theories explored in the previous chapter. It is also interesting in that it has an affinity with some of the postmodern approaches we study later in the book, as well as the constructivist sensibility we covered in the previous chapter. All in all, CT is difficult to 'place' as a self-contained theory about IR because in both its scope and its methods it transcends many of the other theories of IR you will study on your course. Here is just a flavour of the problems IR theorists had 'placing' CT:

- Mark Rupert identifies CT so strongly with Marxism that they share a chapter in his contribution to one leading textbook (Rupert 2007).
- In Jackson and Sørensen (2007: 189–92), CT is referred to as 'neo-Marxism' and integrated almost seamlessly into a chapter on Marxism.
- Sterling-Folker (2006d) puts CT nearer the postmodern end of the spectrum and includes it in a chapter with that approach to IR.
- Hutchings (1999: 88) helpfully suggests that we use CT in the singular to refer to the Marxist and/or neo-Marxist variant explored in this chapter, but reminds us that it can be used in a plural sense to cover any 'non-orthodox' theoretical perspective. This is why CT also goes by the name 'International Political Theory' because its methods can be used to study international politics and social and political theory (that is, theory of the state) more generally.

> Summing up, Hutchings observes that the terminology used to refer to this array of critical perspectives 'can be somewhat confusing' (Hutchings, 1999: 88, note 3). You will have to be careful in essays and exam answers to state exactly what you mean by CT and how you see it relating to other positivist and normative theories of IR.

This chapter begins by introducing you to the origins of CT with an emphasis on the work of Jürgen Habermas. It goes on to study how CT has been accented in IR using the work of Robert Cox and Andrew Linklater.

INTRODUCTION TO CT

To use the terminology we have been working with throughout this book, CT is most definitely a normative theory. As Christopher Hobson writes (2011b: 1919): 'There is an onus to acknowledge the normative and political dimensions of our work, and to seriously consider how it may impact the world being studied'. Here we see constructivist thought shining through in the sentiment that things could be different if we think and act in ways that go against custom, convention and prevailing norms. Like Marxism, feminism and postmodernism, Devetak writes, CT's main concern is with emancipation, defined as 'a quest for autonomy, for self-determination' and this involves it in a critique of the 'impediments' and 'impositions which unnecessarily curtail individual and collective freedom', theoretically and in the realm of practice (Devetak 2009a: 168).

FIRST-GENERATION CT

First-generation CT emerged in Germany in the years between the First and Second World War among the so-called Frankfurt School, which included thinkers such as Max Horkheimer, Theodore Adorno, Walter Benjamin, Herbert Marcuse, Erich Fromm and Leo Lowenthal (see Peoples 2009: 7–18).

> Note how CT emerged in Germany at exactly the same time as E.H. Carr and others were expounding the virtues of Realist thought over Liberal thought in the UK. Why do you think CT took so long to make itself felt within the discipline of IR?

These writers aimed 'to salvage Marxist thought from its orthodox, political manifestations' (Sterling-Folker 2006d: 158), which restricted its emancipatory potential by centring the debate almost exclusively on economic relations. The concern for the Frankfurt School was, rather, 'to comprehend the central features of contemporary society by understanding its historical and social development, and tracing contradictions in the present which may open up the possibility of transcending contemporary society and its built-in-pathologies and forms of domination' (Devetak 2009a: 160).

Production, they argued, is more than a function of economic relations, it is inherently constructed. Ideas, intersubjective meanings, norms, institutions and social practices all influence the where, when and how of the production of material goods (Sinclair 1996: 9). In other words, the Frankfurt School wanted to use Marxist ideals but to build upon them in new ways to challenge the view that the state was the natural or normal basis on which societies should be organized. In short, they interrogated how we have come to *think* about the state.

SECOND-GENERATION CT

Second-generation CT is associated with the work on 'legitimacy' by Jürgen Habermas. His logic is as follows (all from Lynch 2006: 183–4 unless otherwise stated).

1 There are two types of action: 'strategic' and 'communicative'.

2 Strategic action is undertaken to manipulate another person or state via 'threats, incentives or rhetoric'. For example, states use strategic action when they use military force to coerce (compel an opponent to do something they might not otherwise do) or deter (prevent an opponent from doing something they might otherwise do). It is about 'influencing the other through the threat of sanctions or the prospect of gratification' (Crawford 2009: 188).

3 Communicative action occurs 'when actors set aside their self-interest, their relative power, and even their identities in order to seek truth – or at least consensus about the right course of action'. Communicative action 'is oriented to reaching understanding' and is more about consensus building than threats and promises (Neal 2009: 188).

4 Strategic action produces only temporary agreement because it is imposed by one actor on another. Communicative action, by contrast, is more legitimate because both actors have engaged in rational argument in an environment in which 'all affected actors are effectively able to speak and be heard'.

For Habermas, legitimacy for a specific action in the international arena only accrues if there has previously been a full and frank discussion by all actors likely to be affected by that course of action, for example a military intervention by state A in state B. In this forum it is not Realist power or force that wins the day, but 'the rationally more convincing argument' (Sterling-Folker 2006d: 164). According to Habermas, such 'ideal speech acts' are possible. The benchmark by which we judge states' behaviour is as much based on *how* they reach decisions as to what those decisions are.

Habermas' work on communicative action is wide-ranging and complex. It is a form of social theory which mixes philosophy, ethics, politics and linguistics to help us see the potential for a genuinely international public sphere to emerge. Critical Theorists do not just want to explain the world but to critique it and contribute to human betterment by encouraging open and equal exchanges of views about matters of contemporary importance. We shall now see how these variants of CT have been applied within IRT using the work of Cox and Linklater.

CRITICAL THEORY IN IR

The Frankfurt School and the second generation work of Habermas have been felt within the study of IR for at least two decades. We will use the work of two scholars to illustrate this impact: first, Robert Cox, whose major intellectual debt is to Marxism, and, second, Andrew Linklater, who draws more on Habermas' theory of communicative action to chart the possibilities for us to transcend the Realist logic of the state system.

COX ON SOCIETIES, STATES AND ORDER

As described by Timothy Sinclair, Cox's research programme has two elements to it. On the one hand he wants to understand how a relationship, institution or process operates on a day-to-day basis. On the other hand, Cox wants to understand the wider ramifications of the processes by which these things work, 'the contradictions and conflicts inherent in a social structure ... and the nature and extent of structural change that is feasible' (Sinclair 1996: 8).

Note here how Cox combines positivism (explaining the nature of a relationship/institution/process) with a normative agenda (how can we alter that relationship/institution/process in the future?)

CT is all about understanding aspects of the prevailing order, but also takes a much broader perspective. It views that initially contemplated part as 'just one component' and seeks 'to understand the processes of change in which both parts and whole are involved'. It is a guide to 'strategic action for bringing about an alternative order' rather than a 'guide to tactical actions' which sustain the order (Cox 1996b: 89–90).

In his article 'Social Forces, States and World Order', first published in 1981, Cox rethought what he saw as a narrow and overly deterministic Marxist conception of 'structure'. A structure, he suggests, does not determine individual actions; people have more room for manoeuvre than that. Sure, individuals cannot ignore structures, but they can resist and oppose them in ways that may bring about structural changes. Here is the constructivist element to Cox's thinking.

What is a 'structure'? For Cox, 'Three categories of forces' interact in a structure (all from Cox 1996b: 98–9), the direction and strength of the interaction being dependent on the particular case at hand.

1   **Material capabilities** – The Marxist element: 'technological and organizational capabilities', including natural resources and the wealth that commands all of them.

2   **Ideas** – Two kinds. To begin with, we have intersubjective meanings that shape our views of the world at a fundamental level. These are historically 'durable' ideas such as the idea that the world is made up of states, which has become something of a social institution in the practice and study of IR. Then we have ideas about the world held by different groups within societies. Whereas the first set of ideas are common throughout a particular historical structure, the existence of competing sets of ideas continually holds out the prospect of change through the establishment of new structures, or the transformation of existing structures.

3 **Institutions** – Are used to stabilize and perpetuate a social and political order. They are the embodiment of all the power relations that prevail at their point of origin; 'are particular amalgams of ideas and material power which in turn influence the development of ideas and material capabilities'. Institutions have social, ideational and material dimensions.

Having identified the components of a structure, Cox goes on to set out his method of understanding 'historical structures' (Cox 1996b: 100–1). The essence of this approach is to establish the nature of the sphere of human activity from a 'study of the historical situation to which it relates', and then to look within it for rival structures 'expressing alternative possibilities of development'. We do this on three interrelated levels:

1 **Social forces** – flowing from the organization of production and the production process.

2 **Forms of state** – as derived from a study of the nature of state/society at the particular historical juncture.

3 **World orders** – the make-up of forces that shape the interactions between states.

The connections between levels means that developments in one realm affect developments in the other two. The task of the Critical Theorist is to capture the totality of the historical process that led to the present configuration of structures on each of these levels, and then to ascertain the possibilities for future change arising from structural change within each level and at the macro levels themselves. Adapting Cox's own diagrams (Cox 1996b: 98 and 101) we can present the gamut of relationships between and within the levels as shown in Figure 15.

In Figure 15 we see the flows of influence between the three spheres of activity he suggests we use the method of historical structures to uncover. Within each level its component structures (ideas, institutions and material capabilities) are constantly interacting with each other. Given the circulation of ideas, institutions and material capabilities across levels as well as within them, the possibilities for transformations in human activity are endless.

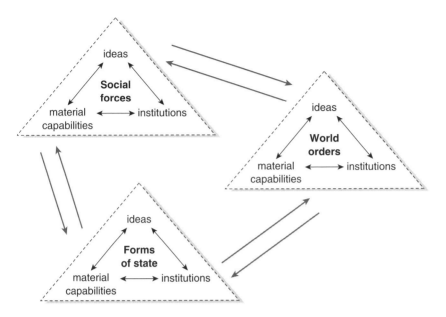

Figure 15 Cox's levels and their internal structures

> Cox sets out an ambitious research programme which invites the student of IR to be a good positivist in order to be a good normative theorist, and this raises interesting questions about the relationship between the two types of theory.

In the rest of the article (Cox 1996b, 102–13) Cox shows how to apply his method of historical structures to understanding the global order prevailing under the ***pax Americana***. Rather than detail the moves he makes here I will leave you to read up on this, and turn instead to his second key article, 'Gramsci, Hegemony and International Relations', first published in 1983, where he developed the concept of **hegemony** in IR in two stages.

The first part of the article was devoted to a reconsideration of the concept of hegemony using the work of Antonio Gramsci (on whom see Rupert 2009). Cox began by arguing that hegemony is not 'dominance of one country over others' or another word for 'imperialism' (1996a: 135). The first definition makes it too focused on state-on-state relations; the second is too far from the Gramscian meaning to make it relevant. The

Gramscian reading of hegemony shifts our gaze from the 'power from above' approach of 'state power' which is rather naked, coercive and bluntly defined. Gramsci's approach to power sees it as 'bottom to top' dealing with the constructed consent, or hegemony, which 'the dominant group exercises through society'. Power in the Gramscian reading is evident in state actions but something more diffuse, operating at a superstructural level in civil society (Gramsci, quoted in Ramakrishnan 1999: 143).

Keep a list of different definitions of 'hegemony' as you come across them in your reading. They will be useful when it comes to writing essays and exam answers on global order and the manufacture of consent in the global political economy.

The only way we can understand the meaning of 'hegemony', Cox suggests, is to study when periods of hegemony begin and end (and therefore when historical epochs can be called 'nonhegemonic'). His categorization of recent international history is as follows (Cox 1996a: 135–6):

- **1845–75: hegemonic** – A world economy with Britain central and holding the balance of power in Europe.
- **1875–1945: nonhegemonic** – Reverse of Period 1. Many other powers challenged British supremacy, two global wars erupted and global free trade collapsed.
- **1945–65: hegemonic** – A world economy with the US central to the promotion of order, but arguably not as stable as during Period 1.
- **1965–83 (Cox's 'present' at the time he first published the article): nonhegemonic** – A fracturing of the US-centred period of hegemony after 1945.

The crux for Cox is that hegemonic periods are not based on naked exploitation or coercion of weak states by the strong, but are formed when the order created is 'universal in conception'. Moreover, hegemony not only emerges from state-on-state relations but is about civil society operating 'on the world scale' (Cox 1996a: 136). The principal tool for the manufacturing of legitimacy behind the dominant mode of production is international organizations, which aid 'the process through which the institutions of hegemony and its ideology are developed' (Cox 1996a: 137). International organizations facilitate hegemony in five ways (Cox 1996a: 138–9):

1 Rules – International organizations make, enforce and change the rules, notably in areas of monetary policy and trade relations. The GATT, the IMF and the World Bank are such institutions operating today at the global level. At the regional level the European Central Bank's (mis?)management of the Eurozone might be a further example.

2 Products – International organizations are generally set up by the state that establishes the hegemony, or at least they have its support. This informal structure of influence might be seen in the role the US plays in IMF decision-making and the role the Permanent-5 (the US, Soviet Union, China, France and Britain) play in decision-making in the UN Security Council.

3 Ideology – International organizations set the parameters for policy discussions, legitimating the approaches and practices of the 'dominant social and economic forces'. The neoliberal agenda at the IMF could be one example of the ideological legitimation function performed by this organization, linking to Marxist critiques of international institutions noted in Chapter 2.6.

4 Elites – Brought in from periphery states, they may wish to change the ideological *status quo* but end up co-opted by it. Thus, writes Cox, 'Hegemony is like a pillow: it absorbs blows and sooner or later the would-be assailant will find it comfortable to rest upon'. This is part of the process of creating a social class that transcends state borders.

5 Absorption of counter-hegemonic ideas – A bit like the co-option of elites in that new ideas or approaches can be sucked into the organizational machinery and regurgitated as hegemony-supporting policies which say one thing but actually deliver another.

Try and bring Cox's model up to the present day by pinpointing periods of hegemony/nonhegemony since 1983. Where would the end of the Cold War fit in? How would you define the world today: hegemonic or nonhegemonic? Which state(s) or supra-state actor(s) are responsible (by accident or design) for promoting international order?

Through his work on social forces, order and hegemony, Cox invites us to get inside the workings of states in order to better understand their internal dynamics and, from an IR perspective, the interactions between them. Using his method of 'historical structures' Cox hopes to show that many of the things we take for granted as existing 'out there' in the world, like states themselves, are not social 'facts' but things we build ourselves. Even though Cox's greatest debt is to Marxism, we can see a strongly constructivist turn to his thinking.

BEYOND REALISM AND MARXISM: LINKLATER

The work of Andrew Linklater comes from a slightly different but related tradition of inquiry into the state of normative theory in IR and how to develop it. We will briefly summarize the essence of his argument to show you how he builds his brand of CT. Linklater set out to write 'a critical international theory which endeavours to incorporate and yet to supersede the main achievements of realism and Marxism' (1990: 7). His rationale was that the three dominant traditions in IR at his time of writing had taken the discipline so far, but that none alone had really solved the conundrum of explaining outcomes in IR as the product of interactions between states and the systems within which they operate. For Linklater (1990: 10–27) the flaws in each tradition were obvious:

- **Realism.** Focuses on the causes and consequences of war within an anarchical system but overlooks other important webs of relations between states, such as their economic relations. Lacks any sort of emancipatory agenda, seeing a system that perpetually reproduces itself from Thucydides to the present and into the future.
- **Rationalism (or the English School).** Incorporates the best features of Realism in a larger framework that accounts for order as well as conflict. In the Rationalist account, world politics is formed out of more than 'strategic competition' between states because solidarity can be engendered through states believing themselves to be members of an international society (Linklater 1990: 15; see Chapter 2.4 in this book). However, it is Western-centric and ignores the possibility that global values and other sources of order and disorder might exist.
- **Revolutionism (or Marxism).** Sees conflict in the international system not as the outcome of nation-state insecurities but as the product of tensions within an international system of economic production that cuts across state borders. The Revolutionist approach therefore underplays military

insecurity and conflict – taking us back to the merits of Realism. Plus it was dealt a huge blow by the end of the Cold War which undermined the possibility of forming a 'socialist' world state system.

Having surveyed the state of the discipline, Linklater's conclusion was that elements of the first and the third approaches (from Realism: geo-politics; from Marxism: capitalism) are vital to a comprehensive under-standing of IR. However, in isolation, neither is sufficiently attentive to the fabric of global history to possess the explanatory force their propo-nents claim for them. As he put it, 'a critical theory of international relations can only be developed by moving beyond the realist and Marxist perspectives' (Linklater 1990: 165).

> The 'world' Linklater sees is neither that of the Marxist nor the Realist. It is a more complex world in which states share the world stage with all sorts of other social forces that cut across state boundaries.

For Linklater, the 'critical' element of CT comes from it seeking to extend our understanding of 'community' through a reinvigorated Marxism, one that takes into account all the drivers of human norms and relations between societies, rather than just class struggle (Linklater 1990: 171).

Linklater's broad concept of IR chimes in nicely with the general drive behind CT identified in this chapter. It takes old concepts and looks at them afresh; it invites us to de-naturalize things about the world we take for granted; and it holds out hopes for a new international ethics which would work for all in the world rather than a privileged few.

QUESTIONS TO PONDER

'Are we living in a period of US hegemony? Answer with reference to Cox's work on world order.'

There are at least two steps you will have to take to devise a compelling answer to this question. First of all you have to define 'hegemony'. Knowledge of the two articles by Cox explored in this chapter will be key, but you can refer to any of his books/articles as long as they are relevant to the question set. Cox does a lot of the work for you in both dismissing everyday definitions of 'hegemony' and then setting out his preferred definition. The better answers will supplement Cox's work with a range of competing definitions of 'hegemony', particularly by Realist writers. If you have made a checklist of these definitions, your task here should be fairly easy. Reading up on Gramsci and his followers would show sound acquaintance with the most complex theoretical formulation of 'hegemony'.

Having explained Cox's understanding of 'hegemony' you then have to judge whether the world today is hegemonic. You could do this in one of two ways. On the one hand, you could use Cox's analysis of the features that have made for hegemonic periods in history and those that have made for nonhegemonic periods and weigh up how the world today looks compared to these ideal-type periods (applied theory). On the other hand, you could avoid the past comparisons and go straight for analysis of the social/material/ideational/institutional forces you see prevalent in the world today and evaluate whether these constitute hegemony. The danger is that you pick and choose the 'facts' to suit your argument, so pay attention to: the start point of your selected period, its ideological underpinnings and the organizational fabric. The best answers will stay close to Cox's idea that hegemony rests on consent more than coercion/force, so avoid offering accounts that focus primarily on US military action around the globe. Hegemony is a product of states, to a degree, but is something altogether more elusive than that in its Gramscian guise, with institutions and organizations co-opted to the cause.

'Do the differences between Critical Theorists undermine our ability to call it a "theory" of IR?'

This is a tricky question because it is inviting you to reflect on the nature of CT as a form of inquiry into IR, as well as to investigate the nature of 'theory' more generally. You will therefore have to scope your answer by paring it down to some basics. On CT, you might pick two or three writers as exemplary of the kinds of debates these theorists have among themselves. The same goes for theory: there are many perspectives on what this term means, so pick one that you think helps you best make your argument.

In terms of essay structure you could go for a yes/no approach. First of all, present the evidence that suggests fragmentation within a theoretical tradition undermines its claim to posit a coherent or unified approach to the study of IR. Then look at the converse view that these theories share enough in common to mark them out from other theoretical traditions in IR. The best answers will allude to the fact that all theoretical traditions have different wings to them and interplay with other theories. (See debates about how to categorize Social Constructivist approaches and how they overlap, for example, with the English School. The same can be said for postmodernism, Postcolonialism and feminism.) Overall, therefore, your argument will turn on your opinion of how much unity we can expect within *any* theory of IR.

You could easily put the argument that many of what are called theories in IRT textbooks are not in fact theories at all but 'sensibilities' – loosely connected sets of propositions about what to study in IR (ontologically speaking), to what end (epistemologically) and how (methodologically). If you advance this perspective you will need to debate the conceptual relationship between words such as 'theory', 'tradition' and 'sensibility/mindset', so be prepared to work the grey cells using engagements with the philosophy of international theory.

REFERENCES TO MORE INFORMATION

Generally on CT:

Stanford Encyclopedia of Philosophy (2005) 'Critical Theory'. Available at: http://plato.stanford.edu/entries/critical-theory/
Excellent overview of CT together with an insight into the debates between writers in this tradition.

Giddens, A. (1985) *A Contemporary Critique of Historical Materialism*. Vol. 2: *The Nation-State and Violence*. Cambridge: Polity.
Held, D. (1980) *Introduction to Critical Theory: Horkheimer to Habermas*. Berkeley, CA: University of California Press.

On CT in IRT:

Ashley, R.K. (1981) 'Political Realism and Human Interest', *International Studies Quarterly*, 25(2): 204–36.
Neufeld, M. (1995) *The Restructuring of International Relations Theory*. Cambridge: Cambridge University Press.
Mittelman, J.H. (2004) 'What is Critical Globalization Studies?', *International Studies Perspectives*, 5(3): 219–30.

Keyman, E.F. (1997) *Globalization, State, Identity/Difference: Toward a Critical Social Theory of International Relations*. Atlantic Highlands, NJ: Humanities Press.
Applies CT to the study of globalization and points ahead to the chapters in this book on feminism, postmodernism and Postcolonialism.

Wyn Jones, R. (ed.) (2001) *Critical Theory and World Politics*. Boulder, CO: Lynne Rienner.
A comprehensive collection that showcases the work of both Marxist and more Habermas-inclined theorists.

Worth, O. (2011) 'Recasting Gramsci in International Politics', *Review of International Studies*, 37(1): 373–92.

Review of International Studies (2005) 'Forum on Habermas', 31(1): 127–209. Includes articles on the Frankfurt School as well as on Feminist Critical Theory.

Review of International Studies (2007) 'Critical International Relations Theory after 25 Years', 33 (special issue).

YouTube (2007) 'Jürgen Habermas Interview', posted 1 February. Available at: www.youtube.com/watch?v=jB16ALNh18Q
Short piece in which Habermas sums up the key themes of his research and how they relate to the contemporary world.

2.8 FEMINISM

[F]eminism defies premature attempts at closure. There are the political-theoretical versions: radical, Marxist, liberal, psychoanalytic feminisms and there are more abstract conceptual visions or versions including a feminist variant on structuralism, world systems theory, feminist standpoint theory ... as well as feminist post-modern theories. (Elshtain 1995: 342-3)

Feminist scholarship came to the discipline of IR in and around the 1980s and 1990s. As with openly normative theories we have covered in the last few chapters of this book it was not IR that produced feminist scholarship. Feminists, rather, entered into conversation with IRT as part of a wider social and intellectual movement that has had a major impact across politics, academia and society over recent decades. In IR a diverse array of feminist scholars has added a vital new term to the language of IR: **gender**. This has gone hand in hand, in many but not all cases, with a reassessment of the fundamental ways in which IR scholars try to make sense of their subject matter. Feminist scholarship can also be referred to as gender theory.

Feminists have therefore achieved two significant things in IRT. First of all, they have 'added' women where previously they were overlooked or invisible in the study of international affairs. Second, they have reassessed definitions and rethought methods of studying central IR concepts such as the state, security and sovereignty. As such, critical branches of feminism share affinities with 'thick' constructivism and postmodernism in that they seek to go beyond hackneyed ways of defining and studying IR to lay bare the power relations in 'doing' IR a certain way. Meanwhile, Postcolonial feminists accent the experiences of 'non-Western' females and other subjects left out, or marginalized by, European and North American narratives of global politics and history. This chapter will begin by introducing the concept of gender and move on to highlight the different variants of feminist scholarship you might encounter on your course in IRT.

> As you read around feminism make a note of the similarities and differences between feminism and some of the earlier theories such as Realism and Liberalism in terms of: subject matter; methods; kind of knowledge produced about IR.

GENDER

Of all the keywords in feminist scholarship 'gender' is probably the one you need to get to grips with first. When we are filling out passport forms, opinion surveys, forms to get National Union of Students (NUS) cards and so on, we are asked to tick one of the two 'gender' boxes: male or female. It is easy to tick the correct box because we all know what the differences between men and women are: men are 'male' and women are 'female'. But what is it, beyond biological differences, that distinguishes masculinity from femininity? It is precisely this question that critical feminist scholars seek to answer through analysis of the constructions of each category and their day-to-day ramifications in the practice and theory of IR.

> Feminists argue that IR has excluded/marginalized women empirically (by not seeing them as valid subjects for study) and theoretically (by constructing the conceptual building blocks of the discipline on concepts associated with masculinity).

Here are two of many definitions of gender that prise open this tricky concept:

- **V. Spike Peterson** (1992: 8): 'the socially constructed dichotomy of masculine-feminine (man-woman, maleness-femaleness) shaped only in part by biologically construed male-female dimensions'.
- **J. Ann Tickner and Laura Sjoberg** (2007: 186): 'a set of socially constructed characteristics describing what men and women ought to be'.

> Masculinity is associated with characteristics such as 'strength, ration-ality, independence, protector and public' and femininity with 'weakness, emotionality, relational, protected and private'.

Note the emphasis Peterson and Tickner and Sjoberg place on the con-structedness of gender categories we commonly take to be givens. Feminist scholarship tries to highlight the artificiality of these supposedly natural divisions, and also shows how masculine characteristics have been privi-leged or looked more favourably upon within IR than feminine character-istics. IR in this interpretation operates a **patriarchal** system that works for men at the expense (literally) of women, not only in practical terms but fundamentally because it shapes our 'modes' of seeing and talking about what is important in this field. As Daryl Jarvis puts it (2001: 105), gender is 'an indispensable ingredient in the study of international politics, a means of understanding not just the systemic basis of the international system, but of the power structures embedded in those relations'.

In the introduction to her edited collection *Gendered States,* Peterson (1992: 9–10) elaborates four reasons why it is useful to 'gender' IR:

1 **Decentring biological explanations** – Conceptions of maleness and femaleness are not fixed over time or across national boundaries. Taking gender constructions as 'given' rather than 'made' obstructs our understanding of the subtle yet powerful part they play in the practice and study of IR. As Charlotte Hooper explains, 'historical and anthropological research suggests that there is no single "masculinity" or "femininity" and that both are subject to numerous and fairly fast changing historical and cultural variations' (2006: 377).

2 **The interdependence of key words** – Here, Peterson concen-trates on the interrelationship of the terms 'masculine' and 'feminine' and their associated characteristics such as 'ration-ality' (masculine) versus 'emotionality' (feminine). They are not mutually exclusive but interdependent, meaning that our under-standing of the one is necessarily dependent on the characteris-tics we attribute to the other. Usually, feminine characteristics are valued less than masculine ones and this highlights the power *in* language to degrade the feminine at the expense of the masculine. An exploration of the power relations at work in representing a notional 'Other' to help define one's 'Self' identity is one of the main ways in which constructivist approaches have been put to work in IRT, whether by gender or Postcolonial theorists.

> Feminism is not just about women or women's concerns. It crucially feeds into social theory and questions about our ways of 'being' in the world, male or female.

3 **Structure and agency** – Feminist scholarship is comfortable working with questions about the 'subjective, everyday', and relating these to historical or structural contents within which these day-to-day experiences are felt. There is no privileging of one level of analysis, as we have, for example, in Neorealist theory which emphasizes the structural determinants of state behaviour. Downplaying the identity/beliefs/idiosyncrasies of the states themselves means Neorealists ignore the human, social and ideational aspects of IR that theorists from the English School, Social Constructivism and related theories find interesting.

4 **Diversity** – Feminists take an inclusive approach to the subject matter of IR by speaking to all of the following issues: power, identity, culture, sexual relations, discourse, the international division of labour, poverty and militarism. This wide agenda gives feminists a distinctive handle on all of the big ontological, epistemological and methodological questions about IR as a discipline, covered in Chapter 1.4 of this book. See Cynthia Enloe (2001) for a good example of the eclectic range of subjects to which this theory speaks.

FEMINIST PERSPECTIVES

By saying there are different strands to feminist thought we are not saying that these are mutually exclusive or that they are somehow in opposition to each other. However, there are distinctive approaches to feminist IR that are worth noting, first because they highlight the porous nature of the boundaries between the theories covered in this book; and second, it illustrates how the capacity for one theoretical tradition can house a diverse array of perspectives. Something of this complexity is captured in Figure 16.

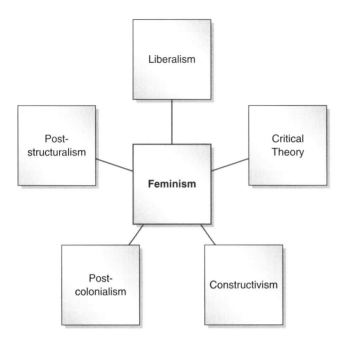

Figure 16   Feminism in IRT

Feminist scholars develop aspects of work in IR and the social sciences more generally. Here we will follow the work of Tickner and Sjoberg (2007: 188–92) who give a breakdown of how these myriad influences show themselves in feminist scholarship. Other textbooks do it differently (for instance, Smith and Owens 2008: 181–5). Note also that their choice of terminology, for example, poststructuralism instead of postmodernism, differs slightly from the terminology used in this book. However, the point is to note the overlap between the various theoretical traditions and this is as good a place as any to seek them out.

That writers cannot agree on how best to capture the field of feminist scholarship says something about the breadth and depth of its concerns. Keep a note of all the variations for use in essays/exams where you have to define 'feminism'.

LIBERAL FEMINISM

Liberal feminists basically accept the conventional framework of IR by looking to add women and women's issues to the IR agenda as it currently stands. This 'add women and stir' approach takes existing subject matters, methods and the positivist epistemologies, and introduces women where previously they were either invisible, forgotten about or glossed over. They do this by documenting 'various aspects of women's subordination' (Tickner and Sjoberg 2007: 188) in economic, political, legal, social and health terms. They seek out women's contributions to society and shine a light on them to make a call for greater equality.

International organizations like the UN and pressure groups such as Human Rights Watch have collected vast amounts of data, statistics and reports on gender (in)equality and women's human rights around the world, and they can be mined for information to help the Liberal feminist cause (Human Rights Watch 2012; UN 1997–2010). A selection of headlines from the Human Rights Watch website in July 2012 shows the diverse issues at stake: 'Saudi women's participation in the London 2012 Olympic Games'; 'Target-driven sterilization of women in India'; 'Child marriage'; and 'Young female deaths from early childbirth'.

CRITICAL FEMINISM

Critical feminists want to go beyond adding and stirring women into existing IR scholarship. Taking inspiration from the work of Marxists and Critical Theorists such as Robert Cox (see Chapter 2.7 of this book), they stress the part perceptions of the key word 'gender' have played in moulding policies and practices in global politics. Gender in the Critical Theory perspective is another structure that shapes (often unwittingly) how men and women interact, and how relations between men and women become infused with power inequalities.

Critical feminists show how all this plays out in the form of material (economic) inequalities, and the maltreatment and exploitation of women. After highlighting these structural inequities, Critical Theorists hope that they can be changed in the future, giving their work an emancipatory edge, or in Kimberly Hutchings' words, 'a productive impact on how international politics are to be understood and judged' (1999: 83). 'Gender' in this perspective is another of those unseen 'structures' that shape the conduct of international affairs without getting any attention from theories such as Neorealism. It is nothing less than a social institution, albeit with culturally relative meanings around the globe and in different eras.

CONSTRUCTIVIST FEMINISM

Following the Social Constructivists, feminist constructivists focus on the ideational rather than the material aspects of global politics. They 'focus on the way that ideas about gender shape and are shaped by global politics' (Tickner and Sjoberg 2007: 190), and are interested in discovering the causes of the ideas that shape our gendered world as well as in the language through which these ideas are expressed. Constructivist feminists work at de-naturalizing divisions between the genders by investigating the ideas that lie behind these constructions and asking: where have our ideas about gender come from; are they just; and how might they be altered?

POSTSTRUCTURAL FEMINISM

This is the widest, most thoroughgoing feminist perspective that questions how we apprehend the world through language, our theories and our 'scientific' ways of studying IR. We have previously seen that gender divisions are constructed around the interdependence of terms such as 'masculine' and 'feminine' and, thereby, the characteristics we tend to associate with each gender. We further noted that these categories and characteristics are imbued with power relations in that masculine characteristics tend to be looked upon as the standard for the rest of humanity to live up to. Things masculine tend to be privileged over things feminine.

Poststructural feminists use the 'gender as power' idea in two important ways:

1 They rethink the very basis of the supposedly objective knowledge claims made by Western science. As Peterson points out (1992: 12–13), Western philosophy has tended to be the preserve of Western elite males where men's experiences are said to be representative of all human experiences; supposed gender differences have been institutionalized in the academy and

policy practice; and the Western phallocentric order privileges masculine qualities over feminine ones (for example, masculine 'reason' is elevated above feminine 'passion').

One of the most famous feminist re-workings of practices in conventional IRT was Tickner's reformulation of Morgenthau's six principles of
'political realism' on the grounds that 'it is a partial description of
international politics because it is based on assumptions about human
nature that are partial and privilege masculinity' (Tickner 1988: 431).
Work through her line of thought to see the depth of the critique poststructural feminists have of IR in its positivist Realist-Liberal guise.

---

2 They apply this to IR by rethinking the ways in which the language
of IR sets up artificial binaries between, for instance, 'civilized/
uncivilized, order/anarchy, and developed/underdeveloped' (Tickner
and Sjoberg 2007: 191). Also consider how regularly terms such as
'good/evil', 'state/failed state', 'secure/insecure', 'terrorist/freedom
fighter' feature in the practice and study of IR. Poststructural feminists invite us to see the real-world implications of what are in fact
artificial binary distinctions which implicitly privilege one of these
terms over the other; they 'seek to expose and deconstruct these
hierarchies' (Tickner and Sjoberg 2007: 191).

Can you think of other artificial binaries commonly used in the practice
and study of IR? Which of the two terms is privileged? What are the
consequences?

POSTCOLONIAL FEMINISM

This branch of feminism makes two contributions to the study of IR.
The first has an affinity with poststructural feminism and the Postcolonial movement more generally (see Chapter 2.10). It highlights the
structured nature of the oppression and/or invisibility of women in
former **colonial** states. Even in states which have formally declared
their independence from their former 'masters' (note the gendered

terminology), Postcolonialist feminists argue that colonial constructions of 'self' and 'other' linger on and denigrate the 'other' as inferior (Tickner and Sjoberg 2007: 192). Like constructivist and poststructural feminists, they highlight the importance of binary categories and therefore see language as a site of oppression and dominance.

The second contribution is more a debate with other feminists. Postcolonialist feminists unpick the fabric of the feminist movement. They argue that feminism has tended to be the preserve of elite Western women, who have made their concerns stand in for the concerns of all women around the globe. Just as feminists criticize the tendency for men's experiences to be held up as representative of humanity as a whole, so Postcolonialist feminists take issue with feminist scholarship that confuses Western women's concerns with those of women from other parts of the world. There is, they say, no 'universal understanding of women's needs', and we need to be aware of cultural, religious and ethnic divergences (Tickner and Sjoberg 2007: 192).

SUMMARY ON FEMINISM

Where Liberal feminists fit into the existing IR agenda, their Critical, constructivist, poststructuralist and Postcolonialist counterparts point to major inequities not just within the world of IR as *practice* but in IR as *theory*. Feminism is not just about raising the profile of women in IR but about raising the profile of the gender-biased nature of IR as an academic discipline. Work on the philosophy of science, on the constructedness of gender and discrimination in the language of IR force us to rethink what IR is all about. We have further cause to rethink these disciplinary practices in our encounter with postmodernism in the next chapter.

QUESTIONS TO PONDER

'Can "gender" concerns be added to the existing IR agenda? Answer with reference to at least two feminist scholars you have studied on your course in IRT.'

Your first task with this question is to scope it by defining the key terms 'gender' and 'existing IR agenda'. With the former you need to give some sense of the constructedness feminists see in the term. Using definitions from key writers such as Peterson and Tickner and Sjoberg, and pulling out the implications, as we did in this chapter, is a good tactic for two reasons. First, it shows that your knowledge of the literature is wide and that you know the meaning of *the* key term in feminist IR. Second, you will immediately produce the names of at least two scholars as directed by the question. It is arguably trickier to define the 'existing IR agenda'. It is open to you to define it how you wish, and one good way is to use the conception of IR prevalent in feminist critiques of its limitations as a discipline. You could also go back to other writers such as Holsti and/or Constructivist writers who present views of the disciplinary 'core' of Neo-realism and Neoliberalism which was dominant until the early 1990s.

Having scoped the essay, you need to come up with a response which will be dependent upon what you see as the mainstream IR agenda. You should ideally try and show that you are aware of arguments that gender and/or women are more than 'variables' which can simply be stirred into IR as part of an ever widening agenda (Liberal feminism). Reference to the more critically inclined variants of feminism will let you show that gender actually subsumes IR by providing a critique of the Western philosophy of science as we conventionally understand it. An 'it depends' answer is no bad approach here because it allows you to talk about the significance of our interpretations of both IR and science as determinants of our position within this debate. The debates within feminism point to its slightly fragmented nature as a cohesive 'theory', and some sense of a loose but identifiable feminist 'sensibility' might usefully feature in your answer.

'"Gender hierarchy is not coincidental to but in a significant sense constitutive of Western philosophy's objectivist metaphysics" (Peterson). Discuss the implications of this statement for IR theory.'

It is always difficult to structure answers to 'Discuss' questions. Some students fall into the trap of writing everything they know about some of the major terms or authors raised in the question. To get past this erroneous approach try and think through why Peterson wrote what she did and how her ideas have been received by other feminists and critics alike.

Your first job is to summarize Peterson's argument: untangle the thrust of her case for your reader in a few hundred words. Ideally you would know where this quote comes from (Peterson 1992), but if not you should have read enough of her work to be able to capture the essence of her argument. The implications are many and varied, and the number you include will naturally depend on the word and/or time limit you have. Normally at undergraduate level you will not be able to cover more than four or five points in depth in the body of an essay or exam answer. You want to try and showcase the point of view that takes 'conventional' IR theory as a sub-set of the positivist, objectivist view of science, and therefore that it can be critiqued on a number of grounds.

Any of the following broad issues could be included, and they would need breaking down: 'gender' and science (science as 'masculine'); feminism as a philosophy of social science; gender and the power of language; IR theory as a masculine pursuit (by men, about men, for men); IR, the public sphere of the international and the neglect of the private (women's realm); is 'gender' a variable? The best answers will do more than explore Peterson's intervention, they will pay some homage to writers who see gender either as irrelevant to, or a pointless distraction from, the core concerns of IR as a discipline, so finding critics of the feminist approach in your course readings will help you out here.

REFERENCES TO MORE INFORMATION

On gender in IRT:

True, J. (2001) 'Feminism', in S. Burchill et al., *Theories of International Relations*, 2nd edn. Basingstoke: Palgrave, pp. 231–76.
   Excellent overview of the contours of feminism and the contribution it has made to IR theory.

Elshtain, J.B. (2006) 'Reflections on War and Political Discourse: Realism, Just War and Feminism in a Nuclear Age', in R. Little and M. Smith (eds) *Perspectives on World Politics*. Abingdon: Routledge, pp. 368–75.
   A feminist deconstruction of the language and assumptions of Realist theory.

Enloe, C. (2009) 'Picking Up the Pieces: Making Feminist Sense of the Iraq War', Lecture at Quinnipiac University, 24 September. Available at: http://www.youtube.com/watch?v=WTFaxobkVps&feature=related (accessed 11 July 2012).

Whitworth, S. (1989) 'Gender and International Relations: Beyond the Inter-Paradigm Debate', *Millennium: Journal of International Studies*, 18(2): 265–72.
   One of the landmark works in feminist IR scholarship.

Whitworth, S. (2005) 'Militarized Masculinities and the Politics of Peacekeeping', in K. Booth (ed.) *Critical Security Studies and World Politics*. Boulder, CO: Lynne Rienner Publishers, pp. 89–106.
Case study of Canadian peacekeeping, illustrating how feminist concerns are central to the study of military values and practices.

Tickner, J.A. (1988) 'Hans Morgenthau's Principles of Political Realism: A Feminist Reformulation', *Millennium: Journal of International Studies*, 17(3): 429–40.
Classic 'standpoint' feminist study which rewrites Morgenthau's work from the perspective of women and in doing so shows the gender bias in this supposedly objective Realist account of IR. Textbooks in IR often feature Tickner's work, so it is useful to have read the original.

Tickner, J.A. (2006) 'Feminist Perspectives in International Relations', in W. Carlsnaes, T. Risse and B.A. Simmons (eds) *Handbook of International Relations*. London: Sage, pp. 275–91.

Blanchard, E.M. (2011) 'Why Is There No Gender in the English School?', *Review of International Studies*, 37(2): 855–79.

Zalewski, M. (2011) '"I Don't Even Know What Gender Is": A Discussion of the Connections Between Gender, Gender Mainstreaming and Feminist Theory', *Review of International Studies*, 36(1): 3–27.

On feminism and gender studies more generally:

Keller, E.F. (1985) *Reflections on Gender and Science*. New Haven, CT: Yale University Press.
Critique of the Enlightenment scientific project which equates 'objectivity' with 'masculinity'.

Mertus, J. (2007) 'Liberal Feminism: Local Narratives in a Gendered Context', in J. Sterling-Folker (ed.) *Making Sense of International Relations Theory*. Boulder, CO: Lynne Rienner Publishers, pp. 252–67.
Good example of feminist theory being put into practice.

Krause, J. (1995) 'The International Dimension of Gender Inequality and Feminist Politics: A "New Direction" for International Political Economy?', in J. Macmillan and A. Linklater (eds) *Boundaries in Question: New Directions in International Relations*. London: Pinter, pp. 128–43.

Lloyd, M. (2005) *Beyond Identity Politics: Feminism, Power and Politics*. London: Sage.

Lange, L. (2003) 'Woman is Not a Rational Animal: On Aristotle's Biology of Reproduction', in S. Harding and M.B. Hintikka (eds) *Discovering Reality: Feminist Perspectives on Epistemology, Metaphysics, Methodology, and the*

Philosophy of Social Science, 2nd edn. Dordrecht: Kluwer Academic Publishers, pp. 1–16.
Demonstrates how an appreciation of gender helps us think critically about the big questions in the philosophy of science and IR.

Spender, D. (ed.) (1981) *Men's Studies Modified: The Impact of Feminism on the Academic Disciplines*. Oxford: Pergamon.

Butler, J. (1999) *Gender Trouble: Feminism and the Subversion of Identity*. London: Routledge.

Steans, J. (2002) 'Global Governance: A Feminist Perspective', in D. Held and A. McGrew (eds) *Governing Globalization: Power, Authority and Global Governance*. Cambridge: Polity, pp. 87–108.

Braunstein, E. (2003) 'Gender and Foreign Direct Investment', in J. Michie (ed.) *The Handbook of Globalization*. Cheltenham: Edward Elgar, pp. 165–75.

Chinkin, C. (1999) 'Gender Inequality and International Human Rights Law', in A. Hurrell and N. Woods, *Order, Globalization, and Inequality in World Politics*. Oxford: Oxford University Press, pp. 95–121.

Review of International Studies (2007) 'Forum: Women and Human Rights', 33(1): 5–103.

2.9 POSTMODERNISM

Key Terms

- Statecraft
- Sovereignty
- Identity
- Deconstruction

- Power/knowledge
- Genealogy
- Discourse

The postmodern vantage point is one of critique. Its aim is to unsettle, to jar, to challenge, and to subject our most fundamental beliefs and principles to intense critical scrutiny. (Shinko 2006: 168)

Postmodernist theory calls for a radical re-thinking of how we think. (Hutchings 1999: 82)

As an intellectual movement, postmodernism swept through the social sciences from around the 1970s onward. Some scholars jumped on board, liberated by the critical tools it offered them. Others have been left confused about what it all means, and some are actively hostile to anything to do with the 'p'-word (Sterling-Folker, 2006d: 165, citing James Der Derian). Critics of postmodernism from within IR have variously called it 'evil', 'dangerous', 'bad IR', 'meta-babble' (Krasner and Halliday, cited in Campbell 2007: 210), or simply questioned the 'novelty of the arguments developed by the proponents of these allegedly new paradigms' (Navon 2001: 612).

James Der Derian notes that French/'continental' philosophy in general has not gone down well in the Anglophone core of the discipline and this has affected the reception of writers such as Michel Foucault: 'The dual imperative of protecting the state and IR theory from any sudden change has always placed a premium on traditional approaches … Taking on many of the shibboleths of IR led to charges of blasphemy' (Der Derian 2009: 70). Bruce Russett's dismissal of newer approaches is emblematic of this scepticism: '"Post-modernism" may have a place in art museums but it should be kept out of the study of international relations' (Russett 1995: 176).

Keep a record of the reasons why different writers you study are supportive of, apathetic about, or hostile to some of the 'newer' IR theories like postmodernism. What informs their views and what does this reveal about the nature of debates about IR theory?

The main thing postmodernism has in common with all the other theories covered in this book is that calling it 'theory' might cause more problems than it solves. There are many variants of postmodernism, just as there are many strands or 'wings' to Realism, Liberalism and the English School. Furthermore, postmodernism is like Marxism, feminism and Postcolonialism in being a broad intellectual movement that cuts across disciplines. Some feminists are postmodernists, but not all; some Marxists are postmodernists, but not all; Postcolonialist writers are renowned for their transgression of all these notional theoretical boundaries. Like Constructivism, postmodernism is difficult to bracket as a theory, because in its ontological and epistemological positioning it is something more like a 'sensibility'. IR is just one site for postmodern work among many.

Postmodernist works come under many names. On your IRT course you might find it called 'poststructuralism' or 'post-positivism' because increasingly tutors are finding that 'postmodernism' is too broad a term or simply inapplicable in the context of IRT (Campbell 2007: 211–12). It does not get any easier when we try and define postmodernism, for as Devetak puts it: 'Postmodernism and post-structuralism are labels with complicated and contested histories' (Devetak 2009b: 183). Although some writers are comfortable using one or both terms to describe their work and methodological approach, others are less so. As we have seen above, some even use the terms as a form of explicit or implied criticism of 'newer' approaches to IR. I have chosen to use the label 'postmodern' in its broadly accepted IR sense to encompass poststructuralist and post-positivist works, even if their authors might take issue with being labelled postmodernists.

How do we identify postmodern texts or do we just know them when we see them? Sterling-Folker goes some way to making this point when she writes 'The postmodern IR scholar also focuses on what the positivist would consider trivial or unrelated to IR, such as the spy novel, football, defense manuals, *Star Trek*, and popular culture' (Sterling-Folker 2006d: 162). It is not only the subject matter that defines postmodernism, however. Postmodernists draw upon an eclectic array of sources, ideas and practices to challenge ontological, epistemological and methodological conventions in IR. In this process, 'readings of Derrida and Foucault have been particularly important' (Hutchings 1999: 77).

As the two quotes at the start of this chapter make clear, postmodernists want to critique things we take for granted in IR, like the idea of the state. In this respect they want to help us reassess not just the world as we see it but the ways in which we think we see the world. While it has obvious affinities with Critical Theory and thicker varieties of Constructivism, as well as an emancipatory agenda that chimes with other openly normative IR theories, postmodernism brings concepts and ideas all of its own to the IR table.

> If you find postmodernism challenging, difficult and unsettling then do not fear! Postmodernists jolt us out of cosy, established ways of thinking and invite us to think the unthinkable.

In this chapter we can only introduce you to some of the most influential ways in which postmodernism has been felt within IR. We will do this, first, by introducing the key concepts and methods associated with postmodernism and, second, we will take you step-by-step through a postmodern study of statecraft by Devetak (1995). By the end of the chapter you should be able to grasp the meaning of basic postmodern terms and be able to spot postmodern IR texts when you see them.

POSTMODERN IDEAS, CONCEPTS AND APPROACHES

Works of IR written in a postmodern vein are built on one, some or all of the following ideas, concepts or approaches inspired by the work of the French philosophers Michel Foucault (1926–84) and Jacques Derrida (1930–2004).

DECONSTRUCTION

Inspired by the philosophy of Jacques Derrida, **deconstruction** is another widely used and abused terms in the social sciences. According to Devetak, it 'defies definition' but 'can be understood as a strategy of interpretation and criticism directed at concepts which attempt closure or totalization' (Devetak 1995: 20). According to Mishra and Hodge, what deconstruction does best is: 'interrupting, intervening, opening up the discourses of the dominant, restoring plurality and tension' (Mishra and Hodge 2005: 386). Postmodern writers who want to jar 'the whole edifice of common-sense notions' (Devetak 1995: 20) use deconstruction in a variety of ways, the technique of 'double reading' being especially popular (see the next section).

Claudia Aradau (2010: 107–8) summarizes it by suggesting that in IR 'a deconstructive perspective has challenged taken-for-granted "truths" about what the international is and how it functions. Deconstruction has helped IR scholars destabilize both hegemonic texts and dominant understandings of the subject'. Especially important has been its unsettling of dichotomies and breaking down the supposed barriers between inside and outside, domestic and international, and self and other.

Maja Zehfuss uses the example of 'gender' to illustrate deconstruction at work. We can attempt to overturn the privileging of supposedly masculine characteristics over feminine characteristics by asserting that 'the (putatively masculine) ability to rationally and objectively assess various options is not as good as the (putatively feminine) ability to take feelings into account'. However, this critique merely reproduces part of the thinking it allegedly overturns, by accepting that 'feminine' can be distinguished from 'masculine'. In being accepting of this artificial distinction: 'The original hierarchy remains possible and can therefore reassert itself'. A second move is necessary to displace this system of thought altogether: Derrida's 'displacement'. A displacement would involve investigating whether 'masculine' can be thought of as separate from and antithetical to 'feminine'. Derrida invites us to reconsider our structures of thought because the dichotomies on which our thought patterns are based, he believes, 'do not work' (Zehfuss 2009: 141–2).

POWER/KNOWLEDGE

Postmodernists investigate the ways in which power is generated by putting artificial closures or limitations on our understanding of the world. Following on from that, they explore how the exercise of power is deeply intertwined with the production and transmission of knowledge around societies.

This focus on power/knowledge comes directly from Foucault's understanding of power, which is quite different from the definition of 'power' many IR scholars work with. To use David Campbell's terminology (2007: 215–16), the conventional meaning of power is essentially repressive and is associated with state power, whether expressed physically in the form of bullets or nuclear warheads, or ideationally in terms of the persuasive power of a political speech, for instance. Repressive power 'from above' involves the imposition of limits or constraints on our thought and actions and often aims, bluntly, at telling us what to do. This is power as threat and control.

Foucault – like Gramsci (see the Critical Theory chapter, above) – sees power as being more productive than repressive. The power of which he speaks is the power to define and impose those limitations in the first place. How, he asks, is language used to limit our thinking about what is normal, legitimate and proper in the world? Who is it that gets to circumscribe our social 'truths'? Productive power shapes things, builds things, describes and categorizes them. Naked power from above might be contrasted both with feminist renderings of the term (for example, Elshtain 1995: 354–6) and a similarly nuanced Foucauldian notion of power from below. 'It is not simply a means of repression or coercion, but rather it flows throughout society in networks'; it is 'not simply possessed but practiced' (Neal 2009: 163).

The X-Files gave us the positivist motto 'the truth is out there'. For Foucault, things are much more complicated. 'Truth is a thing of this world: it is produced only by virtue of multiple forms of constraint. And it includes regular effects of power. Each society has its regime of truth' (Foucault 1991: 72–3). James Keeley summarizes Foucault's appreciation of regimes as intrinsic to the discourse by which they are constituted:

> … a regime gives specific definition and order to a public space or realm of action. It specifies a phenomenon and an issue-area deemed of public interest and in this sense 'politicizes' them. It identifies the relevant qualities of the occupants of that space. It defines the relations within which they see and are seen by each other and in terms of which they conduct the public business with respect to that issue-area. (quoted in Ramakrishnan 1999: 142)

This is a quite different 'regime' from the more or less formal and institutionalized cooperative regimes at work in Neoliberal theory (see Chapter 2.3 in this book). Foucault gets behind the façade of language to ask what sources of power societies have erected under truth, behind truth and around truth to give it authority and legitimacy: to make it *function* as truth and to support socially constituted regimes. How does an always *partial* truth about the world come to parade as *the* truth, to make it appear to hold across time and space?

REPRESENTATION

Foucault's interest in discovering 'regimes' of truth led him to engage with issues of representation: how different regimes of truth call to mind the world to us through language. We are forever using words in the place of things. In the context of IR, 'we are engaging in abstraction, representation and interpretation' when we use words to try and make sense of international affairs (Campbell 2007: 204). Terms such as 'globalization', 'War on Terror', 'freedom', 'international system', even 'humanity', by necessity, relate to objects, people and clusters of things that have happened, are happening and which will continue to happen in some form into the future. The point for Foucault is that our words can only ever *stand in* for, or represent, these social facts; words can never *be* those things. Individual words in this interpretation are more like concepts: always slippery and prone to manipulation and misapplication.

DISCOURSE

To summarize Foucault's line of thinking so far: we have all these words in our respective languages which are routinely used to represent or stand in for the objects they are meant to be neutrally describing. In the process their meanings become slippery and prone to ambiguity. But he does not stop at identifying the gap between the units of language (signifying words) and the essentially unknowable things they represent (for example, signifieds like 'globalization'). Foucault takes this problem with the units of language and applies it to the systemic level of our sentences and paragraphs to demonstrate that at the narrative or discursive level the problems of language relating to things become even more acute.

If we study discourse, Foucault suggests, we see the productive power of language. The study of discourse has become 'a means of gathering the things said and written on a particular subject in a particular context by a particular group of people (often political elites), in order to try to interpret what is being done politically through such statements' (Neal 2009: 166). David Campbell (2007: 216) describes discourse as 'a specific series of representations and practices through which meanings are produced, identities constituted, social relations established, and political and ethical outcomes made more or less possible'. Discourses do not simply describe the world, they 'constitute the objects of which they speak' (Campbell 2007: 216). See also the selection of definitions on offer in Ramakrishnan 1999: 137).

For Der Derian (2009: 71): 'Discursive practices mediate and often dominate IR by establishing what can be said and who can say it with authority'.

> The study of discourse is popular among postmodernists and 'thick' Constructivists, showing something of the blurred boundaries between these heavily overlapping sensibilities.

We can have a discourse about anything, and it will necessarily be positioned, as well as imbued, with power relations. For Miguel Cabrera, discourse is 'the coherent body of categories, concepts and principles by means of which individuals apprehend and conceptualize reality … and through which they implement their practice in a given historical situation' (Cabrera 2005: 22–3). In representing and giving meaning to social action, discourses are inherently performative. In other words, discourses can offer up the power relations that lie behind them for critical scrutiny, but they can just as easily mask them from view and make us believe certain things or ways of 'being' in the world are natural, timeless or universal when in fact they are not. 'A discourse provides a set of possible statements about a given area, and organizes and gives structure to the manner in which a practice, topic, object, process is talked about. In that, it provides descriptions, rules, permissions and prohibitions of social and individual actions' (Kress quoted in Fowler 1992: 42).

So there are discourses of terrorism, security, human rights, international community, climate change, the state. The field of IRT could be treated as a discourse unit if you wanted. Each and every one of these fields can be read 'against the grain' to expose its limits as well as its meaning-making processes.

TAKING IT FURTHER

Writing Security

David Campbell's *Writing Security* starts from the premise that: 'Danger is not an objective condition … that exists independently of those to whom it may become a threat' (1998: 1). Danger, he continues, 'is an effect of interpretation' rather than an objective quality of a given event or set of events (1998: 2). Threats to a state's national security are constructed out of the interplay between conceptions of national identity (and the interests that are said to flow from it) and interpretations of what is, or is not, perceived to pose a threat to the values bound up with that sense of identity: 'the boundaries of a state's identity are secured by the representation of danger integral to foreign policy' (p. 3). The rest of the book is an extended engagement with the principles and assumptions of two prominent explanations for foreign policy actions within IR: Realism and Marxism. Both readings, Campbell asserts, are flawed because they 'maintain that there are material causes to which events and actions can be reduced'. To advance a different perspective of 'dissent', Campbell draws on the work of Foucault to interpret how key terms such as 'danger', 'threat' and 'power' have 'historically functioned within discourse' on US foreign and security policy from the end of the Cold War through to the mid-1990s (pp. 5–6). Particular weight is given to 'moments' such as the Iraqi invasion of Kuwait in August 1990.

Campbell's book treats recent US foreign policy as the product of a series of 'texts' about US identity and its global mission at the end of the Cold War. Policy documents, speeches and the US citizenship test are all mined for insight into the practices of identity creation that have gone into making US foreign policy. Foundational IR texts such as Thomas Hobbes' *Leviathan* are deconstructed or 'read against the grain' to make the argument that foreign policies do not emerge *after* the creation of states, but are 'integral to their constitution' (p. 60). Conjoining 'inside' with 'outside' Campbell echoes writers such as R.B.J. Walker (1993) who challenge the conceptually hegemonic appreciation of the practice of international relations which makes possible the study of IR: the assumption of a domestic, private realm internal to states standing prior to – and separate from – a public, anarchic realm of the international existing 'out there' beyond neatly constructed state borders.

This postmodern reading of the problem of the subject in IR makes the ways IR theorists have come to know the world (rather than the world itself) the object for critical discussion. As Walker summarizes the postmodern sensibility (1993: 6), 'Theories of international relations are more interesting as aspects of contemporary world politics that need explaining than as explanations of contemporary world politics'.

GENEALOGY

In light of the overwhelming power, influence and everywhere-ness of the discourses through which we make sense of the world, Foucault invites us to write not histories but **genealogies**. Genealogy, explains Devetak, is 'a style of historical thought which exposes and registers the significance of power-knowledge relations' (Devetak 2009b: 185).

Genealogy is not history of the beginning, middle and end variety, with a focus on origins and causation to understand how things got the way they are. It is 'a form of history which historicizes those things which are thought to be beyond history, including those things or thoughts which have been buried, covered, or excluded from view in the writing and making of history' (Devetak 2009b: 185). For Jens Bartelson, likewise, genealogy 'is strategically aimed at that which looks unproblematic and is held to be timeless; its task is to explain how these present traits, in all their vigour and truth, were formed out of the past' (quoted in Reus-Smit 2002: 494).

Steve Smith argues that it is important to apply a genealogical attitude to a discipline like IR because 'international theory has tended to be a discourse accepting of, and complicit in, the creation and re-creation of international practices that threaten, discipline and do violence to others' (Smith 1995: 3). A genealogy of IR, says Richard Ashley (1986), exposes the link between the practice of IR and its discourses. It asks how things came to be this way in the discipline and inquires into the politics behind the production and dissemination of academic knowledge about IR. It further investigates how dominant discourses such as Realism emerge and rise to prominence within the discipline, and how scholars set about claiming that their theory or interpretation is the most valid or truthful (covered in Smith 1995: 4–7).

In the work of those writers who investigate the genealogy of IR we can clearly see a postmodern concern to 'unravel history to reveal the multifarious trajectories that have been fostered or closed off in the constitution of subjects, objects, fields of action and domains of knowledge' (Devetak 2009b: 185–6).

That genealogists seek out the positioned nature of knowledge about IR perhaps explains why some scholars in IR are nervous about the advent of postmodernism within the discipline. It radically challenges claims to scientific 'objectivity'.

CASE STUDY: DECONSTRUCTING 'STATES'

Devetak's (1995) book chapter 'Incomplete States' helps us appreciate the impact of the postmodern turn in IR in two ways. First, it flags up the similarities, but, more importantly, the ruptures between postmodern theory and other normative theories covered in this book. Second, Devetak's chapter casts light on the artificiality of IR's disciplinary discourses about the state. The steps Devetak takes are as follows:

1 **Identifies the problem area.** At the beginning of the chapter Devetak notes a paradox: '*there is statecraft, but there is no completed state*' (1995: 19, original emphasis).

2 **Defines statecraft.** Devetak introduces the principle writers on which he draws for inspiration about his conception of statecraft as an ongoing effort to define the state, rather than the result of the settled existence of states. His use of Machiavelli in tandem with Derrida is itself unsettling because the latter is normally used by Realists to support their theories of state behaviour in a self-help system (pp. 20–1).

3 **Challenges Neorealist theory.** Devetak identifies the theories against which he operates (Neorealism and Neoliberalism) and explores Waltz's comfortable assumption that completed states interact in the international system. For Devetak, Waltz assumes too much: we cannot take states as completed entities at all.

4 **Introduces Critical Theoretical approaches.** The argument here is that to understand the 'inside' (states) we have to understand their 'outside' (all the different kinds of structure that help make those states) (p. 25). State boundaries, Devetak writes, are built on social power as well as defined geographical territories. To overlook the former by only concentrating on the latter is to misconstrue the historically produced, 'temporary and provisional' nature of state boundaries (pp. 25–6). Hence, it is insufficient to look to 'sovereignty' as the arbiter of what is internal and external to states when that very concept can be called into question (pp. 27–8).

5 **Poststructuralism and the state.** Here, Devetak uses Hegel to argue for the 'dynamic and ongoing' processes of state construction which we have to account for when we collapse the boundaries between 'inside' and 'outside' (p. 29). It is by overturning the 'inside/outside' distinction that we move out of the realm of Critical Theory and into the realm of deconstruction. Using writers such as Campbell, Ashley and Foucault, Devetak shows how states are never completed entities. Foreign policy discourses, he

argues, are practices that give shape to or help construct states; these discourses are not resorted to by states '*after* their full, completed constitution' (p. 32).

QUESTIONS TO PONDER

'How can taking a genealogical approach help illuminate the study of IR?'

This question invites you to consider the benefits and the costs of writing genealogies of IR. Clearly your first task is to summarize what 'taking a genealogical approach' means by using the work of Foucault or at least a summary of his views as presented by writers who apply him to IR such as David Campbell, Steve Smith or Richard Ashley.

Having defined this, you then have to set out what you think the benefits of genealogy are and can be for IR. All of the above writers (plus many 'thick' Constructivists) cover this issue so you can structure this part of the essay around the three or four that you think are most illuminating in your opinion. Make sure when you introduce new concepts (for instance, 'regime of truth') or use technical terms such as 'discourse' that you pause to define these terms for your reader. You could use a case study such as Devetak, above, to illustrate how the genealogical approach works in practice and to introduce the type of knowledge it can produce.

The most successful essays will not stop at the benefits. They will consider the 'backlash' against postmodern approaches to IR by investigating some of the arguments advanced by writers who think postmodernism is either jargon-filled mumbo-jumbo or a dangerous distraction from the 'real' concerns of IR: war, peace, security, the environment, and so on. Showing that you are familiar with all sides of a debate in this way helps demonstrate wide reading and your critical capability to weigh up different sides of an academic debate.

'Why do you think "postmodernism" has been received with such hostility by some writers in the field of IR? Is their hostility justified?'

Answering this question first of all relies on a robust definition of 'postmodernism', so you should find a writer or writers who define this difficult term and run with their ideas. You could perhaps include a brief analysis of competing terms such as poststructuralism and explain why you either do or do not choose to use the terms interchangeably. However you do it, you need to set off in the essay from a position where the marker knows precisely what you mean by postmodernism.

The next requirement is to demonstrate good knowledge of both postmodernism (briefly, so as not to waste too many words) and the criticisms levelled at it by some IR writers. In Campbell's textbook chapter (2007), he lists five writers who criticize postmodernism, so it is not as if they are thin on the ground. You will need to know not just what they say but why they say it, so read their original works and summarize them. How many you can cover will depend on the word limit you have (for coursework) and time limit (for an exam answer). You could try grouping their critiques of postmodernism. They tend to focus on: questions about its relevance to IR as a field of study; its ethical implications (the slide into various forms of relativism) and its relevance to the practice of international relations (policy relevance).

Having set out the criticisms, you are then invited to evaluate them. Have they depicted the postmodern movement (as you understand it) accurately? Are they misunderstanding the nature of IR to simply write off this huge intellectual movement? At the start and end of the essay remember to set out your core argument: do you agree or disagree with the critics?

REFERENCES TO MORE INFORMATION

Before you read the original works of postmodernist writers, and related, such as Foucault and Derrida it is worth checking out introductions to their thought:

Keeley, J.F. (1990) 'Toward a Foucauldian Analysis of International Regimes', *International Organization*, 16(1): 83–105.

Hoy, D.C. (1986) *Foucault: A Critical Reader*. Oxford: Basil Blackwell.

Danaher, G., Schirato, T. and Webb, J. (2000) *Understanding Foucault*. London: Sage. Especially Chapter 3 on discourses and institutions and Chapter 5 on power.

Andersen, N.A. (2003) *Discursive Analytical Strategies: Understanding Foucault, Koselleck, Laclau, Luhmann*. Bristol: The Policy Press.

Stocker, B. (2006) *Derrida on Deconstruction*. Abingdon: Routledge.

Moi, T. (ed.) (1986) *The Kristeva Reader*. Oxford: Basil Blackwell.

Foucault, M. (1991) 'Truth and Power', in P. Rabinow (ed.) *The Foucault Reader: An Introduction to Foucault's Thought*. London: Penguin, pp. 51–75.

Foucault, M. (1977) *Security, Territory, Population: Lectures at the Collège de France, 1977–78*, trans. G. Burchell. Basingstoke: Palgrave Macmillan.

Vucetic, S. (2011) 'Genealogy as Research Tool in International Relations', *Review of International Studies*, 37(3): 1295–1312.

Chomsky, N. and Foucault, M. (2007) Chomsky vs. Foucault, http://www.youtube.com/watch?v=kawGakdNoT0, 17 April (accessed 11 July 2012). A debate on societal organization and the amorphous nature of 'power'.

Ransom, J.S. (1997) *Foucault's Discipline: The Politics of Subjectivity*. Durham, NC: Duke University Press.

Lloyd, M. and Thacker, A. (eds) (1997) *The Impact of Michel Foucault on the Social Sciences and Humanities*. Basingstoke: Macmillan.

On discourse and deconstruction:

Burnham, P, Gilland, K., Grant, W. and Layton-Henry, Z. (2004) *Research Methods in Politics*. Basingstoke: Palgrave Macmillan.
See Chapter 10 for a brief introduction to discourse analysis.

Howarth, D. (1995) 'Discourse Theory', in D. Marsh and G. Stoker (eds) *Theory and Methods in Political Science*. Basingstoke: Macmillan, pp. 115–33.
In the second edition of this popular text, discourse theory is strangely absent.

Milliken, J. (1999) 'The Study of Discourse in International Relations', *European Journal of International Relations*, 5(2): 225–54.

Fairclough, N. (2000) *New Labour, New Language?* London: Routledge.
Dissects New Labour's domestic and foreign policy discourses from a critical linguistic perspective and shows you how their manifestoes, legislative proposals and policy speeches make sense of the world for their audience.

Wodak, R., De Cillia, R., Reisigl, M. and Liebhart, K. (2003) *The Discursive Construction of National Identity*, trans. A. Hirsch and R. Mitten. Edinburgh: Edinburgh University Press.
Good on how to use methods of critical discourse analysis to investigate national identity construction and then applies that method to the case of Austria.

Bloom, H. et al. (1979) *Deconstruction and Criticism*. New York: The Seabury Press.
A collection of essays by five of the leading proponents of deconstruction.

Norris, C. (1993) *Deconstruction: Theory and Practice*. London: Routledge.
Thorough overview of the will to deconstruction evident in writings by Derrida, Nietzsche, Marx and Wittgenstein.

Nealon, J.T. (1993) *Double Reading: Postmodernism after Deconstruction*. Ithaca, NY: Cornell University Press.
Pin-Fat, V. (2009) 'How Do We Begin to Think About the World', in J. Edkins and M. Zehfuss (eds) *Global Politics: A New Introduction*. London and New York: Routledge, pp. 22–44.

More generally on postmodernism and politics/IRT see:
Hay, C. (2002) *Political Analysis: A Critical Introduction*. Basingstoke: Palgrave. See Chapter 7.

Walker, R.B.J. (1995) 'International Relations and the Concept of the Political', in K. Booth and S. Smith (eds) *International Relations Theory Today*. Cambridge: Polity Press, pp. 306–27.
Deconstructs the 'inside/outside' binary in IR and therefore pulls the rug from under the feet of state-centric theory.

Munslow, A. (2007) *Narrative and History*. Basingstoke: Palgrave Macmillan. Explores the mechanics of representation using Foucault and others to examine how history is made meaningful to us. Also reassesses the concept of 'facts', so useful for your wider readings into the philosophy of social science.

Renwick, N. and Krause, J. (eds) (1996) *Identities in International Relations*. Basingstoke: Macmillan.

Devetak, R. (2005) 'The Gothic Scene of International Relations: Ghosts, Monsters, Terror and the Sublime after September 11', *Review of International Studies*, 31(4): 621–45.
Highlights the importance of language, symbols and imagery in constructing IR as a field of thought and practice.

Ashley, R. (1988) 'Untying the Sovereign State: A Double Reading of the Anarchy Problematique', *Millennium: Journal of International Studies*, 17(2): 227–62.
Der Derian, J. (1995) 'A Reinterpretation of Realism: Genealogy, Semiology, Dromology', in J. Der Derian (ed.) *International Theory: Critical Investigations*. Basingstoke: Macmillan, pp. 363–96.
Ashley, R. (1988) 'Living on Border Lines: Man, Poststructuralism, and War', in J. Der Derian and M. Shapiro (eds) *International/Intertextual Relations: Postmodern Readings of World Politics*. Lexington, MA: Lexington Books.

2.10 POSTCOLONIALISM

Key Terms

- Race
- Ethnicity
- Identity
- Empire

- Knowledge
- Discourse
- Power

Postcolonialism ... offers new ways for thinking about techniques of power that constrain self-determination, whether they emanate from within or without. (Grovogui 2007: 231)

Postcolonialism, like feminism and postmodernism more generally, is another relative latecomer to the field of IR. The reason for its tardy arrival exposes the politicized nature of IR's mode of producing knowledge about the world. It is absent from some IR textbooks (Burchill 2001a; Jackson and Sørensen 2007; Sterling-Folker 2006b), partially incorporated into others (Baylis et al. 2008b) and has a full place in yet more (Dunne et al. 2007). If you have read most or all of the preceding nine chapters in this book, covering each IR theory one by one, ask yourself whose voice or voices we heard most from? There is an argument to be made that IR has – in the main – been developed, taught and put into practice by privileged white Western males.

Postcolonialism exposes the latent bias in existing IR renderings by reminding us of the discipline's blind spots, both in terms of subject matter and the epistemological claims of positivism. As Smith and Owens put it, much postcolonial scholarship highlights 'the important degree of *continuity* and *persistence* of colonial forms of power in contemporary world politics ... a form of "neo"-colonialism' (2008: 188; their emphasis). Ramakrishnan agrees: 'Postcolonialism is useful in understanding the realms of representation and perception. An exposition of postcolonialism is worthwhile as a project which unravels the language of global political economy of control, if not its process' (Ramakrishnan 1999: 163).

Feminists ask, 'Where are the women?' Marxists ask, 'Where are the classes?' Postcolonialists inquire, 'Where is the ethnic diversity?' and 'What forms of control from now absent formal Empires linger on in the world today?'. An interdisciplinary tradition, Postcolonialism explores the power relations that govern IR's ways of representing the world, highlighting race as another global structure too long ignored by the core of the discipline: 'postmodernity and postcolonialism find themselves enmeshed in exploring the very meanings of emancipation and of the consequences, good or ill, that may accrue to it' (Kadir 1995: 20). Postcolonialists produce normatively inclined work that critiques the formal and informal practices of **colonialism** which have given rise to exploitation, alienation and repression of large portions of the globe by a supposedly rational, enlightened European imperialist order.

As with other 'post-ist' approaches that have come to the field of IRT, Postcolonialism resists easy categorization (Abrahamsen 2007; Mishra and Hodge 2005: 379). As R.S. Sugirtharajah has written, 'postcolonialism is interdisciplinary in nature and pluralistic in outlook … it is attracted to all kinds of tools and disciplinary fields, as long as they probe injustices, produce new knowledge which problematizes well entrenched positions and enhance the life of the marginalized' (quoted in Kumar 2011: 654). Postcolonial writers take inspiration from literary theory, philosophy, history and new approaches to anthropology and ethnography.

As with IR, Postcolonialism has a 'problem of the subject' all of its own because 'postcolonial theory is not concerned with a unified "problem"' (Kumar 2011: 665). In general, however, it is activist, and whichever form it takes it 'continues in a new way the anti-colonial struggles of the past' (Young quoted in Huggan and Tiffin 2007: 8). We will consider the dynamics of Postcolonialism mainly using the work of Edward Said, but with the usual proviso that his work is one of hundreds we could use to illustrate this diverse tradition, which like all theories has its critics as well as its proponents (for instance Eagleton 1998). Mark Salter's pithy definition helps appreciate how Postcolonialism can be applied to IR: 'the set of inquiries into historical and contemporary colonial relations of power' (Salter 2010: 129); let us see how.

POSTCOLONIALISTS FIND THEIR VOICE

In 1978, Edward Said published *Orientalism*, a book in which he traced how the 'West' had tried to place, use and direct the 'rest' of the world through the production of knowledge about it. In the Preface, Said (2003: xii) explained that: 'History is made by men and women, just as it can also be unmade and re-written, always with various silences and elisions, always with shapes imposed and disfigurements tolerated, so that "our" East, "our" Orient becomes "ours" to possess and direct'.

Here we see several features of the postcolonial approach to IR (see also his *Culture and Imperialism* (Said 1994)):

- **Things can be different.** Constructivists promote the idea that structures in the international system that we take for granted, such as 'anarchy', are in fact made by states, and more importantly by the social interactions that every day constitute the idea of the state. Said makes this point when he notes that history and the events that have unfolded in the past are made by people. Our accounts of history refer to a past 'back there', but there are, in the final analysis, only ever representations of that past, not a resurrection of the past itself. These events can be 'unmade and re-written', just as all social norms can be, if we possess the means, the imagination and the will to do so.

Said used the term 'Orient' to apply to various regions of the world notably the Middle East and parts of Africa and Asia. The terminology is in a constant state of flux: what do you think we mean by the 'West' and 'the rest' today? Are the supposed divisions down to geography, politics, economics, culture or identity?

- **'Ours' is not 'theirs'.** Postcolonialists investigate who it is that tells us about the world and what they say about its nature. For Said, the West has generally spoken for the rest in that Western scholars dominated the study, categorization and education about world peoples during the past two centuries or so. In the process, Western voices dominated other voices in the world; Western representations of these 'other' indigenous peoples who had their own stories to tell were simply drowned out. The stories the West developed about the character of these peoples, their politics and cultures, arguably tell us more about Western beliefs and prejudices than they reflect the reality of those other worlds.

> We noted in Chapter 2.8 that postcolonial feminists criticized their Western counterparts for writing works that implied that feminists shared the same or similar concerns the world over. This debate within the feminist movement tells you a lot about the postcolonial agenda: encouraging awareness of diversity.

- **Discourses are power.** Said suggests that in becoming 'ours' the West can direct the rest of the world: note the suggestiveness of the implication that control and domination are the result of producing knowledge about the Third World. Later in the book, Said is even more explicit: 'The relationship between Occident and Orient is a relationship of power, of domination, of varying degrees of a complex hegemony … a sign of European-Atlantic power over the Orient than it is a veridic discourse about the Orient' (Said 2003: 5–6). Said notes that within supposedly disinterested scientific discourses that the West has produced about the rest of the world, reside complex mechanisms of domination and an imperialist mentality. This does more than a disservice: it does a gross series of injustices to the 'reality' of life in the non-Western world. Here we see the obvious debt to Michel Foucault, with the Orient brought into being discursively and this affecting the way it was 'experienced and dealt with' (Varadarajan 2009: 296).

'Power' in *Orientalism*

TAKING IT FURTHER

Near the beginning of *Orientalism*, Said (2003: 12) sets out the different dimensions of power that infuse discourses about the 'Orient':

1 Power political: the establishment of colonial structures for governing foreign territories. The administrative elites from 'core' countries sent to 'peripheries' to arrange economic and social life in the interests of the core.

2 Power intellectual: the subjection of the Orient to study by linguists, historians, scientists and so on. Involves measuring, naming, ordering and placing the 'other'.

3 Power cultural: orthodoxies, canons of taste, texts and values.

(Continued)

(Continued)

4 Power moral: ideas about who 'we' and 'they' are, as well as how 'we' and 'they' think. Implied in the language – the discourse – put in place to describe and evaluate the colonized peoples.

Said's concept of power is Foucauldian. IR in its formative years as a discipline concentrated on repressive power: the power, for example, of one state to compel another to do its will by the threat or actual use of force. Power for Foucault and Said is productive and creative: it is the power that comes from being in a position to tell others the way the world works; the power that comes from knowledge. In the above typology Said's first dimension of power is repressive, the remaining three are productive, and it is no coincidence that the vast bulk of *Orientalism* is given over to studying those dimensions.

LANGUAGE AND POSTCOLONIALISM

And postcoloniality is the twisted grimace of an unrelenting colonialism whose pertinacity clones itself with aberrant vehemence in new regimes of power. (Kadir 1995: 19)

Feminist scholars implicate language directly in the patriarchal domination of women by men. A large part of their critique involves analysis of the binary oppositions within language used to compare masculine/feminine characteristics: for example 'rational/irrational', 'detachment/commitment' and 'brutality/compassion'. In each case the former term is privileged and it is no coincidence they are all associated with Western constructions of positive masculine qualities. The latter feminine qualities are not regarded as highly, so that the universal benchmark or standard for humanity is essentially masculine. This language infuses everything from scientific methodologies to the attributes of states as unitary rational actors.

When you spot different theorists using the same ways of defining or critiquing a particular aspect of IR make a note of it because it helps you see the similarities across apparently different theoretical traditions.

Bill Ashcroft, Gareth Griffiths and Helen Tiffin (1994: 7) remark that imperial oppression came in part via the 'control over language' as 'the medium through which a hierarchical structure of power is perpetuated, and the medium through which conceptions of "truth", "order", and "reality" become established'. Their book traces how Postcolonialism has been stimulated by the reclaiming of English by indigenous populations, resulting in innovative and new forms of postcolonial literatures. Just as Marxism inspires theoretical work as well as practical action in the form of the anti-globalization movement, so Postcolonial literature is an expression of the wider anti-imperial resistance movement: 'an example of effective dissidence' (Smith and Owens 2008: 189).

How has this control over language been exerted? Said (2003: 40) remarks on the binary oppositions that Western speakers traditionally set up in their discourse to frame the characteristics of 'Europe' and the 'Orient'. Despite saying nothing about Postcolonialism in the original version of *Orientalism* 'the work nevertheless provided scholars with many registers with which to address and interpret both Orientalist, self-serving, colonial discourses (within which are embedded a European compulsion to confine the other) and the highly adventurous, indeed agonistic, discourses of anticolonial struggles' (Mishra and Hodge 2005: 375). Table 3 shows Said's binaries in operation.

Said recommends that we pay attention to the language through which we represent ourselves and others because this process of identity construction has dangerous implications if it is built on prejudice. As Gordon Pruett has remarked, 'Western identity, and especially its sense of superiority, depends upon the denigration of that which is not itself. A single term for such a view when applied to persons is racism' (quoted in Ramakrishnan 1999: 156). In Orientalist discourses, the European characteristics are held up as positive, while Orientalist characteristics are criticized and/or undervalued. Perhaps even to portray

Table 3   Said's binaries

European	*Oriental*
Rational	Irrational
Virtuous	Depraved
Mature	Childlike
Normal	Different

them as in Table 3 is to downplay the violence these hierarchies deliver to our representations of the Oriental.

> Note in Figure 17 how the 'Oriental' is said to be 'irrational' – very much in the same way as feminine characteristics are looked down upon in gendered discourses of masculinity and femininity. Europeans are, it seems, 'better' than Orientals because they are more masculine.

What Said and the Postcolonialists question is the basis these supposedly timeless qualities have in 'reality' and the moral values inherent in privileging one of the terms over its supposed opposite. In Figure 17 we can see how the European characteristics are both stronger (bolder) and deemed to be of a higher order than their Oriental counterparts. They are enlightened/Enlightened. This assumption, and the manifold subjugations and silences imposed on the rest of the world by linguistic practices and new forms of postmodern governance by 'the West' have been carefully picked apart and opened to critical scrutiny by Postcolonial writers.

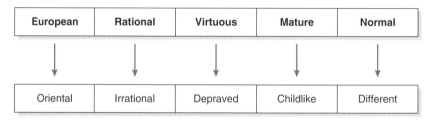

Figure 17   **Power and oppression: Said's binaries in operation**

QUESTIONS TO PONDER

'What are the affinities between postmodernist, Constructivist and Postcolonial approaches to IR?'

Your initial task in planning an answer to this question is to arrive at a suitable definition of each theory – no easy task. Using your knowledge of each tradition, you might want to stress the diversity but also the common themes and issues across writers, using illustrative quotations and reference to a few authoritative scholars to back your case. You will not have much space for this given the demands of the question, so be sure to focus on the central themes and ignore the detail of each theory or the temptation to write everything you know about them.

You then have to weigh up the similarities between the three approaches to IR – one way might be to remove them from the realm of discrete 'theories' and use the language of loosely rated 'sensibilities'. In this chapter we referred to Said's take on language, representation, the role of ideas and education in constructing the Orient in the West – his point being that the Orient has been 'made' by human endeavour, it is not necessarily an accurate portrait of the 'reality' of that world. You could therefore link his work to thick Constructivism and some postmodernism. A standard answer would stop there. The highest achieving answers, however, will go on to note that, if anything, Postcolonialism shares just as much with other theories of IR such as feminism and Marxism in terms of its identification of structural inequalities in IR. It all depends on the space and time available to you as to how far you can investigate these other overlaps. But if you can convey your sense of the nature of the interplay between Postcolonialism and these other theories, then you will get credit for exhibiting a thorough knowledge of the fabric of these normative theories of IR.

'"… an exercise in cultural strength". What are the implications of Said's description of *Orientalism* for the study of IR?'

The nub of this question is to explain what Said means by talking of Orientalism's exercise of 'cultural strength', and to link that with a discussion of the dynamics of the Orientalist tradition more generally. For Said, Orientalism highlights the repressive dimensions of power but is far more about the productive dimensions of power whereby individuals in the West defined, delimited and 'named' the Orient. In the process, they helped legitimize various techniques of colonial repression and exploitation, based on everything from race to the embellishment of cultural hierarchies. Said's 'cultural strength' is therefore about the exercise of various forms of power and the best essays will do more than concentrate on the naked military or political forms of power. They will look at the reinterpretation of power by the likes of Said, Gramsci and Foucault.

Tracing the implications for the study of IR will involve assessing the impact of Said's work on the evolution of Postcolonialism as an intellectual movement. It is interesting that Said's early work did not mention Postcolonialism but it encouraged an identifiable body of work to develop around this label, rather like Marx and Marx-inspired writers. You will not need to know in detail the sociology or politics of Postcolonialism as an intellectual movement, but you can tell how important Said and other writers are in this canon by the number of references to their ideas in textbook chapters and the like. Having established Said as a key writer you should be in a position to draw out three or four implications of this quote for the study of IR. Set out those you feel are most crucial and alert the reader to other points as you see fit. The kinds of implications you can consider would include: issues of race, ethnicity, identity, language, power, discourse, exploitation, systemic level structures, oppression and the politics of disciplined knowledge.

The best answers might allude to the interplay between Said's approach and those taken by postmodernists, Marxists and feminists.

REFERENCES TO MORE INFORMATION

Fanon, F. (1968) *The Wretched of the Earth*, trans. C. Farrington. New York: Grove Press.
Opened up windows on the repressive practices of colonialism not just physically but also in terms of the knowledge that Europe's imperial masters produced about the world.

Spivak, G.C. (1987) *In Other Worlds: Essays in Cultural Politics*. London: Routledge.
Chowdry, G. and Nair, S. (eds) (2002) *Power, Postcolonialism and International Relations: Reading Race, Gender and Class*. London: Routledge.
Bhaba, H.K. (1994) *The Location of Culture*. London: Routledge.

Bush, B. (2006) *Imperialism and Postcolonialism*. Harlow: Pearson Education.
Explores the history, concept and dynamics of imperialism, together with, in Chapter 6, the Postcolonial move in studies of Empire.

Darby, P. (2000) *At the Edge of International Relations: Postcolonialism, Gender and Dependence.* London: Continuum International Publishing Group.
Good on the wide-ranging challenge postcolonialism poses for 'conventional' IR theory.

Darby, P. and Paolini, A.J. (1994) 'Bridging International Relations and Postcolonialism', *Alternatives*, 19(3): 371–97.

Ferguson, Y.N. and Mansbach, R.W. (1991) 'Between Celebration and Despair: Constructive Suggestions for Future International Theory', *International Studies Quarterly*, 35(4): 363–86.

Mohanty, C.T. (1988) 'Under Western Eyes: Feminist Scholarship and Critical Discourse', *Feminist Review*, 30(3): 61–88.

Hoogvelt, A. (2001) *Globalization and the Postcolonial World: The New Political Economy of Development*, 2nd edn. Baltimore, MD: Johns Hopkins University Press.
Parts I and II refresh you on the Marxist take on the global political economy, while Part III works the postcolonial dimension region by region.

Walker, R.B.J. (ed.) (1984) *Culture, Ideology, and World Order*. Boulder, CO: Westview Press.
Especially the chapters on civilizations, hegemonies and world order and the hegemony of Western reason.

Krishna, S. (1993) 'The Importance of Being Ironic: A Postcolonial View on Critical International Relations Theory', *Alternatives*, 18(3): 385–417.
A review essay themed around works by critical and postmodernist scholars such as David Campbell and James der Derian.

Ling, L.H.M. (2001) *Postcolonial International Relations: Conquest and Desire Between Asia and the West*. Basingstoke: Palgrave Macmillan.
Challenges the 'clash of civilizations' thesis as a process of 'othering' that downplays the complex global interactions that shape cultural and individual identities.

Geore, J. and Campbell, D. (1990) 'Patterns of Dissent and the Celebration of Difference: Critical Social Theory and International Relations', *International Studies Quarterly*, 34(3): 269–93.

Krishnaswamy, R. and zHawley, J.C. (eds) (2008) *The Post-colonial and the Global*. Minneapolis, MN: University of Minnesota Press.
Wide-ranging collection covering everything from the politics of disciplined Western knowledge to World System Theory and resistance to Empire in a globalized world.

Sankaran, K. (2008) *Globalization and Postcolonialism*. London: Rowman and Littlefield.

Loombe, A. (1998) *Colonialism/Postcolonialism*. London: Routledge.

Sajed, A. (2012) 'The Post Always Rings Twice? The Algerian War, Poststructuralism and the Postcolonial in IR Theory', *Review of International Studies*, 38(1): 141–63.

2.11 GREEN THEORY

Key Terms

- Environmental justice
- Ecocentrism
- Ecological security
- Regime

- State
- Ecoanarchy
- Ecological citizenship

Environmental questions cannot be neatly boxed off from other political questions. (Paterson 1995: 214)

In Chapter 2.8 on feminism we saw how the concerns raised by this big social movement fed into IRT throughout the later 1980s and 1990s in the form of 'gender' perspectives on world politics and international society. We found it far too simple to portray feminist writings as somehow being tacked on to the existing core of the discipline. The critically inclined feminist literature challenges the fundamentals of what it means to say we study IR (the ontology of the discipline) and argues that the dominant methods and epistemologies of the discipline are inherently positioned in ways that marginalize women and women's experience. 'Gender', they say, is not a variable that can be added or removed from IR when we like, but it is always there and demands attention whenever we think about matters international.

As you can appreciate from Matthew Paterson's quote above, Green theorists have much the same approach to IR. They do not see questions relating to the environment, ecological sustainability and development as ones that can be adequately answered by existing state-centric structures, either in the theory or practice of IR. Instead, they call for a thoroughgoing reassessment of the ways in which we think and act in terms of the environment, calling into question the role of the state and its approach to human security in the process. While Green theorists take a variety of positions and enthusiastically engage in debates amongst themselves, 'they share at least one core premise – that *our received wisdom about the relationship between nature (the natural environment) and culture (the human environment) must be questioned'* (Weber 2010: 192; original emphasis). In this chapter we explore this normative challenge to IRT in three parts: Green approaches to IRT; ecocentrism as ontology; and the idea of ecological citizenship.

IR AND GREEN THEORY COLLIDE

Issues and debates surrounding the contemporary environment are constantly in the media and political spotlight as communities grapple with the problem of providing development at a pace that is sustainable at a global level over the long term. For example, environmental concerns are part of the remit of the UN, under its Division for Sustainable Development which aims to meet present needs while simultaneously promoting the ability of future generations to meet their needs (UN 2009); climate change is an ongoing bone of political contention and scientific contestation.

The environment has also featured on the agenda of regional organizations such as the EU for a number of years. For instance, in 2006, the member states affirmed their commitment to a sustainable development agenda in words echoed precisely by the UN in 2008 (Council of the European Union 2006: 2). At the national level various types of 'green' party have flourished in many countries over the past three decades. In the UK, for example, the Green Party is now a multi-issue party centring on creating a healthy environment for the present and in the years ahead, but with more than an eye on the international dimensions of its normative platforms (Green Party 2010).

It should be obvious from the number of environmental issues on the contemporary global agenda that theorizing them is no easy business. When we choose to buy re-usable carrier bags for our supermarket shopping, or when we donate money to charities providing clean water in desertified regions of Africa, we are responding to issues raised directly by the Green movement, which has grown rapidly since the 1960s (Eckersley 2007: 249). In deciding to go for re-usable carrier bags and giving money to the African water charity, we are responding to the popular environmentalist call to 'think globally, act locally'. This urge acknowledges the likelihood of an impending global sociological crisis (Paterson 2009: 260), and highlights the ways in which Green theorists cause us to rethink the state's role in dealing with environmental issues.

A useful way to get to grips with the goals of Green theory is to summarize its take on the pitfalls of mainstream IR; we will do this using the work of Paterson (1995: 213–18; see also Hovden 1999):

- **A narrow agenda.** To use the terminology developed earlier in this book (see Chapter 1.4) Green theorists see flaws in the ontological starting point for mainstream IR: state behaviour at the international level. Paterson identifies a problem with any approach that begins by asking what we can do internationally to, say, combat waste pollution of our rivers: it overlooks the domestic sources of those problems and the potential solutions to them. We can only 'think globally, act locally' if we either forget or reform the central place states occupy in dealing with environmental matters.

For the purposes of Green theory as Paterson developed it in the 1990s, 'mainstream' IR meant Neorealism and Neoliberalism. Do you think these theories still constitute the core of the discipline today?

- **Flaws in Neoliberal assumptions.** The knock-on point concerns the agreements states make about the environment, such as the Kyoto Protocol of 1997 (for the text of the treaty see UN (1998)). In making these agreements, Paterson argues, the first assumption is that the signatory countries will want and be able to implement those agreements through appropriate regulation at the domestic level. What this overlooks, he remarks, is the influence of powerful corporate lobbies at the domestic level which can affect national climate policies against the spirit of international agreements (for example, the oil and coal lobbies). It is, he concludes, 'politically naïve' to ignore the impact of these organized interests and therefore theoretically flawed to talk about IR as the exclusive preserve of state actions and decisions.

  The second assumption is that scientists can provide 'objective' advice on the environment. The criteria they develop and the measurements they use to develop these criteria will always be politically skewed in some way. In the true spirit of normative IRT, says Paterson, beware anyone who claims to be value-free or objective about any issue, however supposedly technical the subject matter.

TOWARDS ECOCENTRISM

The objections Green theorists have to Neoliberal regime theory lead them to offer 'an alternative analysis of global ecological problems'. Their work exposes the problematic nature of Neoliberal assumptions and ethical values and encourages us to think about the environment in new ways which 'expand the menu of state development options' (Eckersley 2007: 256). In raising these questions about mainstream approaches, Green theorists 'see' a different world compared to the **anthropocentrism** of the Neoliberals (Dalby 2009), which 'only values the human species and is therefore only concerned with the survival of the human species' (Weber 2010: 193). Against this human-centred approach, an 'ecocentric' philosophy sees the world as made up of 'the larger web of life, made up of nested ecological communities at multiple levels of aggregation (such as gene pools, populations, species, ecosystems)' (Eckersley 2007: 251). They see a world in which humans are not the only sentient beings for whom policies on the environment should be made. Rather, humans are 'part of nature, not above nature', the fate of the one hinging directly on the fate of the other (Weber 2010: 193).

Where feminists argue that IR theory has been 'gender blind', Green theorists argue that IR theory has been 'Green blind', with a significant emphasis on a feminist 'ethics of care' informing their appreciation of the dynamics of world politics.

In the spirit of shifting our focus to the world and its long-term health and survival, Green theorists think through the best way to respond to ecological challenges in ways that transcend the state-centricity of traditional IR approaches. The 'IPE wing' of Green theory (Eckersley 2007: 255) has already been discussed. It takes its cue from the flaws in Neoliberal IRT and proposes an alternative account of the causes and solutions to global ecological problems.

The 'green cosmopolitan' wing of Green theory brings together individuals and groups committed to articulating new ways of thinking about ecology and proposing solutions 'at all levels of governance' above and below the state (Eckersley 2007: 255). Their commitment is to the creation of new norms of 'environmental justice' which means (adapted from Eckersley 2007: 253):

- Ecological risks affect more than human beings alone and more than citizens of states, but all peoples around the globe.
- Participation in decision-making on the environment should be massively expanded and democratized to include representatives of all those affected by such decisions.

- A minimization of risks vis-à-vis the wider community.
- All risks must be acceptable and they should be gauged democratically and with the input of all affected parties (a form of Critical Theory's theory of communicative action; see Chapter 2.7 above).
- Those suffering as a result of ecological problems should have adequate recourse to redress and compensation.

Paterson identifies a lively debate within the Green tradition between two strands of thought on how best to generate environmental justice (Paterson 2009: 263–73). The first strand is what could be seen as the more conservative approach: maintain states in their present form but reform their role to give more say over environmental issues for regional and international organizations. In this approach, the state retains its central role in IR but its role is modified to help humans 'think globally, act locally'.

The second strand is the 'ecoanarchist' strand. Ecoanarchists believe the state should be dismantled, with decentralization of decision-making power and authority promoting the existence of 'global networks of small-scale self-reliant communities'. These communities would not be based on hierarchical, consumer capitalist lines, but on horizontal 'libertarian, egalitarian, and participatory grounds' (Paterson 2009: 269. (For an appreciation of how the study of Anarchist thought can contribute to IRT more generally see Prichard (2007, 2011).) From within the 'green cosmopolitan' wing of Green theory there has emerged in recent years the notion of ecological citizenship and we can consider that to pose the most fundamental challenge yet to state-based understandings of IRT; this is the theme of the next section.

ECOLOGICAL CITIZENSHIP

Earlier forms of Green theory were associated with rationalist microeconomic assumptions about the behaviour of states towards the environment in international organizations. The ontological positioning of this work was in line with what could be considered the 'core' of the discipline to the early 1990s. More recently, Green theory has reflected postmodern (in this case post-state) trends in the discipline. It has departed from a focus on the costs and benefits of cooperation at the international level to consider environmental attitudes and practices at the level of individual humans as well as non-state actors. Inspired by the work of Alan Dobson (2003) this sub-field of Green theory has developed around an attempt to rethink and in many cases go beyond

cosmopolitan ideas and ideals (Dobson 2006b). Particular attention has been paid to new understandings of citizenship and the ways in which actors across the levels from humans to states, to non-state and supra-state actors 'manage' their behaviour by recasting the balance between rights/duties and responsibilities/obligations.

For example, Neil Carter and Meg Huby do a good job of showing that actors such as ethical investors (individuals, businesses and fund managers) have sprung up around the globe in recent years and acted as ecological citizens. They are motivated by concerns such as nuclear power, ozone layer degradation, the Third World, armament proliferation and animal testing (Carter and Huby 2005: 262). They further show that while it is harder for companies to be 'black boxed' as ethical citizens in their own right, 'their activities are crucial to the achievement of ecological citizenship goals'. By engaging in practices such as Corporate Social Responsibility (CSR), companies can provide the organizational rules and institutional norms for the promotion of ecological citizenship (Carter and Huby 2005: 262).

In turn, CSR has been encouraged by government laws and regulations. For instance the UK Department of Trade and Industry (DTI) defines a 'responsible' organization as doing three things. First, recognizing that its activities inevitably impinge upon the society in which it operates. Second, in response, it takes account of the economic, social, environmental and human rights impacts of its activities across the world. Finally, it seeks to achieve benefits by working in partnership with other groups and organizations (DTI cited in Carter and Huby 2005: 269).

Can you discover examples of firms trumpeting their concern with CSR? Why is it in companies' interests to take CSR seriously and how does this help illustrate the relationship between rules and norms in IR?

This and related work on ethical investment and CSR being undertaken way outside conventional IR's disciplinary boundaries (see Palacios 2004; Hellsten and Mallin 2006) makes a compelling empirical case for theorizing ecological citizenship in tandem with the study of capitalism in the global political economy. The next section will show how this theorizing has been undertaken with special reference to the challenges it poses to state-centric accounts of IR at the notional 'core' of the discipline.

DEFINING ECOLOGICAL CITIZENSHIP: JUSTICE AND ORDER BEYOND STATE AND TIME

One way of understanding ecological citizenship is to contrast it with traditional conceptions of democratic citizenship in political theory, whereby 'citizens should be under no duties and obligations towards the environment other than those laid down in political decisions resulting from just and legitimate processes (Martinsson and Lundqvist 2010)'. Beyond politically driven motivation for action we have morally driven motivation, because 'the ecological crisis demands a new type of citizenship built on "non-reciprocal" morally derived responsibilities applicable to all human action'. Note the production of billions of ecological footprints the world over every day (Martinsson and Lundqvist 2010: 531). In this thicker conception of citizenship human beings can aspire to live 'the good life' but they have morally binding obligations 'to take personal responsibility for restoring global justice'. An ecological citizen is one 'who embraces green values and attitudes and carries these out in practice' (Martinsson and Lundqvist 2010: 519–20).

Thus, ecological citizenship 'focuses on understanding the motivations and reasons for responsible actions' as far as the environment goes (Smith 2005: 16). It brings a feminist ethics of care into dialogue with solidarist conceptions of and universal human values, as well as work on globalization and inequality we associate with the English School and Marxists/neo-Marxists. Perhaps more than any other IRT we study in this book, this approach is forward looking rather than an attempt (Neorealism for example) to freeze time and explain power configurations between major and minor powers at a given historical juncture. Ecological citizenship certainly deals with the present but stretches our horizons well beyond it. For example, the effects of deforestation highlight the need for justice on the plant now and in the future; water quality issues 'prompt awareness of our immediate successors', while the disposal or storage of nuclear waste 'raises obligations to distant future generations' (Smith 2005: 19).

We can summarize the core tenets of ecological citizenship with the help of Carter and Huby (2005: 256–7):

- First, it is **non-territorial**. Environmental problems such as acid rain do not stop at state borders, so ecological citizens have to operate within and beyond the state to achieve their collective goals.
- Second, it **takes place within the public and private realms**. Where conventional IRT focused on state interactions 'out there' in the realm of 'the

international', ecological citizens are aware that their low-level day-to-day actions have public ramifications; for example using plastic bags instead of recyclable multi-use canvas shopping bags.

- Third, ecological citizenship is associated with **'virtues that enable citizens to meet their obligations'**, notably the social justice needed to ensure a just distribution of ecological space for all humanity, and compassion.

- Fourth, it entails **non-contractual responsibilities**, for instance to ensure that ecological footprints are sustainable, without expectation that there will be reciprocity. In other words, do not expect you will get anything much in return for acting as an ecological citizen. By definition, future generations cannot pay you or thank you in advance!

EMPIRICAL AND NORMATIVE ASSUMPTIONS

The idea of ecological citizenship has been developed to provide an answer to the 'practical question' that animates Green theorists across the board: 'of how a sustainable society might be brought about' (Dobson 2006a: 450) when environmental concerns more often than not clash with perceptions of economic, political or material self-interest (Dobson 2007). What is right can conflict with perceptions of our immediate wants/needs/interests.

At its heart are empirical concerns with the nature and scale of the 'ecological footprint' we leave behind: as humans going about our daily lives; as companies in the process of manufacturing and distributing goods and services; and as states *in toto* in terms of the regulation and discussion of environmental concerns at the international level. Its normative concern comes through in its concentration on the political and moral obligations coming from individuals being united across national borders in a common humanity.

Dobson describes the three commitments of cosmopolitanism as follows (all in Dobson 2006b: 167–8 unless otherwise stated):

1 **Scope: who is obliged and to whom?** In principle the scope is universal across all human beings. As Dobson points out, this universalist conception is well covered in Andrew Linklater's *The Transformation of Political Community* (1998). The problem cosmopolitans encounter is practical: we might be cosmopolitans in theory but find it difficult or impossible to put the theory into practice (Dobson 2006b: 169).

2 **Nature: what are we obliged to do?** Harder to capture but writers coalesce around the following themes prevalent in Linklater's work: avoid deception and harm; cultivate and exercise certain virtues, for example compassion; and work towards the creation of open communities of discourse. Thomas Pogge adds that we should refrain from involving ourselves in unjust institutions and Charles Jones suggests we should do justice wherever possible.

3 **Source of obligation.** Links to the motivation of human action. Legal sources are rule-bound obligations (fear of sanctions or reprisals for example). Dobson calls these 'perfect' obligations. 'Imperfect' obligations are ethical obligations and these are not sanctionable.

ECOLOGICAL FOOTPRINTS

Ecological citizenship provides a related but slightly deeper account of the ties that bind present and future generations and the codes of justice that apply to our interaction with the environment. Dobson looks to go beyond a 'thin' approach to cosmopolitan citizenship by introducing the idea that people are better motivated to act on an appreciation of their cosmopolitan responsibilities when they can be persuaded or made to feel causally responsible for the suffering of 'real' or 'imagined' others. This sentiment entrenches the appreciation of 'connected selves' because it encourages humans to feel morally responsible for injustice or harm (Dobson 2006b: 172). Recognition of environmental degradation and resource depletion caused by global warming could be one example of an issue that in our globalized world 'produces literally *global* relations of causal responsibility' (Dobson 2006b: 175).

Our chances of generating 'thick' cosmopolitanism of the sort that transcends a 'thin' appreciation of our membership of a global human community thus turn on the extent to which we believe our (individual, corporate and state) ecological footprints bring with them a sense of justice – not just to other humans living on the planet now, but those billions who will live with the effects of our actions for centuries into the future.

> The idea of the ecological footprint enables us to think of the material impact we have on the biotic (including human) and abiotic [non-living] elements of the environment that lie within – or beneath – it. No one can avoid having an ecological footprint, and so everyone impacts on someone or something, all the time. (Dobson 2006b: 176–7)

Ecological citizenship encourages us to think beyond IR's conventional notions of space and time and to collapse the public–private distinction as a way of making better sense of our 'being' in a globalized world of scarce resources.

QUESTIONS TO PONDER

'Are Green issues outside the remit of IRT?'

To organize your response to this question you will have to take a clear stance and back it up using evidence from two sets of literature. One is on the appropriate subject matter or central agenda of IRT; the other literature you will need to know is Green theory – its ontological positioning (what it studies) and how it can contribute to IR debates more generally. Your answer will turn on your definition of both the key concepts in the question: what are 'ecocentric issues' and what is 'the remit of IR'? What type of Green theory do you take to be representative of those concerns: the 'reform the state' approach of writers such as Robert Eckersley, the 'do away with the state' approach of the ecoanarchists such as Murray Bookchin (see References for more information), or the ecological citizenship ideas of Dobson? You might have to allude to the commonalities across their thought as well as the divergences, so some general knowledge of the textbook chapters on Green theory will help you see into the different agendas at work.

As for the remit of IR, you could reasonably take the conventional 'Neo-liberal' position as representing an orthodox interpretation of IR's agenda. What Greens question, in common with Marxists, feminists, postmodernists and other normative theorists, is the extent to which this agenda addresses issues in 'world politics' today. If you agree that normative theory speaks more to our contemporary concerns than the positivist, state-centric approaches of Realism and Liberalism, then you will not think Green theory is outside the remit of IR but fundamental to it.

'Critically evaluate Dobson's idea of ecological citizenship as an approach to IRT'

Dobson's work on ecological citizenship has spawned a dedicated body of work in its own right. You can legitimately focus on Dobson whilst perhaps in the early stages of the answer showing how he links to Green theory more widely (for example, he goes beyond anthropocentrism; he contributes to work on cosmopolitanism; and he theorizes along the lines of a feminist ethics of care).

Many of the marks in this answer will be gained by showing a good depth of knowledge on this concept of 'ecological citizenship'. Before you launch into criticisms of any theory you need to patiently establish your position by setting out exactly what you understand the theory (theorist in this case) to be saying. A robust understanding of ecological citizenship requires: one or more definitions from the relevant literature; an explication of its core concepts such as the ecological footprint; and a general statement of its normative positioning within key IR debates about, for instance, the role of the state and the dynamics of contemporary international society in the era of advanced globalization.

The amount of marks you can pick up for the 'critically evaluate' segment will then rest on the extent to which you can present Dobson's case in the context of IRT more widely. Who agrees with him? Who disagrees with him? Why? Do you think that Green theory 'fits' within what we might reasonably consider is encompassed by the 'field' of IR? Does it deal effectively with IR topics such as the role of the state, order and justice? You can bring to bear as many other theories as you like in making your argument, and as long as you do so from a position of strength you can get mileage from any of the theories you cover on your course.

REFERENCES TO MORE INFORMATION

Vogler, J. (2008) 'Environmental Issues', in J. Baylis, S. Smith and P. Owens (eds) *The Globalization of World Politics: An Introduction to International Relations*, 4th edn. Oxford: Oxford University Press, pp. 350–68.
More conventional treatment of Green theory than you will find in Paterson and Eckersley's critically inclined approaches.

Doran, P. (1995) 'Earth, Power, Knowledge: Towards a Critical Global Environmental Politics', in J. Macmillan and A. Linklater (eds) *Boundaries in Question: New Directions in International Relations*. London: Pinter, pp. 193–211.
Uses Foucault's idea of discursive regimes to expose the limits of environmental practices and policies put in place by states and international organizations.

Lövbrand, E. and Stripple, J. (2006) 'The Climate as Political Space: On the Territorialisation of the Global Carbon Cycle', *Review of International Studies*, 32(2): 217–35.

Smith, M.J. (1998) *Ecologism: Towards Ecological Citizenship*. Buckingham: Open University Press.
Opening chapter useful on the anthropocentric/ecocentric distinction.

Dobson, A. (2007) *Green Political Thought*, 4th edn. London: Routledge.

Wall, D. (2005) *Babylon and Beyond: The Economics of Anti-Capitalist, Anti-Globalist and Radical Green Movements*. London: Pluto.
Ecoanarchist take on Green theory, also useful for your understanding of Marxism and Anarchism.

Bookchin, M. (2005) *The Ecology of Freedom: The Emergence and Dissolution of Hierarchy*, 4th edn. Oakland, CA: AK Press. Leading ecoanarchist writer. Or try Bookchin, M. (2007) *Social Ecology and Communalism*. Oakland, CA: AK Press.

Eckersley, R. (2004) *The Green State: Rethinking Democracy and Sovereignty. Cambridge*, MA: MIT Press.
The state-led approach to promoting environmental justice. Conflicts with the ecoanarchists' view of how to achieve the same ends.
Paterson, M. (1996) *Global Warming and Global Politics*. London: Routledge.

On the nature and limits of inter-state approaches to the environment.
Kegley Jr., C.W. and Wittkopf, E.R. (2001) *The Global Agenda: Issues and Perspectives*, 6th edn. New York: McGraw-Hill.
Part IV contains ten chapters on various aspects of ecology and politics.

Haas, P.M., Keohane, R.O. and Levy, M.A. (1993) *Institutions for the Earth: Sources of Effective Environmental Protection*. Cambridge, MA: MIT Press.
Conventional IR approach using regime theory to explain environmental outcomes.

Young, O.R. (1989) *International Cooperation: Building Regimes for Natural Resources and the Environment*. Ithaca, NY: Cornell University Press.
As with the Haas, Keohane and Levy book, critiqued by writers such as Paterson who advocate a wholesale rethink of the ways in which we view the contemporary environment and act to sustain it into the future. For a regime-centric approach, see also:
Mitchell, R.B. (2006) 'International Environment', in W. Carlsnaes, T. Risse and B.A. Simmons (eds) *Handbook of International Relations*. London: Sage, pp. 500–16.

On ecological citizenship and cosmopolitanism:
Brown, G.W. and Held, D. (2010) *The Cosmopolitanism Reader*. Cambridge: Polity Press.

Dobson, A. and Bell, D. (eds) (2006) *Environmental Citizenship*. Cambridge, MA: MIT Press.

Gabrielson, T. (2008) 'Green Citizenship: A Review and Critique', *Citizenship Studies*, 12(4): 429–46.

Hailwood, S. (2005) 'Environmental Citizenship as Responsible Citizenship', *Environmental Politics*, 14(2): 195–210.

Hutchings, K. and Dannreuther, R. (eds) (1999) *Cosmopolitan Citizenship*. Edinburgh: Edinburgh University Press.

Smith, M. (1998) *Ecologism: Towards Ecological Citizenship*. Buckingham: Open University Press.

Walzer, M. (1994) *Thick and Thin: Moral Argument at Home and Abroad*. Notre Dame: University of Notre Dame Press.

PART III

LECTURES, SEMINARS, COURSEWORK AND EXAMS

The highest achieving students on any module are usually those who manage their learning by taking responsibility for it. In an era when students are asked to pay substantial fees for the privilege of going to university (in England, for example), the potential is there for some students to believe that because they fork out money they have a right to obtain a degree of their choosing. Nothing could be further from the truth. Whether we agree that universities should charge fees or not, your yearly payment is for the right to study the degree, not to be given one for doing nothing!

In most universities the marks you receive for the first year of your degree programme do not count towards your overall degree classification – they are about assessing your ability to progress to Year 2 and beyond. Do not see this as an excuse to slack in the first year. Use that time to learn good work habits which you can put into practice straight away in the second year. In a competitive job market employers increasingly want to see transcripts of Year 1 marks to help them decide between potential graduate employees.

Just like owning a car, you are buying the right to take *ownership of your learning* on your degree programme. Some car owners are careful with their vehicle and take every care to keep it cleaned, polished and roadworthy. Others have a slap-dash approach to car maintenance which means that in time their car becomes something of a dangerous, un-roadworthy rust bucket. It is up to you to decide what kind of owner of *your* learning you want to be. Your university tutors, friends, parents and relatives can help to a certain extent, but your final degree classification will tell potential employers exactly what kind of owner of your learning you have been. The earlier you take responsibility and the greater responsibility you take, the better you will fare on your journey through university.

The following chapters give you tips and advice on how to take control of your learning. The first three help you get the best out of your lectures, seminars and feedback. The remainder consider how to succeed at essays and exams, including a chapter on how to avoid sloppy academic practice and plagiarism.

CORE AREAS

3.1 How to Get the Most Out of Lectures
3.2 How to Get the Most Out of Seminars
3.3 Using Feedback
3.4 Essay Writing
3.5 Good Practice in Essays
3.6 Plagiarism and How to Avoid It
3.7 Exam Revision
3.8 Exam Tips

3.1 HOW TO GET THE MOST OUT OF LECTURES

This chapter discusses one of the most widely used methods of delivering information at university: the lecture. You can maximise your learning in lectures by taking a three-phase approach, covering: preparation for the lecture, learning during the lecture and consolidating your learning after the lecture. Thinking seriously about managing your learning in all three phases will certainly help you get the most out of lectures, which otherwise can become an impersonal and overwhelming experience.

> Lectures are one small part of the overall learning process. Taking ownership of your learning means knowing the advantages as well as the limitations of learning in lectures.

PREPARATION

Your tutor will use lectures and the accompanying printed and online module documentation and reading lists to set the scope of your learning on your module (see Part I of this book). Depending on the structure of your course you will normally have anything up to two lectures on IR per week and usually some accompanying seminars through the semester.

ATTENDANCE

The most obvious way to get the best out of lectures is to attend them! Given the learning technologies available today, the classic stereotype of an academic lecturer standing at the front of a vast, dark, soulless lecture theatre droning on to a slumbering mass of students could not be further from the truth (in the vast majority of cases at least). All lecturers differ in their approach, style, use of visual aids such as hand-outs and PowerPoint, but they all have one thing in common: they are passionate about their subject and will want you to be passionate about it too.

Common Pitfall

It is a mistake to believe lectures are only useful for subject-specific material that you can get from any old textbook. Attending lectures is the best way to 'get inside the head' of your lecturer and get a feel for how they approach the subject.

If you begin a course not attending lectures it becomes psychologically harder and harder to attend as the course goes on, either because you feel embarrassed about your non-attendance, or because you simply get in the habit of missing them. So, make sure you attend the very first lecture of the course and maintain your participation through the module. By hearing the lecturer talk first hand you will gain a major advantage over students who do not attend regularly or at all.

In academic year 2009/10, I conducted a statistical analysis of the relationship between lecture attendance and marks achieved on my IRT module. I found that those students who frequently attended lectures almost always scored better coursework and exam marks than regular non-attendees.

READING

Your course tutor will either give you, or publish electronically, a list of suggested readings for each lecture on your course. Sometimes this will be in the form of a long list of sources. More often than not your tutor will divide the list week by week and/or into 'essential', 'desirable' and 'further/wider' reading.

Most tutors will recommend one or two essential textbooks as 'course reading' and you should start with the relevant chapters from these. See the Introduction in this book for a selection of IR books you will probably find recommended as course textbooks.

Before your lecture you should aim to read at least the essential reading and as much of the desirable reading as you can. There is no set amount that each tutor expects, but as a rough guide if you are reading at least five book chapters and/or journal articles before each lecture you will stand a very good chance of grasping the fundamental points your lecturer will want you to take from his/her lecture. You will have time after the lecture to put the icing on the cake with further reading.

One way to approach your reading might be:

- Begin with general textbook sources to get a feel for the key themes and then move on to the tougher journal articles and monographs.
- Set yourself realistic reading targets.
- Learn how long it takes you to read one average textbook chapter and one average journal article and plan your reading on that basis.
- Learn *where* you read best: in your room, in the department or in the library?
- Find somewhere without too many distractions where you can concentrate and take focused, organized notes.
- Make a note of concepts/issues you do not understand and root around for further information on them. If necessary, contact your tutor who will be happy to discuss them with you and advise where you can find information to enhance your understanding.

Most tutors make their lecture notes and/or PowerPoint presentations available to you. Print them out and read them before your lectures so you can pay particular attention in the lecture to the areas you understand less well.

DURING THE LECTURE

The two most important things you can do to get the best out of lectures are, first, to go prepared and, second, to see them as an opportunity to engage actively with the subject matter.

> The whole set-up of a lecture unfortunately tends to encourage the idea that the style of learning on offer is passive (lecturer talks; you listen). You need to think of ways to remain actively engaged over the course of the lecture. Taking a bottle of water in can help you maintain concentration.

NOTES

If notes are available to you prior to the lecture, make sure you have read through them and identified any difficult concepts or ideas you do not understand. You can make additional notes either on these printouts or make your own notes from scratch. Either way, be sure to label your notes with the date and subject matter of the lecture so you can organize them easily. A simple A4 file with your notes divided by topic will help you stay organized and find what you want to when putting together essays and revising for exams.

Lecture notes should represent a *legible* account of the main ideas presented in the lecture, together with the odd point to follow up and perhaps references to key writings the lecturer mentions which are not on the reading list, or which come particularly recommended. Lecturers will usually present the 'big' picture in lectures and focus only on key concepts and ideas. It is up to you to put the flesh on the bones of the topics covered through preparation and post-lecture consolidation (see below).

> If a lecturer mentions an author or text that is not on the reading list do not be afraid to ask him/her to spell out the author's name (by email after the lecture if you prefer) so you can trace the source easily in the library.

Lecturers will usually explain the meaning of new or difficult terms related to each topic they cover. If at the end of the lecture you are still unfamiliar with a term, you have two options to clarify your thoughts. First, try and find the term defined in the reading (glossaries are useful here). Second, contact your lecturer who will be happy to explain its meaning or at least give you some help locating a relevant definition. If many writers define the same term differently, keep a record of all their definitions for use in essays and exam answers.

NOTE-TAKING

There is no one recipe for success as far as taking notes in lectures goes. If you try and take too many notes, you will miss some or lots of what is said. If you take too few you will not generate a detailed enough picture of what was said for later reference. Do not worry if you do not capture everything that was said; the important thing is that you were present and that you leave with an idea of the big picture. Use your first-year lectures in particular to work out a note-taking strategy that works for you, and which gives you the optimum balance between listening attentively and recording what was said.

If your lecturer talks too fast, he/she should not mind if you ask to record the lecture to playback at your leisure. But remember: you do not need to tape every lecture and religiously copy out what was said.

AFTER THE LECTURE

Possibly the least recognized element of lecture-based learning is the post-lecture phase in which you consolidate and develop your knowledge.

CONSOLIDATION

This is all about establishing your grasp of the basics of the topic by confirming that you understand core concepts, foundational terms and so forth:

- Take time to read through your notes after the lecture.
- Re-write any lecture notes that are illegible.
- You could re-write the entire set of notes in a format that is clear and simple to understand. This option is useful if you want to make it easy to retrieve information from an ordered, clearly structured stock of information at a later stage.
- Make a summary of the lecture in a series of bullet points at the top of your notes. This will help you establish your understanding and make it easy to find the relevant material at a later stage.

- Make a note of any points made in the lecture that you are still unclear about.
- Make a list of any further reading mentioned by the lecturer.

Form a small study group (3 to 5 people) to review your notes, pool ideas on difficult concepts and consolidate your understanding of the main issues covered in each lecture.

DEVELOPMENT

Having consolidated your knowledge of the lecture you are now in a position to develop that knowledge. You can do this in several ways:

- Do any essential or further reading you did not do prior to the lecture.
- Trace and read sources mentioned in the lecture but which were not on the reading list (contact your tutor if necessary).
- Research around difficult concepts or ideas raised in the reading and lecture. A small study group helps with this.
- Marry your lecture notes with notes from your reading. For example, if your lecturer talked about different theoretical traditions approaching an issue in IR from different perspectives, could you name writers who represent each of those traditions? If not, would you know where to look to find out?
- Practice questions: take a look at past exam papers for your course. Could you now attempt an exam question on the lecture you have just listened to? If the answer is '*no*', you need to do more reading and research around the subject.

Spend half an hour or so each week planning and drafting a 1,500 word answer to a past exam or essay question. This will be invaluable practice for the real thing. Very few students will do the same so your tutor would happily give you feedback on your answers.

3.2 HOW TO GET THE MOST OUT OF SEMINARS

Seminars offer you the opportunity to explore various perspectives on a given topic in depth. They expose you to different styles of learning and encourage you to think creatively around problems individually and in groups. Despite these benefits seminars are not always well attended by students, which seems strange when, in the same breath, students will say that contact time at universities can be insufficient for their perceived learning needs! This is a great shame because the seminar environment encourages you to develop subject-specific expertise as well as transferable skills for use outside the learning environment.

> If you aim to get the best out of seminars in IRT, you are giving yourself the best chance of succeeding at your coursework and exams as well as developing vital communication and teamwork skills for the long term.

In this chapter we will consider the nature of the university seminar and how you can get the very best out of your seminar time, with particular reference to seminar learning, effort and presentations.

SEMINAR LEARNING

Lectures are usually held up to be the cornerstone of academic programmes in the social sciences and what we most associate with university level learning. Yet seminars play a vital part in helping you generate depth to your understanding of a given subject in a way that lectures rarely can. In IRT terms, the lectures will more than likely present a broad-brush overview of the main assumptions and explanations put forward by each school of theory. In seminars you will have time to consolidate your understanding of the basics, as well as debating the relative strengths and weaknesses of different theorists' interpretations of IR. Seminars in IRT are where you can get prepared to do the basics well and develop your critical faculties to get you towards the higher end of the marking spectrum.

Initially, seminar learning can seem a daunting prospect. You are often working with students you may not have met properly before and may be asked to tackle questions you had not thought about prior to the seminar. Teaching and learning in seminars assume many forms and you will probably not know how you are going to be learning before you actually get to the seminar room on the day.

Common Pitfall

Do not let the relative uncertainty about how you will learn in seminars put you off attending. See it as a challenge and a way of proving that you are flexible and adaptable. Your tutor will look positively on those students who throw themselves wholeheartedly into seminars.

Here is a small sample of the kinds of seminar learning you might experience at university:

- **Individual summaries/critiques.** You might be given a short extract from a key text and asked to spend 10 minutes reading it and summarizing/critiquing the main points it raises. Some tutors might ask you to pre-prepare summaries in advance of the class, so keep a regular check on your university email account in case you need to turn up with this work ready to go.
- **Pair work.** Discuss a problem/perspective/issue with the person sitting next to you.
- **Group work.** Discuss a problem/perspective/issue with a small number of other students in the seminar, possibly leading to a 'group' answer which you present and defend to the rest of the class.
- **Pyramid work.** All students start with the same issue to consider for five minutes. Then you work in pairs for five minutes and finally you discuss your ideas in groups for five minutes. It is called pyramid work because the number of 'units' involved decreases as the seminar progresses, building

up from a base of lots of students thinking about a problem to fewer pairs and finally even fewer groups.
- **Class debate.** As in parliaments you may be split into groups and asked to propose or oppose a motion. As an example, in recent years I have split my seminar groups into two teams to debate the motion: 'This House believes the study of gender is vital to the study of IR', with one team proposing the motion and the other opposing it. Debates are good for helping you consider all sides of a problem because not only do you have to work out your own position, you have to think about how to counter what the opposing team might argue.
- **Whole group discussion.** Most common at the end of seminars. A chance to wrap up big issues, ask questions, iron out any lingering misunderstandings and consolidate your knowledge from the lecture and seminar readings.

All tutors organize seminars differently and some can be set in their ways! If there are styles of seminar learning you find particularly helpful, your tutor will consider using them if you politely alert him/her to your preference.

YOU GET BACK WHAT YOU PUT IN

As with lectures, you tend to get as much out of seminars as you put into them. Here are some very basic tips on the kinds of things you can do to work confidently and rewardingly in seminars:

- Do a realistic amount of preparatory reading. If your tutor has identified essential reading you should at least complete that.
- Take all your notes with you to each seminar, plus pen and paper to jot down further notes during the seminar.
- If you are not sure you understand something – ask.
- Make sure you try and say something relatively early on in a seminar, even if only to ask a basic factual question. Studies show that the longer you go without speaking, the harder it becomes to intervene as the seminar progresses.
- At the end of the seminar check through your notes to make sure they are legible, and for any issues you may want to follow-up on.

Sometimes, the problem is not that you have come to a seminar unprepared but that you are frightened of interjecting into a debate. In this case, remember the following:

- Very few people feel totally at ease at speaking in public, especially on subjects that are relatively unfamiliar to them. Most academics I know still get nervous before giving lectures, even if they have been doing it for 20 years. Students are no different, and even if they *appear* confident you can be sure they are nervous inside.
- There really are no stupid questions. If you are unclear about something you can be sure you are not the only one.
- Your tutor is not there to tell you what to think. At university level tutors are less like school teachers than facilitators for your learning.
- Disagreements among students in the seminar group will be many and varied. This is entirely to be expected.
- There are no right or wrong answers to questions about IRT. We may prefer one theory over another but no one can shoot a theoretically informed opinion down by saying it is definitely 'wrong'.
- Learning how to disagree and how to conduct rational arguments in a seminar environment will help sharpen your critical thinking and communication skills, and is a vital transferable skill to take away with you from university to the world of work.

> In pretty much any career you pursue after graduating you will have to speak in public in some environment, whether one-on-one with a boss or colleague, or to larger groups at conferences, for example. Use the university environment to generate confidence at public speaking.

PRESENTATIONS

Standing up and talking about academic matters can be a stressful business. In seminars for IRT you may be asked to give a presentation on your own, or to work in pairs or groups and then to present your combined results. Either way, here are some tips on how to plan and deliver an effective presentation:

PLANNING YOUR PRESENTATION

- Spend time preparing as thoroughly as you can and get started as early as possible, especially if working as part of a group.
- If working in pairs or a group, apportion work evenly and set realistic targets for each group member. Set deadlines and stick to them.

- Decide if you want to use visual aids such as hand-outs, PowerPoint or online sources such as YouTube, and prepare these in advance.
- Clearly structure your presentation and centre it on one core argument or theme. Signpost your argument at least once during the talk.
- Read as widely as you can and show you have a good knowledge of the field.
- Build practice time into your schedule, especially if you are using visual technologies such as PowerPoint. Whether presenting on your own or in a group, run through the entire presentation at least once to check that it flows well and that you cover the ground you need to in the allotted time.

DELIVERING YOUR PRESENTATION

- Stick to the allotted time. It is better to be slightly under than over.
- Make eye contact with everyone in the audience at least once during the talk.
- Use a script if necessary but try to avoid simply reading out a monologue or you will lose the audience's attention.
- Try and look and sound enthusiastic and confident (even if you are not!)
- If using PowerPoint do not turn around to talk to the screen – remember it is an aid, not the object of the talk, or the audience for it.
- Make sure your talk follows the structure of your hand-out or order of the PowerPoint slides (practicing in advance is critical here).
- Summarize the main argument of your talk at the end in a concluding section.

In seminars you have a huge opportunity to establish confidence in your knowledge of the subject matter of IRT. The skills you develop there will be of great value in other seminars and when you enter the world of work. Take them seriously and you will benefit enormously from them.

REFERENCES TO MORE INFORMATION

Here are some books dedicated to improving your seminar communication and presentation skills:

Bradbury, A. (2006) *Successful Presentation Skills*, 3rd edn. London: Kogan Page.

Stott, R. (2001) *Speaking Your Mind: Oral Presentation and Seminar Skills*. Harlow: Longman.

Barrass, R. (2006) *Speaking for Yourself: A Guide for Students to Effective Communication*. London: Routledge.

Kroehnert, G. (1999) *Basic Presentation Skills*. Roseville, NSW: McGraw-Hill.

Bonnett, A. (2001) *How to Argue: A Student's Guide*. Harlow: Pearson.

Van Emden, J. and Becker, L. (2004) *Presentation Skills for Students*. Basingstoke: Palgrave Macmillan.

3.3 USING FEEDBACK

The best way to improve as a student of IRT – or any subject – is to know what your strengths are and how to consolidate them, and what your weaknesses are and how to address them. If you cannot or do not understand your knowledge base and how to enhance it then you need to take steps to do so, so that you can take constructive ownership of your learning. This brief chapter will explain the feedback at university level and give you some tips on how you can get the best out of it.

WHAT IS FEEDBACK AND WHERE CAN I GET IT?

Feedback comes in a variety of forms: numerical or summative; narrative or formative (including 'feed forward' or areas for improvement); oral or informal feedback. Feedback also comes from a variety of sources. University tutors are where you look principally for feedback on your performance, but fellow students can also give feedback on your thinking, in, for example, a seminar exercise where you get to exchange interpretations of a given topic or theoretical approach. Being open to feedback is the way to improve your critical edge and get a head start in essays and exams.

SUMMATIVE FEEDBACK (YES, MARKS IN THE 70s AND ABOVE ARE UP FOR GRABS)

This is the 'grading' element of feedback. The summative mark you are awarded for a piece of work tells you in a very quick and easy way where you are on the scale of achievement on a module. The lower down you are on the scale, the more time you will have to spend working out what you need to do to improve. For example, if you receive a mark in the 40s you probably have to address your skills across the board: making sure you do sufficient reading, structuring your thoughts, developing an argument, and honing your communication skills. If you score in the 50s you know what to do in an essay but have not executed the piece of work very effectively, or the analysis is over-simplistic. Marks in the 50s are usually given for work that lacks focus, direction and much reading of key sources. Presentation skills are usually a problem too.

If you are operating in the 60s, generally, you will have a decent grasp of the skills across the board and should be concentrating on the detail as a way of moving forward by fine-tuning your wider reading, generating more critical depth in your work, and presenting it technically correctly. If you achieve a mark of 70 plus you can be confident of repeating that standard of work in the future with the same level of preparation and attention to detail. Things are never guaranteed though, so do not rest on your laurels. Now the task will be to fine-tune your skills to reach for the 80s plus, which are – despite rumours – within reach for the best students.

Common Pitfall

When you receive hard or online copies of assessed work back do not simply look at the mark and throw the essay away. Check through the general and specific feedback so you know what you did well, and where you need to enhance your skills or knowledge base.

In sum, as your marks move higher up the scale, the better your tutor judges you to be at meeting the essential and desirable learning outcomes for the module. But how do you know where to improve? This is where formative feedback comes in.

FORMATIVE FEEDBACK

Summative feedback tells you where you are; formative feedback tells you how to get where you want to be. In other words, summative feedback is your mark; formative feedback justifies why you were awarded that mark narratively. It should, if delivered effectively, flag up the positive things the tutor liked about your work and spell out where you were weaker. Some formative feedback sheets invite the tutor to theme his or her comments around set headings such as 'structure of essay', 'logic or argument', 'analytical content and sources', 'presentation, including referencing' and 'area(s) for improvement'. Assessment sheets that give the tutor scope to range freely over the essay can be harder to 'read' off, as it were, but do not let this deter you. All tutors look for the same kinds of qualities in university-level work (see Chapter 3.4), and, even if idiosyncratically, they will try to help you understand where you went right and wrong in a piece of work.

Perhaps the most important element of a feedback sheet is the 'area(s) for improvement' box. This is where your tutor will spell out very clearly the skills you need to work up to improve for the future, taking your essay as a representative case of your hardest effort to achieve your potential. If your tutor writes that improvement has to come from reading some IRT, structuring an answer and presenting your work according to department guidelines, you probably will not have got a great mark because these are foundational skills. If, however, you are invited to read a few more authors to give you some depth and are asked to tidy up the presentation of your bibliography you have demonstrated a robust grasp of the essay basics and will have obtained a decent mark. This is more about fine-tuning than anything else.

Even if hard copies of essays are returned to you with formative cover-sheets attached, some tutors will also have commented on your writing as they marked it. In those comments you will get a little bit of extra useful detail about what they liked and what they disliked, and you will appreciate a bit better how you can improve for that tutor next time around. Tutors are happy to discuss the 'meaning' of written feedback should you be confused, but I would be wary about asking them to change your mark upwards!

ORAL FEEDBACK

Very simply, this is the informal or 'hot' feedback you get from tutors in conversation in and around lectures and seminars, and probably more likely in the seminar room during presentations and group work, for example. It is a form of formative feedback not always valued that highly by students. However, if you listen carefully to what tutors say to members of a seminar group – not just on your own work – you will find a feast of hints and tips. What the tutor says 'off the cuff', as it were, will inform your understanding of the subject matter and how to impress that tutor in assessments (another reason to attend seminars regularly). You may well receive formal summative and formative feedback on oral presentations (see Chapter 3.2,) but oral feedback often comes more conversationally. It is particularly useful when you do non-assessed work where you can test whether you are on the right path by taking such feedback seriously and seeing if your work passes muster with your tutor.

There is another vital opportunity for you to receive feedback which in my experience all but a very few students take: one-to-one chats about your academic progress with the module tutor. This could be about a draft essay plan, formative feedback on assessed work, or even exam performance, which tends to be known to you in mark form only. Making an appointment to discuss your performance for quarter of an hour with your module tutor might make the difference between a 2:2 and a 2:1 in your overall module mark, or better still a 2:1 and a 1st class mark. It all adds up.

SUMMARY

If you think strategically about your learning at university you will take every scrap of feedback you can garner and put it to its very best use. In this chapter we have surveyed the three main types of feedback you will receive: summative, formative and oral. Assessed work is where you receive the bulk of the feedback, but there are many opportunities to get feedback from your tutors in a non-assessed context. If you take feedback on the non-assessed elements of your course seriously you will be better prepared to succeed when it comes to the real thing. Feedback in all its forms should be an integral part of your learning about IRT.

3.4 ESSAY WRITING

... there are several practices widely recognized as essential to good research. Among these are clarity of purpose, logical coherence, engagement with alternative arguments and the provision of good reasons (empirical evidence, corroborating arguments, textual interpretations etc.). (Reus-Smit 2012: 532)

Essays will probably be a huge part of the assessed workload on your degree programme. Exams and/or seminar presentations may feature too, but inevitably you will have to tackle a formal, fully referenced essay at some point on your course, ranging from anything between 1,500 and about 4,000 words. Recognizing what makes for a successful essay is vital at university level. The sooner you can develop the techniques for producing coherent, flowing and concise written responses to questions, the better you will fare on all your modules. Christian Reus-Smit's description of the tenets of good academic research are exactly what tutors look to see you working at in your written submissions.

> The main components of a good coursework essay also make for good exam answers, so think of them as requiring the same skills. The only thing missing from exam answers are formal references and a bibliography.

In this chapter I want to suggest that the process of putting together a successful essay takes three things: sound preparation and planning, a structured approach to writing and presentation, and a solid amount of evidence to back up your claims. I will flesh these out below, then in the next chapter we will see hard examples of best practice in IR theory essay technique.

PLANNING AND PREPARATION

KNOW YOUR ENEMY

Your initial undertaking from a planning perspective is to know the precise requirements to be met in your coursework. These will be available from your tutor either at or near the start of the module and are usually included in the module guide. The key things to take note of are:

- **Essay deadline.** Coursework delivered after the deadline is either subject to the removal of penalty marks or given zero. Set yourself a realistic completion target and aim to finish at least one day before the deadline to give yourself time to proof read the essay for errors, omissions or ambiguities in your argument or written English.

> Getting a friend or relative to read through your essay before you submit will help iron out any obvious problems with it. Their outsider perspective helps them spot things you may have missed because you are so 'close' to the essay.

- **Deadline extensions.** If you have a valid claim for an extension contact your module tutor well in advance of the deadline. Check your department's guidelines on what you need to support a claim for 'mitigating circumstances' and keep all the relevant supporting evidence, for example, a doctor's note if you have been ill.
- **Length of essay.** It is important to stick to the word limit set. Check with your tutor if you are allowed to go slightly above or below the word limit and how far these bands extend. Up to ten per cent above or below is sometimes permitted but it will depend on your tutor's and/or department guidelines.
- **Presentation and submission requirements.** Check your departmental undergraduate handbook for full details on how to format your essays, how to provide and present references, and where to submit your work. Tutors get bombarded with emails in the week leading up to the submission deadline and it does not look too good if you ask simple questions that are all answered in the handbook!

- **Lecture and seminar insights.** In lectures and tutorials, tutors will often hint at ways of approaching essays that they feel pay dividends. This is another reason to attend lectures and seminars regularly.

> Attending lectures and seminars helps you learn more about the subject matter and also gives you a feel for what your tutor expects to see in essays and exam answers.

PLAN YOUR ARGUMENT

Having oriented yourself to the requirements of the essay you need to set about planning it. To get to this stage you will need to have carried out at least the essential reading on the topic, and preferably the desirable and as much wider reading as possible. You can always carry on reading while you write, as long as you have most of the research completed before you begin planning it.

> When tutors mark a big batch of essays, they get used to seeing the same authors and ideas rehashed over and over again. Doing wider reading will help your essay stand out from the crowd.

When you feel comfortable that you know the basics about the subject and are ready to put finger to keyboard, here are some tips on how to keep the essay focused, manageable and persuasive:

- **Core argument.** Your essay should hang together around a central argument, point of view, interpretation or opinion that you advance consistently through the narrative. This should preferably be in the form of a direct response to the question set and should appear as the focal point in your introductory section. Your central theme will be tailored to suit the essay question, but the key thing is that you *have* a central argument and can explain it clearly and concisely. Without the focus a core argument provides, you will not be able to give direction to the essay and the reader will not be sure of where you are going either. Wandering around a range of topics hoping something of relevance might emerge is not the way to approach writing.

> It sounds formulaic but you could even begin the essay by writing 'This essay will argue that … '. Few students have the confidence to lead off with their argument but it helps a tutor to see exactly where you intend to go from the outset.

- **How many points?** Undergraduate essays vary in length, usually from 1,500 words upwards, so there are no hard and fast rules that will work in every situation. Assuming the introduction and conclusion combined are approximately 10 per cent each of the entire word count, in a 1,500 word essay this would leave 1,200 words as the 'body' of the essay. This is not a lot of words. You will not be able to cover more than four or five main points, so you will have to be selective about what to include and what to ignore. The less successful essays tend to be those that try to cover every single point made about a particular topic in the reading, or which rehash cursory summaries of the relevant lecture. Being selective is critical at the planning stage. Learning when to leave material out (or delete chunks of what you have just written) is a big part of developing effective writing techniques. It takes confidence and firmness of intent to stick to only the essentials that help you advance one core proposition.
- **Getting your own opinion across.** Some students worry if they do not include any of their own opinions in coursework essays. Do not agonize about this. You are not expected to develop new theories of IR or never-thought-of-before critiques of the theories you examine in an essay. Your approach to the subject matter will come through in your main argument and the structure you give your answer. The 'originality' of the essay is, therefore, inherent in an essay that you have planned and written in your own words, and backed up by quotes and evidence from established sources.

> Remember that the same essay question can be answered in an infinite number of ways. By devising your response, writing mostly your own words, and structuring your answer yourself, your work counts as original.

ESSAY STRUCTURE

If you ask any university student about essay structure they all know what it means: beginning, middle and end. In my time teaching IRT I have increasingly come to the conclusion that this only tells a very small part of the story about essay structure; in fact it might actually obscure as much as it reveals. Students usually grasp this basic 'macro' structure, but what about the middle or body of the essay? The essence of a robust structure is not just that the essay is in three parts, but that the various segments or paragraphs that make up those parts are also structured. It is at the micro level structure that the vast majority of students trip up. The classic feature is an essay that starts with a coherent introduction and ends with a workable conclusion, but in the middle jumps around at random with ideas, authors and concepts cropping up all over the place. The student has structured the essay at the macro level but forgotten about the micro level.

> If you think essay structure is all about introduction, body, conclusion, think again! There is much more to it than that. Structure applies on two levels: macro and micro, and successful essays pay attention to both levels.

EVERYONE KNOWS ABOUT MACRO STRUCTURE!

I will not dwell on the macro structure needed to write a successful essay. Suffice to say that you should be familiar with the basic idea and your tutor will usually be happy to look over a plan that comes in this format as a way of assuring you that your answer looks like a logical response to the essay question set. Figure 18 presents the essence of a 'macro' essay structure.

WHAT IS MICRO STRUCTURE?

Less familiar might be the idea of micro structure. This is the structure of the individual sections themselves, particularly the body of the essay. Why is this important? The whole idea of an essay is that you are showing your tutor you are organized, well informed, and able to construct a logical argument that flows nicely through the piece. If you do not structure at the micro level as well as the macro level you risk losing your reader because they will probably not be able to follow where you go in the body of the essay.

> One way to structure the body of an essay is by using headings and sub-headings. This helps the reader see how you have organized your answer.

INTRODUCTION

- Aims of essay
- Core theme/argument
- Essay plan

BODY OF ESSAY

- The key points that help you advance your central case
- *Micro structure*

CONCLUSION

- Reminder of central argument
- Wider issues raised by essay

Figure 18   Macro essay structure

Concentrating on micro structure is essential at both the planning and writing stages. You need to structure each section of your essay from introduction through body and conclusion, and this means making sure the various paragraphs that make up each section follow logically from the one to the next.

Because it is the most difficult aspect of writing a good essay let's concentrate on how a well structured body of the essay might look, in theory, from a micro perspective. We will assume an essay is in four main parts, top and tailed by an introduction and conclusion. Depending on the word limit of the essay, each point in the body of the essay would be developed in roughly two to three paragraphs. Figure 19 sets out the micro structure of an essay.

Figure 19 reads quite formulaically, but do not be put off by this. Your tutor will be reading dozens, sometimes hundreds of essays and will want to be told precisely what your argument is, how you put the case in your essay, and to know that *you* know why you travelled where you did in the answer. If you make this structure explicit you will definitely stand out from the vast majority of students who will keep the marker guessing about their intellectual journey.

The basic requirement of a good essay is that you take your reader on a journey that you have planned in advance. If you cannot (or do not) explain your journey from start to finish then do not expect your tutor to be able to follow you through it, not without getting frustrated or annoyed at any rate.

> INTRODUCTION
>
> - Aims of essay
> - Core theme or argument you will make
> - Essay plan: what you will cover in points 1 to 4
>
> BODY OF ESSAY
>
> - POINT 1
>   - Summarize essence of point 1 (*S*)*
>   - Make point 1
>   - Explain how point 1 helps you advance your core argument and where you are going next in the essay (*B*)**
>
> - POINT 2
>   - Summarize essence of point 2 (*S*)
>   - Make point 2
>   - Summarize upshot of points 1 and 2 (*S*) and say where you are going next in the essay (*B*)
>
> - POINT 3
>   - Summarize essence of point 3 (*S*)
>   - Make point 3
>   - Summarize key findings from points 1, 2 and 3 (*S*) and say where you are going next in the essay (*B*)
>
> - POINT 4
>   - Summarize essence of point 4 (*S*)
>   - Make point 4
>   - Summarize key findings from point 4 and recap how they relate to points 1, 2 and 3 (*S*)
>
> CONCLUSION
>
> - Reminder of central argument
> - Where you went in points 1 to 4
> - Wider issues raised by essay

Figure 19   Micro structure of an essay

Notes:
* (*S*) denotes a signpost section (see below)
** (*B*) denotes a bridge section (see below)

TECHNIQUES TO HELP YOU DEVELOP YOUR ESSAY'S MICRO STRUCTURE

You only develop essay planning and writing skills through practice. Here are a few things you can try to structure your essays clearly and explicitly.

> Try implementing some or all of these techniques in your next essay. Also, try and identify good structuring techniques from the reading you do. Borrowing tips from the experts is a great way to develop essay skills.

- **Signposts.** Quite literally, you should point the reader's way through the essay. Think of it like following road signs on a car journey. When they are in plentiful supply and easy to understand, it is easy to find your way to your destination. However, when there are no signs, or if they point the wrong way, or if they are unclear, then it becomes difficult for you to follow them. By inserting signpost sentences regularly, you give the reader the pointers they need to navigate their way through your thinking in the essay.
- **Bridges.** These are similar to signposts in that they give the essay direction, but they are used specifically to help the reader cross between two distinct parts of an essay. In the example above, bridging sections would be used to take the reader from the introduction to the body of the essay, from point 1 to point 2, from point 2 to point 3, from point 3 to point 4 and from point 4 to the conclusion. Hence, while signposts are used at the start of new sections or paragraphs to point the way ahead or recap a central theme in the essay, bridges are less frequent but play a crucial role in getting your reader into and out of sections.

SUMMARY ON SIGNPOSTS AND BRIDGES

There are three main varieties of signposting (Redman 2006: 64): (1) at the beginning of a new section to summarize what you will argue in it; (2) at the end of a section to recap the central theme of the section; and (3) where necessary to remind the reader of the subject of your essay – especially useful when you get to the later stages of an essay.

> We will see practical examples of signposting in IR theory essays in the next chapter.

Signposts and bridges are very similar in some respects because the idea of both is to help the reader through an essay. You can happily combine the two together if you wish. Say you are tackling the essay question: 'Realism is the "common sense" theory of IR. Discuss'. This essay naturally falls into two parts: those who agree with that statement and those who disagree with it. At the end of all the 'for' points you could write, *'Having discussed three reasons why Realism is said to be the common sense approach to IR,* **the essay will now consider the arguments against this view by looking at the work of Liberal and Feminist scholars**'. This sentence contains both a signpost (italics) and a bridge (bold). Feel free to experiment with signposts and bridges and find what works best for you. The important thing is that you will get credit for trying because you will be showing your tutor that you are organized and have thought seriously about how to write 'academically'.

EVIDENCE

Successful essays and exam answers are built on a solid block of evidence. Academics use evidence to provide them with information about a subject and as a point of reference within a given debate. In IR, theorists get their evidence from many places: history, contemporary politics and other theorists, for example. Your tutor will recommend a series of readings for your course and the first place you should look is there, but feel free to go beyond the recommended readings. Being creative with your research on a topic is a sign of initiative and your tutor will notice your work more if you have put in the effort to look beyond the basic texts.

> A successful essay requires both technical proficiency and an in-depth knowledge of the subject matter.

By providing authoritative evidence you are showing your essay is built on more than a passing acquaintance with the subject or what you heard your friends talking about in the Students Union bar the night before you submitted it. Through the evidence you provide you are demonstrating a thorough engagement with the key literature, a familiarity with the technical concepts and an active involvement in the debates that take place between writers in the field. In sum, you are showing that you have made every effort to get inside the heads of the writers you have been asked to study on your course. You can only do this by reading widely and providing full references to the sources of information you used to construct the essay.

Common Pitfall

Students routinely fail to provide evidence to back their assertions. You do not need a reference for every fact presented in an essay if it is common knowledge. For example, saying that the Second World War ended in 1945 would not need a reference. However, you do need to show the provenance or origin of every major argument, interpretation or point of view you discuss in an essay. For instance, if you set out the key assumptions of Realism or alluded to different varieties of Critical Theory, you would need a clear reference to your source because these are NOT common knowledge but your interpretations drawn from other people's texts. We will come back to referencing in Chapter 3.6 on plagiarism.

USING EVIDENCE

You can use evidence from your reading around IRT in a variety of ways:

- **Quotes.** Use these if a writer makes a particularly succinct, cutting comment on a given issue, provides a suitable definition for a difficult concept, or has come up with an interpretation, theory or model that critically shaped a debate within a field. Try and limit the amount of quotes you use in an essay so that enough of your own words still come through. Quotes should support your ideas, not the other way around. Common pitfalls with using quotes are that they are too long and/or become just a series of unrelated sentences from writers with no explanation for why they appear where they do. If quotes are not referenced you run the risk of being accused of plagiarism (see Chapter 3.6).

If you are quoting a writer who uses italics or bold font in their original work, make sure you tell your reader that the emphasis in your essay has not been inserted by you but appears in the original. This level of technical detail is critical if you want to get the best marks. Faithful reproduction of original texts and sources is the key.

- **Paraphrase/summary.** You may not always want to quote directly from authors but instead paraphrase them, usually in the form of a summary of their arguments. This is an equally valid way of introducing evidence from established sources into your essay. Remember that even if you do not quote directly you will still need to include a reference to the original source.
- **What to cite?** When providing references you only need to cite the source where you located the information. If you got all your information about postmodernist writer X from textbook authors B and C, then your reference will be to textbook writers B and C. If you cite the original work by writer X your tutor will mistakenly assume you read the original. Do not pretend you have read an original work of IRT if you have not. If you got all your information about a theory from a textbook be honest about it. It is sloppy practice to claim to have read things you have not, and is usually pretty obvious to the tutor.

REFERENCING

Before you start writing an essay acquaint yourself fully with your department's style guidelines on how to set out references and bibliographies. As a general rule you are likely to be asked for the following:

- If a reference appears in the essay it will need to appear in the list of references at the end in a format that makes it easily identifiable to the reader.
- A bibliography includes all the sources you used to research an essay; a list of references only includes those sources you refer to in an essay.

Do not be tempted to 'pad' a bibliography with sources you did not read!

- Make sure you achieve consistency with dates, spelling of surnames and so on in your essay references and bibliography.
- Arrange your bibliography or list of references alphabetically by surname, and always start on a new page at the end of the essay.
- When referencing online sources do not include the full web address in the text the essay, save it for the bibliography. In the essay you need a shortened reference fully traceable in the bibliography. For example, if you wanted to refer to UN Secretary-General Ban Ki-moon's statement to regional groups of the UN in January 2008, this is available online. In your essay you would summarize or quote from it and your reference would read (Ki-moon 2008). Save the full title and web address for the bibliography, so that the reader can find it if they look under 'Ki-moon 2008'. Some websites contain no author and/or date. In that case you simply say 'anonymous' or 'no date' where applicable.

Give your marker as much information as possible so that they are able to trace your sources.

REFERENCES TO MORE INFORMATION

There are many general texts on good practice in essay writing. Try any of the following:

Redman, P. (2006) *Good Essay Writing*, 3rd edn. London: Sage.
  Written specifically for social sciences students and contains lots of examples of good practice.

McMillan, K. and Weyers, J. (2007) *How to Write Essays and Assignments*. Harlow: Pearson Prentice Hall.

Fowler, A. (2006) *How to Write*. Oxford: Oxford University Press.

Hennessy, B. (2002) *Writing an Essay: Simple Techniques to Transform your Coursework and Examinations*, 4th edn. Oxford: How To Books.
  Good on both the macro and micro sides of essay writing.

Kirton, B. (2007) *Just Write: An Easy-to-use Guide to Writing at University*. Abingdon: Routledge.

Price, G. and Maier, P. (2007) *Effective Study Skills: Unlock Your Potential*. Harlow: Pearson Longman.

Includes writing skills in a discussion of good academic practice more generally.

Rose, J. (2007) *The Mature Student's Guide to Writing*. New York: Palgrave Macmillan.

Levin, P. (2004) *Write Good Essays!: A Guide to Reading and Essay Writing for Undergraduates and Taught Postgraduates*. Maidenhead: Open University Press.

Creme, P. and Lea, M.R. (2000) *Writing at University: A Guide for Students*, 2nd edn. Buckingham: Open University Press.

Bailey, S. (2006) *Academic Writing: A Handbook for International Students*, 2nd edn. London: Routledge.

There are also texts on writing specifically for political science students:

Scott, G.M. and Garrison, S.M. (2006) *The Political Science Student Writer's Manual*, 5th edn. Upper Saddle River, NJ: Prentice Hall.

Part I on writing and referencing competently is excellent.

Harrison, L. (2001) *Political Research: An Introduction*. London: Routledge.

Chapter 9 is on writing a politics dissertation, but the same principles apply there as in an essay, so well worth a look.

3.5 GOOD PRACTICE IN ESSAYS

This chapter contains extracts from genuine student essays on IRT which show you how three students more or less successfully deployed some of the essay techniques discussed in the previous chapter. All the essays responded to one question: 'How "scientific" is IR theory?' These were submitted in academic year 2006/7 and I am grateful to the students concerned for letting me use their essays. I have transcribed the extracts exactly as they appeared in the originals, including typographical errors, spelling/grammar errors and references.

MACRO STRUCTURE: INTRODUCTIONS

Compare the opening paragraphs of each essay.

Student 1

Purely by definition one could certainly suggest that students of International Relations theory undertake a very scientific approach to their studies. Indeed, the theory of any study could be deemed scientific, although outside the boundaries of how society would usually call a fact based science, those being, in general terms, biology, chemistry, physics and, to a certain extent, maths … [*student then introduces definitions of 'science' from Reader's Digest Universal Dictionary*] … However, it would be very easy to argue over definitions without coming to any conclusions as to whether a study of theory has the right to be called a science or is simply an argument made without any evidence to support it. Some would say that without this actual, factual grasp on

---

a subject a theory cannot be a science. Others would argue that the very approach to the production of a theoretical analysis earns it the right to be called a science. In today's world this is what we would call a social science, that is 'The study of society and of … relationships in and [relating] to society' (Reader's Digest Universal Dictionary 1987, p. 1443).

Student 2

This essay critically investigates the debate on 'How "scientific" is IR theory?'. I will start by outlining what the term 'scientific' means and then use this definition to question whether IR theory is a science, and if so, to what extent? As well as who supports or opposes this relatively new look on the subject to come to a qualified conclusion.

Student 3

'Until the late 1980's, most social scientists in international relations (IR) tended to be positivist' (Baylis *et al.* 2001: 274). However, from then on numerous post-positivist theories have emerged, attacking positivist methodology, epistemology and ontology, questioning the validity of the underlying assumptions of positivism. Arguably, the discipline of IR is 'scientific' in nature and this essay aims to investigate and evaluate the nature of IR by exploring the construct and meaning of 'scientific', with respect to social and natural phenomena, and the underlying assumptions of positivist explanatory and post-positivist constitutive perspectives.

You can see three very different approaches here. Which do you think works best as an introduction? If you were the marker, which introduction would persuade you that the student was on top of the material being presented?

- **Central argument.** Student 3 is the only student to set out a core argument: 'Arguably, the discipline of IR is "scientific" in nature'. Student 2 states that he intends to answer the question but forgets to tell us what his answer will be. Student 1 barely provides an introduction in the sense that he dashes into the different definitions of science and related debates without giving us any pointers to where he will go in the essay.

- **Essay structure.** Student 3 clearly identifies how his central arguments will be advanced. In the final three lines of the paragraph he says that his argument that IR is 'scientific' will be made first by considering the definition of 'scientific' and then by considering the positivist versus post-positivist debates. Student 2 gets as far as saying that he will define 'scientific' but there the clues run out. Student 1 does not provide any direction but rushes off into the definitions themselves. Here we see the best essay *signposting* in Student 3's piece. Student 1 gives no signposts at all, and Student 2 manages just a smattering.

- **Subject matter expertise.** Two of the introductions give early indications of the level at which the student is operating. Student 1 relies on two quotes from the Reader's Digest, while Student 3 uses an authoritative source in a chapter from Baylis and Smith's *The Globalization of World Politics*. Even after reading just the introductions the marker would be persuaded that Student 3 was more on top of the reading than Student 1, even if the final judgement would wait until the end of the essay. However, first impressions are important and it helps if you can establish an authoritative position early in an essay.

Individual departments and tutors have differing opinions on the utility and validity of students using online dictionaries and resources such as Wikipedia. Check your course handbook and with your individual tutor to see if he/she has preferences. If in doubt, avoid.

- **Technical aspects.** Students 2 and 3 write in plain, unambiguous English. Student 3 references correctly and it is easy to follow his thoughts in the introduction. The quality of Student 1's written English is lower for the following reasons:

  - First, why does the definition of IR suggest that students of the subject take a 'very scientific' approach to the subject? The logic is contentious and the meaning of 'very scientific' is unclear. Can a method of studying a topic be 'quite scientific'?!
  - Second, Student 1's use of 'Some would say …' and 'Others would argue …' smacks of imprecision. At the very least, a source would have

been needed to clear up the confusion. Overall it adds to the impression that the student is not yet on top of the reading material on this topic.

o Third, Student 1's references are incorrectly presented according to what were then my departmental guidelines on the Harvard system of referencing. Presentation of your notes and bibliography, as we have seen, is a key thing to get correct in essays. If you can spend time getting it right, you will show your tutor that you can present work 'academically' and you will be given your credit accordingly.

SUMMARY ON INTRODUCTIONS

Having read these introductions the marker will be thinking that Student 3 is the most organized, well-prepared and logical student who can, moreover, express his ideas clearly and unambiguously. Student 2 is some way to understanding the basic requirements of an essay, while Student 1 is getting there but seems to be the least technically proficient student.

MICRO STRUCTURE

We have seen how important it is to structure essays at the micro as well as the macro level. Here are some examples of signposting and bridging from the three submissions which helped the students organize the body of their essays.

STRUCTURING AROUND QUESTIONS

Student 1 [opening paragraph of body of essay]

But how do we undertake such an approach to studying issues as complex as classifying a state's identity in the contemporary world to understanding the balance of power and war and the significance of 9/11?

While there is a lot going on in the sentence, we can see that Student 1 is setting up the next paragraph or two by posing a question which, on being answered, should help him answer the essay question.

> ## Student 2 [after defining 'science']
>
> In the purest meaning of the word is IR theory 'science'? Can IR be seen objectively and with only fact and figures?

The student goes on to analyse writers in the 'yes' camp, such as E.H. Carr. My feedback on this part of the essay was that the student did not spend enough time looking at the 'no' camp.

NUMBERED POINTS

> ## Student 3 [in section on empiricism]
>
> The positivist or naturalist 'scientific' perspective on IR has four main underlying assumptions, which are largely drawn from the main assumptions of logical positivism (Smith et al. 2006: 19). Firstly, they believe in the unity of science … Secondly, facts and values are distinguishable… Thirdly, positivists hold the social world to contain regularities … Lastly, they hold the neutral nature of facts … (Baylis et al. 2001).

Most works list the fourfold characteristics of positivism in this way. You can see how replicating the numbered approach helps Student 3 take the reader smoothly through them, and he backs his case with reference to two authoritative sources. Providing micro structure to paragraphs first helps you organize your thoughts; second, helps you write in well balanced paragraphs; and third, makes it easy for the marker to follow your thinking as it develops through a paragraph.

MICRO STRUCTURE: SIGNPOSTS AND BRIDGES

> ## Student 1 [on the different strands of Realist thought]
>
> First, the concept of 'procedural realism' stated that the rose-tinted view of the world that liberals so readily adopted 'must be succeeded by a stage

of hard and ruthless analysis'. 'Scientific realism' continued claiming that 'no political utopia will achieve even the most limited success unless it grows out of political reality' and finally 'ideological realism' argued that 'realism is the necessary corrective to the exuberance of utopianism'.

Despite the fact that these are two of the most dominant theories in the world of IR, we can see that they are also just a fraction of the number of theories that do surround this study.

Unfortunately we have to ignore the total absence of sources in the above. You can see that it is a distilled version of Gregory Crane's analysis of Realism (explored in Chapter 2.2 of this book) which in turn quotes E.H. Carr. As such, the student needed at least one reference to show the origin of his ideas.

Overlooking the bad practice vis-à-vis references, focus on the transition between paragraphs. After the summary of different types of Realism, the text does not just jump to a new point without warning. The student carefully explains where he goes next by alluding to the fact that there are many other theoretical perspectives on IR, providing a bridge for the reader to cross from one paragraph to the next.

In a perfect essay every break between paragraphs would be accompanied by a line either at the end of one paragraph or at the start of the next explaining the journey being taken. This is what Student 3's essay did so effectively.

Student 3

In the same manner as evolutionary biologists, explanatory theorists claim that by using theories as a starting point events can be reconstructed and explained … [*summarizes explanatory theory*].

Conversely post-positivist theories are constitutive in nature. In this perspective theory is viewed to be a construct of the world [*summarizes constitutive theory*] … Claiming that facts are neutral is 'simply a reflection of an adherence to a particular view of epistemology' (Baylis *et al.* 2001: 274).

Note here the improved use of quotes and reference to a key source compared to Student 1. Each paragraph is themed: the first covers explanatory theory, the second covers constitutive theory. These themes are clearly set out for the reader at the beginning of each paragraph, while at the end of the second paragraph there is a useful recap quote summarizing the nub of the matter.

The use of 'Conversely' at the start of the second paragraph is a pithy way of showing that the interpretation explored in paragraph 2 contradicts that set out in paragraph 1. The student is demonstrating that he has located divisions within the literature and is able to set these down clearly for the reader. Equivalent techniques you can use to show differences of opinion between writers include:

- 'By contrast ...'
- 'On one hand ... On the other hand ...'
- 'Some writers argue ... Others suggest ...'. Make sure if you use this approach you provide references. Do not leave the reader guessing who you mean, otherwise it comes across as lacking evidence and rather as a 'straw man' approach to essay writing.

Taking time to wrap up at the end of a section is a great way of helping guide the reader through your essay. You can either use a quote or spend a line explaining the essence of your thinking in that section and relating it to the overall argument you are making.

MACRO STRUCTURE: CONCLUSIONS

Now take a look at the conclusions by Students 2 and 3.

Student 2

In Conclusion then a broad consensus is upon us as regards to International relations being a science in the broadest definition of the meaning but one must be cautious. International relations is a science with it's limitations. It would be wrong to approach politics purely from this angle without also understanding the human emotion behind the politics also. And I believe scientific realism does account for this ambiguity in that it accepts that one application of methods in one science is not necessarily the optimal method for other sciences.

Student 3

In conclusion, the discipline of IR can claim to be 'scientific'. The social world and natural world differ with respect to the nature of the units and system of inquiry, implying that the epistemology and methodology of natural sciences are not necessarily applicable to study social phenomena. In the same manner, what constitutes a 'scientific' inquiry into natural phenomena does not necessarily constitute a 'scientific' inquiry into social phenomena. The term 'scientific' essentially represents valid and justified knowledge rather than certain epistemologies or methodologies and critical to this notion is the nature of the knowledge generated; it must contain objective elements. Essentially, the 'scientific' nature of IR is rooted in the communication of such knowledge. Even as theories operate with different epistemological, ontological and methodological perspectives the knowledge they generate can be viewed as constructive and applicable to the discipline of IR as a whole.

As with the introductions earlier, which conclusion do you think is better? If you were the marker, which conclusion would persuade you that the student knew how to debate effectively the issue of IR as a 'science'?

- **Recap.** Student 3 summarizes the gist of his answer better than Student 2. It is clearly in line with the argument put forward in his introduction (see p. 287) and it explains the rationale as to why that was the answer given. Student 2 talks about scientific realism. However, the student does not reinforce an argument from the introduction where scientific realism is never mentioned and where we were in fact left guessing about the answer to be given in the essay. Student 3 knows where he is going from the outset, whereas Student 2 seems to have achieved his answer as the essay progresses rather than before he started writing the essay. Student 3 thus provides the more logical macro structure as a function of his research design skills.
- **Subject matter expertise.** Note the comparison in the language used in the two conclusions. Student 3's conclusion reads much more like an 'academic' piece of work, using terminology and expressions of which he has demonstrated ample knowledge in the preceding essay. Student 2 raises new issues such as the 'human emotion' behind politics which were absent from the preceding essay. You should play it safe in conclusions by only bringing in concepts/themes/ideas you have thoroughly explored in the essay. Student 3 thus provides the more authoritative conclusion.

Common Pitfall

Only use long or technical words if you are absolutely sure you know what they mean and have defined them for your reader. Trying to blind a marker with multisyllabic words (like 'multisyllabic' in fact) will never convince him or her if you do not demonstrate an in-depth understanding of these long words and the meanings and conceptual disagreements lying behind them.

- **Written English.** The clarity of Student 3's conclusion is better than Student 2's. First, there are no typographical mistakes as in 'International relations' or 'it's limitations'. Second, the quality of expression is greater, helped by sharper sentence construction (note the need for punctuation in the opening sentence of Student 2's conclusion). Finally, Student 3's conclusion is nearer the length expected for an essay of 1,500 words. Student 3's conclusion thus shows greater all round technical proficiency than Student 2's.

REFERENCING AND BIBLIOGRAPHY

Providing enough references and setting them out correctly are basic features of an essay. Your tutor will expect to see you getting this crucial feature right and you will be penalized if you cannot reference correctly (see the next chapter on plagiarism and sloppy academic practice). Of the three essays only Student 3 managed to present his references correctly. Student 1 routinely quoted without providing references, or set the references out incorrectly. Student 2 provided more regular references but set them out incorrectly. On the quality of references we have already noted the comparison between Students 1 (dictionary) and 3 (key text on IR from reading list). Student 2 also used a dictionary definition of 'science'.

There is no simple correlation between the number of sources in a bibliography and the quality of an essay. However, certain inferences are possible from the three essays explored here. The most successful essay (Student 3's) had ten sources listed in the bibliography. All of these were referred to at least once in the essay, and two of the articles cited were not on the module reading list, showing that the student had read around the subject. The submissions by Students 1 and 2 relied on about half that number of sources and this was reflected in the relative lack of critical depth they injected into their answers.

The last chapter discussed the theory behind referencing and bibliographies, so here I will remind you of the very basic points:

- Check how to set your references in your departmental handbook and/or module guide. If in doubt, check with your tutor.
- Reference only the place where you first found a piece of information.
- Every source you cite in an essay must appear in a list of references.
- A bibliography is wider than a list of references in that it can contain all sources you read when preparing an essay, even if you do not refer to them directly in the submission.
- A general rule is that better essays tend to be based on more sources. Through wide reading, the author is able to generate balance and critical depth to an answer.

FINAL REMARKS

All of these essays had different strengths and weaknesses. Student 3 scored a mid-first mark in the 70s; Student 2 scored a mid-2:1 mark in the 60s and Student 1 scored a mid-2:2 mark in the 50s. You can see that to get a top grade Student 3 did the basics very well and was able to demonstrate, even in this relatively constricted word limit, that he was organized, logical, had good knowledge of the subject and could communicate his ideas effectively in plain English. Both the other essays showed promise but they slipped up on basic presentational points as well as showing a weaker grasp of the subject matter. A successful essay in IRT requires technical proficiency and an in-depth knowledge of the field.

3.6 PLAGIARISM AND HOW TO AVOID IT

Plagiarism has been a growing concern for university staff for several years now. The advent of new technologies and the availability of an ever wider range of electronic sources on all academic subjects has increased the opportunity and, unfortunately, the temptation for some students to try to pass off other people's work as their own. It is becoming increasingly common to pass student essays through electronic plagiarism detection software such as Turnitin, which provides detailed reports on the provenance of written submissions as far as electronic material is concerned.

Being poor at referencing or not knowing how to set references out is one thing; trying to claim you wrote something when you did not is an academic crime of an altogether different nature, and you are liable to be accused of being a plagiarist if you take this route. Beyond all this there is a basic ethic at work: it is cheating, and it is a pretty hollow success to get a good mark for a piece of work that has been plagiarised even to a limited degree. Many tutors I know refuse to write job references for students who have charges of plagiarism on their academic records.

SLOPPY ACADEMIC PRACTICE

Spending so much time reading about violence, Original Sin and humans' failings towards each other make scholars of IRT perhaps as well aware as anyone that no one is perfect. It would be a strange world if we were. The whole point of university-level teaching and learning is to develop research skills, subject-matter expertise and transferable skills to take to the job market. Tutors understand that it can take time to grasp the detailed niceties of how to present academic work to the highest degree. Students that they see trying to do the right thing will be cut a lot of slack. Sloppy academic practice (formally known as bad academic practice) is usually quite easy to spot and shows a student not necessarily intending to deceive, but one who has not yet learnt how to acknowledge the sources of his or her knowledge correctly. Take the example of an essay which discusses anarchy in the international system. Student A has taken notes from the section in Kenneth Waltz's *Theory of International Politics* in which he dissects the difference between anarchy and hierarchy.

The relevant section of the student essay reads as follows:

> Anarchy is difficult to define. Those who view the world as a modified anarchy do so, it seems, for two reasons. First, anarchy is taken to mean not just the absence of government but also the presence of order and chaos ... Second, the two simple categories of anarchy and hierarchy do not seem to accommodate the infinite social variety our senses record. Why insist on reducing the types of structure to two instead of allowing for a greater variety? That said, many scholars do seem to work with these two poles as their guiding influence (Waltz 2010: 114).

Reads quite well you might think, and you would be correct. This is because most of those words are from Waltz himself. This is how that section should have looked.

> Anarchy is difficult to define. 'Those who view the world as a modified anarchy do so, it seems, for two reasons. First, anarchy is taken to mean not just the absence of government but also the presence of order and chaos ... Second, the two simple categories of anarchy and hierarchy do not seem to accommodate the infinite social variety our senses record. Why insist on reducing the types of structure to two instead of allowing for a greater variety?' (Waltz 2010: 114). That said, many scholars do seem to work with these two poles as their guiding influence.

In the first extract Waltz's words are masquerading as the student's own; in fact the vast majority of that extract is from Waltz's book, and even though a source has been provided the lack of speech marks is hiding the fact that Waltz wrote those words, not the student. You might agree with a writer and believe that they can express an argument far better than you can, but if you quote directly from them you *must* give them the credit for expressing themselves in the manner they did.

Notice in the second extract I have moved the actual reference to just after the quotation itself rather than the interpretation that might be seen to flow from it, which Waltz might or might not have gone on to draw in his text. This clearly shows the delineation between the original text and my reading of it as a student of IR.

The reason I think most tutors would consider this sloppy practice (perhaps it might be classed minor as opposed to major plagiarism in some universities) rather than plagiarism (at least on a first offence) is that the source of the quotation has not been hidden from view. The student is telling the reader that he/she has read Waltz, but, we trust, simply failed to convey that this was a direct quotation from the original.

Barring evidence to the contrary we would hope this was a problem with note-taking rather than intent to deceive. When you take notes from any source be sure to make clear what is a direct quote and what is a summary or your own opinion, so that when you reference you do not end up falling into the trap Student A did here.

PLAGIARISM

On the last two occasions when I had to interview students charged with plagiarism they blamed time pressures for their crime. They were poorly organized, had not done enough reading and just threw the essay together at the last minute before hand-in. They had gone to an e-book and Wikipedia and cut and pasted whole chunks from a biography of Hans Morgenthau and an article by Stephen Walt, which ended up being detected by the Turnitin software. They were found guilty of plagiarism and punished accordingly.

> While they all agree on the principle, each university has a slightly different plagiarism policy and means of dealing with academic misconduct. Make sure you are clear on what constitutes plagiarism at your university before you submit assessed work. If in doubt ask someone!

Take another scenario. Student B has been caught short of time on an IRT essay. She has left her essay until the last minute and is panicking that she does not know anything much about anarchy in the international system and its impact on international relations in the Cold War. However, she recalls that Kenneth Waltz does know something about IRT and the following segment of text appears in her essay:

Those who view the world as a modified anarchy do so, it seems, for two reasons. First, anarchy is taken to mean not just the absence of government but also the presence of order and chaos ... Second, the two simple categories of anarchy and hierarchy do not seem to accommodate the infinite social variety our senses record. Why insist on reducing the types of structure to two instead of allowing for a greater variety? Anarchy often leads to a balance of power. As a theory, balance of power predicts that rapid changes in international power and status – especially attempts by one state to conquer a region – will provoke counterbalancing actions. For this reason, the balancing process helps to maintain the stability of relations between states. A balance of power system functions most effectively when alliances are fluid, when they are easily formed or broken on the basis of expediency, regardless of values, religion, history, or form of government.

Quite appropriately the student is moving around anarchy and the balance of power proposition that Waltz advances in his *Theory*. Unfortunately there are no speech marks or references to indicate that almost all of the words above are someone else's. The student has effectively claimed a deep knowledge of anarchy and the balance of power, when in truth the appreciation is entirely someone else's.

The paragraph should have read:

'Those who view the world as a modified anarchy do so, it seems, for two reasons. First, anarchy is taken to mean not just the absence of government but also the presence of order and chaos … Second, the two simple categories of anarchy and hierarchy do not seem to accommodate the infinite social variety our senses record. Why insist on reducing the types of structure to two instead of allowing for a greater variety' (Waltz 2010: 114). Anarchy often leads to a balance of power. 'As a theory, balance of power predicts that rapid changes in international power and status – especially attempts by one state to conquer a region – will provoke counterbalancing actions. For this reason, the balancing process helps to maintain the stability of relations between states. A balance of power system functions most effectively when alliances are fluid, when they are easily formed or broken on the basis of expediency, regardless of values, religion, history, or form of government' (The IR Theory Knowledge Base 2012).

The student has contributed precisely eight words to the paragraph, linking the two quotations with '*Anarchy often leads to a balance of power*'. There is no acknowledgement that the first quotation is in fact a quotation, or that Waltz was the author. The second quotation is from a website of basic IRT definitions, but again there is no indication either that these are someone else's exact words or that the student has used the website as a source of information.

Clearly the essay would need to be looked at in the round, and if Waltz and the IR Knowledge Base did not at least appear in the bibliography the student would be on very sticky ground. Even if they did feature, and especially if the essay was replete with the same practice as here, this student could easily be accused of either bad academic practice and/or plagiarism – trying to present other people's ideas as her own.

TIPS FOR AVOIDING PLAGIARISM

Avoiding plagiarism and/or sloppy academic practice is as easy as shelling peas. Simply know how your department wants you to present your assessed work, stick to those accepted guidelines for presenting academic work and you will not go far wrong. Unintentional plagiarism is still plagiarism.

Here is a list of just some of the most obvious ways you can take steps to avoid falling into this awful trap:

- Leave yourself plenty of time to write the essay and proof read it before submission. This has the advantages of: not putting you under the kinds of pressure where you might be tempted to cut and paste texts as your own; and it gives you time to proof read your finished product to check you have referenced everything you need to, and presented the references correctly.
- Keep your notes organized and written up in such a way that it is very clear when your notes are direct quotes, summaries of an author's interpretation of IRT, or just your own musings on a book or article. Both of the first two would need referencing. Be certain to reference specific page numbers if quoting from a book or journal article. In the above example (Waltz 2010) is too vague for a reference. A specific quote or summary of a particular passage demands (Waltz 2010: 114).
- Do not include too many or too long quotations. An essay should be an expression of *your* intervention in a given set of debates. By all means use authors in walk-on roles to scaffold your argument and to show where you looked for evidence and definitions, but the majority of an academic essay has to be in your own words. At the very least, 85/15 in favour of your own words is probably where you need to be. Large parts of the '85' will of course be you summarizing others' ideas – in which case you will still need to reference them, even in the absence of direct quotations.
- You can under-reference an essay but, in truth, I have never worried if students over-reference. If you are unsure about whether to include a reference to a 'fact', for example, then include it and let your tutor tell you it is unnecessary – they will not mark you down for it. If you under-reference an essay you run the risk of being accused (rightly or wrongly) of plagiarism or at the very minimum, bad academic practice.

SUMMARY

Quite simply, don't be tempted to the dark side; take pride in your work. It is unethical, intellectual theft and unbecoming of upstanding citizens such as students are supposed to be – the next generation of global leaders no less.

Or, put yourself in the place of an academic who has spent decades developing and refining an approach to IRT. They struggle to gain a book contract and when they do, all their hard work and the hours they spent drafting and re-drafting their work fifteen times gets passed off as someone else's work in the blink of an eye. Hobbes' dictum that life is nasty, brutish and short may be true, but it is surely not too short to develop a working knowledge of a topic and to convey it in your own words.

3.7 EXAM REVISION

Your IRT assessment schedule will likely feature a coursework element (essay and/or presentation) and an exam element. Exam periods at university are stressful times and your performance can be badly hampered if you suffer from serious exam nerves. A bit of adrenalin and anticipation will help your performance under pressure, but full-blown panic will do you no good whatsoever. The way to avoid hitting the panic button is to approach your work on the module as a whole in as organized, logical and structured fashion as you can. That way you are not starting to build up your subject knowledge and essay skills from scratch at the last minute, but simply applying them in new ways. In preparing for exams you should continue to practise the good working habits you have developed over the unit as a whole.

START FROM DAY ONE

Revision for exams is not something that starts after a module ends, as if exams are somehow separate from the rest of the work you do on the course. As the final assessed element of the module, the capstone exercise if you like, exams should feature in your thinking throughout the module. Everything you do on the course should help gear you up to prepare for and sit the exam paper in IRT. As Nicholas Walliman (2006: 169) explains, 'You should be like the squirrel that stores up nuts for the winter. Do not waste any lecture, tutorial, seminar, group discussion, etc. by letting the material evaporate into thin air'. When you are reading over your notes at the end of each lecture and seminar make a list specifically for revision. On the list you could include:

- a list of key writers in a theoretical tradition
- a list of the critics of each theory or theorist
- a brief summary of the big debates that surround each theory covered
- the main concepts/definitions that kept cropping up.

Early preparation will save you masses of time later on, allowing you to concentrate on the really important things like practising exam answers and following up gaps in your knowledge in the library.

ORGANIZE YOUR NOTES

Put every note you take from reading, lectures and seminars in a folder or ring binder, clearly separated by course topic or week. This will help you capture the sense of everything you learned and enable you to locate notes quickly and easily. If you are feeling really organized you could put together, electronically or by hand, a glossary of IRT key terms which you update each week with new entries.

PAST PAPERS

These will normally be made available in the module guide or in the online resources for your course. They will give you an idea of the kinds of themes that crop up most often, and the ways in which questions tend to be framed. Keep copies of these in with your notes and pay particular care to the recent papers and those set by the tutor that convenes your course.

Common Pitfall

Do not learn model answers to questions from past papers and regurgitate them wholesale in the exam. Every year the 'twist' to a question on a given theory varies slightly and you will not receive good marks for answering the question from last year's paper!

IDENTIFY GAPS IN YOUR KNOWLEDGE

If you prepare thoroughly for each lecture and seminar you should have a suitably and critically informed knowledge base from which to work at the start of the revision period. When re-reading your notes for the first time, note any areas where you consider your knowledge to be a bit sketchy. You might have gaps in your knowledge base if:

- You do not know the main claims of a given theory of IR.
- You cannot define a key term.
- You have not read an essential text.
- You do not understand a concept that featured in the reading or lecture.

Make time in your revision timetable to research these areas. It is tempting to ignore them and concentrate on revising the topics with which you are most comfortable. However, but you will reap the rewards if you work on your weaknesses and aim to turn them into strengths, because this will give you more flexibility when it comes to choosing which questions to tackle in the exam.

GROUP STUDY

Pooling ideas can be a great way of helping you consolidate and advance your knowledge. Get together with a small group of friends to go over key theories and discuss questions circulated in advance. For example, you could all practice writing an answer to the same exam question and then when you meet explore the relative merits of your approaches. The aim of group revision is not to generate 'model' answers or the same approach to a theory, but to help you think through the basics of each issue and how best to communicate responses to exam questions on a given topic or theory.

PRACTICE EXAM QUESTIONS

Group study can be an effective aid to individual study, but remember that, in the final analysis, it is you who has to sit the exam and write the answer on your own. One of the best ways to prepare for the discomfort of sitting alone with an exam paper in front of you and a blank sheet of paper to fill, is to get used to being in that situation beforehand. You could therefore try the following:

- Empty your room of friends, all turn off your television, radio, mobile, Facebook, Twitter account and electronic gaming devices.
- Get a past exam paper or practice essay question from an IR textbook.

- Give yourself 15 minutes to plan your answer: identify your central argument and essay structure.
- Write a 200-word introduction to the answer.
- Write a two-line summary of each of the main points you would cover in the essay.

It is impossible to replicate exam conditions out of an exam hall but by answering practice questions on your own in a quiet room you will get a feel for the pressure of sitting the exam.

VARY YOUR REVISION SCHEDULE

Although you need to be organized and methodical in your approach, revision can become tedious and unrewarding if you do the same things every day. Strike a balance between routine and monotony by varying your strategies (for example, alternating between group revision and self-directed study), and consider the following:

- You do not need to revise 24 hours per day. Try and keep to your usual waking, eating and going to bed patterns.
- Take regular exercise between revision sessions.
- Do not become a hermit! Make time for periods of relaxation and going out with friends.
- Learn which times of day you feel most active and when you work most effectively, and tailor your revision programme to coincide with those peaks.
- Find out when the exam is and, if possible, write your practice exam answers in that same period to get yourself in the habit of thinking and writing during that part of the day.

Remember, it is not only the naturally intelligent or gifted people who succeed at exams. Grafting hard through a module and paying close attention to what the examiner looks for in a good exam answer is the key, whatever you think your 'natural' level of ability is. Delivering logical, well evidenced, well communicated and critically incisive answers to the question set is the crux.

3.8 EXAM TIPS

I am not an expert on the psychological effects of stress, but from my experience of sitting exams and now working in a relatively stressful job I have learnt that the best way to deal with stress is to think about two things: (1) its causes and (2) ways to combat it. From the students I have spoken to, exam nerves are generally brought on by a combination of lack of preparation and lack of confidence in their ability to write under pressure.

Everything I have said so far in this book has been geared to making the exam period as stress-free as possible by seeing exams as another opportunity to put into practice the good working and writing habits you have developed through the module. Integrating the exam into your overall approach to learning about IRT will help you leap the psychological barrier exams can sometimes become. In this chapter we will consider a few of the tips you can use to get the very best exam mark you can.

THE BASICS

Find out as early as you can where you will be sitting the exam, at what time, and what materials you can take into it with you (if any). Invest in a good alarm clock or ask friends to come and knock on your door if you are frightened of sleeping in for an early morning exam. Amazingly, some students fail to show up for exams, or arrive half an hour into it: this is a recipe for disaster. Make sure you have a good supply of pens that work and all the other stationery you will need. Arrive at the exam in plenty of time so that you can calm yourself down before entering the hall; the last thing you need is to be rushing in late all hot and bothered.

PLANNING YOUR TIME

Find out before the exam how many questions you will have to answer. Typical exams are something in the region of two questions in two hours or three questions in three hours. In both scenarios you have one hour per answer. A good essay plan can take anything up to 10 minutes to put together. Do not mistakenly believe you are falling behind your peers if you do not start writing straight away.

> Have confidence in your ability to structure the exam to suit you. Know how much time you want to allocate to each part of the paper and stick to it.

If your exam is not all about writing essays, make sure you have worked out in advance how long you want to allocate for each part of the paper. For instance, there might be a multi-choice element, or a short summary element where you define key terms. However the paper is structured, make sure you leave enough time for each segment and that you have time at the end of each paper to read and correct each answer. When the exam begins try and get into your own little bubble ('in the zone' as the pro sports saying goes) to block out what is going on around you. Concentrate on the tasks ahead of you and manage your time accordingly. Aim for an occasional but not obsessive eye on the clock.

WRITING YOUR ANSWERS

Spend a few minutes at the start of the exam deciding which questions you want to tackle. Pay attention at this point to the phrasing of the questions. There might be topics you are very familiar with but where the question is phrased in a complex or difficult way. Think carefully about what kinds of structure you could use for each question on offer, and which of those structures helps you communicate your argument clearly and concisely given the stock of knowledge you possess about the relevant theory(ies).

Know before you go in whether you want to plan all the answers at the start of the exam and then write them, or whether you want to plan and write the answers one at a time. A practical advantage of the latter approach is that you give your writing hand a break while you plan the next answer. Whichever method you deploy keep an eye on the clock so that you do not spend too much time on one answer at the expense of the others.

It is always tempting in an exam to spend disproportionate amounts of time on the question(s) you feel you know really well. However, a very long, overly detailed answer to one question will never compensate for short, thin answers elsewhere. Balance is vital.

The essence of a good exam answer is that it is structured well, flows nicely from start to finish and is supported by a good range of authoritative evidence. Your tutor will want to see that you have thought critically about the themes and issues raised by the question and that you can devise logical, well-reasoned responses to the questions you tackle. As in a coursework essay you are encouraged to use quotes from the books you have read. Make sure you refer to key authors on whose work you have drawn to frame your arguments. If you can go beyond the basic course texts and into advanced and wider reading you will stand out from the vast majority of students who will churn out standard names, sources and interpretations.

Common Pitfall

The classic mistake in exams is to write everything you know (or can remember) about a given subject. The 'scatter-gun' answer, as it is known, is a giveaway that a student has not prepared well for the exam. Sound revision and a robust essay structure will help limit the time you spend wandering off the subject.

Try not to repeat too much information from one answer in another because this indicates a thin knowledge base. Consider a two-questions-in-two-hours exam: if you can show the examiner that you know, in detail, three or four theories of IR across your two questions, this looks better than if you can only demonstrate knowledge of two theories which you rehash in both answers.

In sum, the best exam marks go to students who do the following:

- Show sound knowledge of the subject matter.
- Answer the questions set rather than the question they want to see.
- Structure their answers around a few key points.

- Signpost their writing (see Chapters 3.4 and 3.5).
- Use appropriate evidence to back their arguments. This can be presented in the form of short quotes or summaries of writers' arguments.
- It is an IRT exam so make sure you can reference theories of International Relations! Waffling on about the Iraq War, 9/11, the Eurozone crisis or the Libya intervention will only be relevant in the context of a theoretically informed approach.

REFERENCES TO MORE INFORMATION

Cottrell, S. (2006) *The Exam Skills Handbook*. Basingstoke: Palgrave Macmillan.

McMillan, K. and Weyers, J. (2007) *How to Succeed in Exams and Assessments*. Harlow: Pearson Prentice Hall.

Levin, P. (2004) *Sail Through Exams! Preparing for Traditional Exams for Undergraduates and Taught Postgraduates*. Maidenhead: Open University Press.

Tracy, E. (2002) *The Student's Guide to Exam Success*. Buckingham: Open University Press.
   The focus here is on the emotional and psychological aspects of preparing for and sitting exams.

Holmes, A. (2005) *Pass Your Exams: Study Skills for Success*. Oxford: The Infinite Ideas Company.
   A 'tips' book with useful advice on building up your confidence and playing the exam game and passing.

PART IV
ADDITIONAL
RESOURCES

GLOSSARY

Actor   In this context does not mean Will Smith or Angelina Jolie. In IR it means the unit of analysis or agent (for example, the state or a supranational organization) whose behaviour theorists try to explain. Different theories tend to emphasize the significance of different actors in international affairs.

Aesthetics   The branch of philosophy dealing with the nature/appreciation of beauty and the beautiful. If you like the look of a piece of art, you could say it is aesthetically pleasing. There is a view that individuals are drawn to certain interpretations and theories about IR on aesthetic grounds as much as anything else.

Agency   There is a big debate within Politics and IR about the extent to which we explain people's/states' behaviour with reference to their own actions and ideas. Some people believe in the priority of agency over structures others make reference to the impact of the structures that shape the lives and worlds of those people and states (agents).

Anarchy   When applied to IR, means lack of an orderer in the international system. This 'orderer' could be something like a world government but does not have to be as formal or powerful as that name implies.

Anthropocentrism   The idea that humans are the only creators of meaning in the universe and the only life form worth considering when we take decisions and make policies.

Authorship   I am the author of this book. I brought it into existence conceptually and wrote it myself. But I also conceptualized it with the help of my editors at Sage and the colleagues who commented on earlier drafts, as well as indirect 'conversations' with the theories I have covered over my years teaching IRT. Authorship is a complex social process. Authorship in IR is all about who brings what into existence and relates to wider questions of decision-making power and influence in the international system.

Social constructivists, for example, argue that states 'author' anarchy; anarchy does not 'author' states.

Balance of power   Centrepiece of Neorealist theory developed by Kenneth Waltz to explain how the structure of the international system explains the interactions of the units within it.

Bretton Woods System   Named after the place in the US where the leading industrial powers met in 1944 to hammer out the rules for the management of their commercial and financial relations. Collapsed in 1971.

Colonialism   Has both formal and informal aspects. Formally it means the practice of one country controlling another by military, economic and/or political means, usually with the use of, or threat of, violence and local territorial infrastructures. Informally it can mean the exploitation or oppression of less developed and weaker countries by more developed and stronger ones through global structures such as international institutions. A key component of Marxist and postcolonial theories of IR.

Commensurability   Popularized by Thomas Kuhn. Two theories are commensurable if they can be compared to determine which is better. In order to achieve this, it must be proved that the two theories 'see' the same world and use the same language to describe/explain that world. If they do not, then they are incommensurable – it is impossible to compare which is better.

Cosmopolitanism   A political theory that denies the relevance of the state in determining individual morality and justice. Usually contrasted with communitarianism which charges states with a central place in shaping individual attitudes on these issues.

Deconstruction   Associated with the thought of Jacques Derrida, deconstruction is a vital tool for postmodernist IR scholars who use it to probe, unsettle, unhinge and pull apart supposedly settled core IR concepts such as the 'state' and 'sovereignty'. One of the most popular ways they achieve this is through the double reading of texts.

Defensive realism   A Realist approach focusing on states seeking security in a balance of power. Kenneth Waltz's Neorealism is a good example. Critiqued by the offensive realists (see below).

Determinism The philosophical proposition that human beliefs, actions and decision are causally determined by prior events and circumstances. In IRT the debate plays out between those who believe the structure of the international system decisively shapes state behaviour (the determinist position) and those who believe states themselves have the capacity to 'author' the international system (Constructivists and postmodernists for example).

Diplomacy The official conduct of relations between two or more states, or two or more groups of states. Usually carried out by government ministers and civil servants, or diplomats, it entails negotiation, communication and the drawing up of treaties, agreements, and the like. Can also include unofficial dimensions such as cultural exchanges. Political disagreements between countries can mean diplomatic ties being cut as a sign of disapproval by one state at the actions of another.

Discourse Means much more than a conversation between two people. Associated with the work of Michel Foucault, it refers to the way in which language is used to structure our accounts of, and give meaning to, the social world. The study of discourse is usually undertaken for critical purposes, the identity of 'speaker' and 'spoken about' and to pull back the veil on hidden power relations in a society or set of human relationships.

Empiricism A theory of knowledge that suggests knowledge should be generated through direct observation and other sensory experience.

Epistemology Theory about how we know things and what is regarded as hard and fast knowledge in a given discipline; or the origins and legitimacy of knowledge.

Essentially contested If we say an object, event or process is essentially contested it implies that while it has been observed to exist there is no agreement on its meaning, implications or potential uses. For example, we might all assert that the 'Arab Spring' has changed the conduct of national politics in countries such as Egypt, but the wider meaning of the Arab Spring is itself much harder to pin down – its origins, impact and likely future outcomes. The 'Arab Spring' is an essentially contested concept.

Etymology The study of the origin, development and derivation of words.

Falsification   The process of proving a theory to be flawed, for example, because a prediction generated through its application turns out to be wrong.

Functionalist integration theory   Developed by David Mitrany. Explains how economic and social integration increases levels of interdependence between states and can therefore lead to peace and security for the states involved.

Genealogy   Associated with Michel Foucault, an investigation into the historical practices which create subjects through discursive closures, exclusions and marginalizations. Not a history in the conventional sense of understanding how things come to be. In IR we undertake genealogies to probe how the discipline makes sense of the world: what has IR had to forget or overlook to make knowledge about international affairs seem like the 'truth'?

Gender   The social meanings given to the concepts 'male' and 'female' and the supposed characteristics that flow from them in terms of those that are held to be 'masculine' and those we associate with 'femininity'.

General Agreement on Tariffs and Trade (GATT)   Set up at the Bretton Woods conference in 1944 to promote the reduction of barriers to international trade such as tariffs and quotas.

Generic skills   See *transferable skills*

Globalization   Extremely difficult to define in a few words! Widely taken to imply the widening, deepening and/or intensification of economic, political, technological, cultural, social and environmental interactions across state borders. Products of globalization include rolling 24–7 news media and social media such as Twitter which have sped the pace of cross-border communication.

Hegemony   Concept used in IR to chart the relative position of states in the international system, measured by their power (loosely defined). For example, the USA is said to have been a hegemonic power since the end of the Cold War, especially but not exclusively in military terms. In Critical Theory the definition broadens so that it is less about dominance by force than subtle forms of consent and consensus-building. In this interpretation hegemony becomes the dynamics of order that comes from states getting into positions whereby their ideas/practices are accepted by other states without the threat or use of force. Includes the use of international organizations to spread norms and thereby shape the system in subtle ways, for instance the International Monetary Fund (IMF).

Hypothesis   A prediction about the state of the world and/or relationships between variables within that world. For example, we might want to test the hypothesis that students who attend more lectures and seminars/tutorials achieve higher marks in essays and exams than those who attend fewer lectures and seminars/tutorials. We would test this hypothesis by studying attendance registers and correlating them with the marks achieved for each student. If marks generally rise as attendance rises we have proved the hypothesis.

Ideational   That feature of the study of IR dealing with ideas that transcend state borders and which can come to be shared either as tight value sets or influences on state behaviour. Linked to later Liberal, Neoliberal, English School and Constructivist thought on international institutions and the spread of norms in international systems/societies.

Interdependence   The idea that the political, economic and social connections among states or groups of states have reached a point where the actions of one or other of those states directly affect the other states, intentionally or not. Linked to the concept of globalization and usually contrasted with independence.

International organization   A body created by states to which they delegate authority to carry out action at the international level. The United Nations is the most comprehensive global international organization operating today.

International regime   A term associated with Neoliberal IRT. Encompasses the argument that international cooperation is about more than the formalized, rule-bound cooperation we see in the establishment of international organizations. Institutions and international organizations also promote informal modes of inter-state cooperation via regimes.

International system   All the states that exist in the world today constitute the international system. IR scholars disagree about the nature of this system. Some (e.g. Realists) see the system as inherently conflict ridden, others (e.g. Liberals and English School theorists) argue that even without a world government, state behaviour tends to be structured and regulated, thus avoiding the worst excesses of perpetual war and violence.

Metatheory   Theory about theory; theory about the rules and standards by which theories count as theories, how they make sense of their subject matter, and how we measure theoretical contributions to a given field. Metatheory focuses on the philosophical assumptions underlying theories, so is explicitly concerned with questions of ontology, epistemology and methodology.

Methodology   In the social sciences, the procedures by which we generate knowledge. For example, research using quantitative methods interprets statistical data whereas qualitative research interprets meanings, beliefs and attitudes of subjects. In the natural sciences, rules and guidelines on how to set up experiments and interpret the data.

Multinational corporation   A company or business that has headquarters, offices and/or means of production such as factories located in different countries around the world, such as Barclays Bank, McDonald's and Coca-Cola. Used interchangeably with 'transnational corporation' and sometimes shortened to 'multinational' or MNC.

Nation-state   Used interchangeably with 'state' in much IR literature. Has a specific meaning whereby members of a territorially bounded population share more in common than merely their land borders. This includes ethical codes of conduct and values which come from them sharing a common language, tradition and sense of history: who they are and where they are going, collectively speaking.

Naturalism   The view that the social world and the natural worlds can be studied using the same methods. It was arguably the dominant theoretical approach within IR until the 1980s (especially as practised in the US) when normative theory became more prominent within the discipline.

Norm(s)   Norms are socially shared sets of understandings and expectations about how it is appropriate to behave for agents with given identities. Norms are not always written down but they can be formalized in laws, for example governing the relations between states on the global stage. They feature prominently in theories of IR such as Liberalism, Neoliberalism and Constructivism.

Normative theory   Presents a challenge to positivist ways of viewing the world and studying it. Critiques the view that social scientists can produce objective knowledge by emulating the methods used by natural scientists – a detached observer and a world to be observed. Normative theorists try to understand the role played by values, morality and ethics in international relations.

Offensive realism   The 'human nature' image of international relations in which the innate lust for power combines with the security dilemma in anarchy to give rise to constant instability in the system. This is the insurmountable 'tragedy' of international politics for writers such as Mearsheimer.

Ontology   Theory connected with the things, properties and events that exist in the world; what exists to be investigated.

Paradigm   Popularized by Thomas Kuhn's 1962 book *The Structure of Scientific Revolutions*. Scientists who work in a particular research paradigm 'are committed to the same rules and standards for scientific practice' and work to continue that particular research tradition (Kuhn 1996: 11). IR theories can be likened to Kuhnian paradigms in that they set down precise research agendas and validate work against certain benchmarks and practices.

Patriarchy   A system of rule or governance by men. Such systems can be openly patriarchal where men have greater legal, political, religious and social freedoms than women. Or they can be covert, in that women are discriminated against institutionally, in the workplace (in terms of pay and conditions), and so on. Feminist scholars have deepened our understanding of the overt and covert sources of patriarchy in IR both within states and in the international system at large.

Pax Americana   Describes the period of relative international peace (or absence of world war) since 1945. Replaced the *pax Britannica* evident in the mid-nineteenth century centred on the 'order' provided by the British Empire.

Pluralism   A position within English School theory concerning the appropriateness of contravening state sovereignty to achieve ethical ends, for example the humanitarian intervention in Libya in 2011. The debate revolves around normative positions taken on such values as order and justice in IR and pluralists believe order trumps justice except in acute emergencies. See *solidarism* for the countervailing view.

Positivism   Both a philosophy about scientific research and an episte-mological approach to the study of IR. Positivists try and apply the methods and practices of the natural sciences to the social sciences. They assume we can produce objective knowledge about the world through the careful application of the scientific method of observation, reporting and testing the properties of a world external to us.

Post-positivism   Refers to the approach taken by a range of writers who critique but do not necessarily seek to overthrow positivist ways of generating knowledge. Some of them we explore in this book, such as Critical Theorists, feminists and poststructuralists. In some literature is called 'reflectivism'.

Reductionism   Using the behaviour of a component part to explain the behaviour of the environment or system within which it operates. For example, Realist IR theorists explain the behaviour of states by treating them like humans in a state of nature, implying that in a given situation states act as humans would do. This is a contested approach to explai-ning IR because it privileges interests, takes them as given, and ignores the identity-driven sources of foreign policy action.

Reflectivism   A catch-all term used to describe the very loose commu-nities of scholars who reject or critique positivist approaches to the study of International Relations. In this book the terms reflectivist could be used to describe 'thicker' Constructivists, Feminists, Critical Theorists, Green Theorists, Postcolonialists and Post-structuralists.

Reification   The process of attributing to some phenomenon (for example, 'anarchy') human, living or 'real-life' properties which it can-not or does not possess. In IR, Social Constructivists say that Realist scholars 'reify' anarchy; in other words, Realists take this abstract, liter-ally nonexistent thing to be something real and tangible, when it does not exist out there at all, only 'in our heads'.

Security dilemma   Classic Realist concept whereby a state seeking to maximize its security makes other states in the international system feel less secure. Constant fear of the 'other' is what, for Realists, produces and reproduces patterns of global conflict over long periods of time.

Solidarism   A position within English School theory concerning the appropriateness of contravening state sovereignty to achieve ethical ends, for example the humanitarian intervention in Libya in 2011. The debate revolves around normative positions taken on such values as order and justice in IR. Solidarists believe the needs of basic justice for humanity override the necessity to maintain a sovereign state order. See *pluralism* for the countervailing view.

Sovereignty A state is said to possess internal sovereignty when it exercises ultimate legal and political authority over a named territory. It possesses external sovereignty when other states respect its jurisdiction in these matters. Proponents of humanitarian intervention suggest that state sovereignty can and should be violated in cases of urgent need, such as crimes against humanity or genocide.

State Used to refer to two things: a bounded, populated territory and/or the body that governs that particular territory. Said to have emerged with the Treaty of Westphalia in 1648, the modern state is sovereign when it and it alone has the right to pass laws to regulate its own affairs and population. The state was held to be the main actor in international relations by many early theorists such as those writing in the Realist and Liberal traditions. Newer approaches in IRT think about the implications of global politics conducted 'beyond' (above, below and alongside) the state.

Subnational actor One that operates at a level below that of the state of which it is a part. Local councils in England are subnational actors.

Supranational actor A body set up by states to advance their common political, security and economic interests by making and executing legislation that affects the signatories. The European Union is an example of a supranational organization.

Theory Systematically describes aspects of the world, categorizes these aspects and considers their interrelationships with the intention of making sense of complexity and developing law-like generalizations.

Transferable skills Also go by the name of generic skills or employability skills. Generally encompasses the following: reading, writing and arithmetic; listening, speaking, thinking; time and project management; information skills; design and presentation; problem identification, definition and solving; and personal knowledge. It is useful to keep a log of these skills that you acquire during your degree programme to enhance your CV and employability prospects.

REFERENCES

Aalberts, T.E. (2010) 'Playing the Game of Sovereign States: Charles Manning's Constructivism *Avant-la-lettre*', *European Journal of International Relations*, 16(2), 247–68.

Abbot, K.W. and Snidal, D. (1998) 'Why States Act Through Formal International Organizations', *The Journal of Conflict Resolution*, 42(1), 3–32.

Abrahamsen, R. (2007) 'Postcolonialism', in M. Griffiths (ed.) *International Relations Theory for the Twenty-First Century*. London: Routledge, pp. 111–22.

Adler, E. (1997) 'Seizing the Middle Ground: Constructivism in World Politics', *European Journal of International Relations*, 3(3): 319–63.

Alker, H. and Biersteker, T. (1995) 'The dialectics of world order: notes for a future archaeologist of international *Savoir Faire*', in J. Der Derian (ed.) *International Theory: Critical Investigations*. Basingstoke: Macmillan, pp. 242–76.

Anievas, A. (2010) 'On Habermas, Marx and the critical theory tradition: theoretical mastery or drift?, in C. Moore and C. Farrands (eds) *International Relations and Philosophy: Interpretive Dialogues*. London: Routledge, pp. 144–56.

Aradau, C. (2010) 'Derrida: Aporias of Otherness', in C. Moore and C. Farrands (eds) *International Relations and Philosophy: Interpretive Dialogues*. London: Routledge, pp. 107–18.

Ashcroft, B., Griffiths, G. and Tiffin, H. (1994) *The Empire Writes Back: Theory and Practice in Post-Colonial Literatures*. London: Routledge.

Ashley, R.K. (1986) 'The Poverty of Neorealism', in R.O. Keohane (ed.) *Neorealism and its Critics*. New York: Columbia University Press, pp. 1–26.

Ashley, R. (1995) 'The Powers of Anarchy: Theory, Sovereignty, and the Domestication of Global Life', in J. Der Derian (ed.) *International Theory: Critical Investigations*. Basingstoke: Macmillan, pp. 94–128.

Axford, B., Browning, G.K., Huggins, R. and Rosamond, B. (2006) *Politics: An Introduction*, 2nd edn. London: Routledge.

Babst, D.V. (1964) 'Elective Governments – A Force for Peace', *Wisconsin Sociologist*, 3: 9–14.

Bailey, J.L. (2008) 'Arrested Development: The Fight to End Commercial Whaling as a Case of Failed Norm Change', *European Journal of International Relations*, 14(2): 289–318.

Bain, W. (2000) 'Deconfusing Morgenthau: Moral Inquiry and Classical Realism Reconsidered', *Review of International Studies*, 26(3): 445–64.

Barnett, M. (2008) 'Social Constructivism', in J. Baylis, S. Smith and P. Owens (eds) *The Globalization of World Politics: An Introduction to International Relations*, 4th edn. Oxford: Oxford University Press, pp. 160–73.

Baylis, J., Smith, S. and Owens, P. (2008a) 'Introduction', in J. Baylis, S. Smith and P. Owens (eds) *The Globalization of World Politics: An Introduction to International Relations*, 4th edn. Oxford: Oxford University Press.

Baylis, J., Smith, S. and Owens, P. (eds) (2008b) *The Globalization of World Politics: An Introduction to International Relations*, 4th edn. Oxford: Oxford University Press.

Bellamy, A.J. (ed.) (2005) *International Society and its Critics*. Oxford: Oxford University Press.

Blair, T. (1999) 'Doctrine of the International Community', Speech, Chicago, 24 April, http://www.britishpoliticalspeech.org/speech-archive.htm?speech=279 (accessed 20 July 2012).

Blair, T. (2001) Leader's speech, Brighton, 2 October, http://www.britishpoliticalspeech.org/speech-archive.htm?speech=186 (accessed 20 July 20).

Blair, T. (2006) Speech to Foreign Policy Centre, 21 March, http://www.guardian.co.uk/politics/2006/mar/21/iraq.iraq1 (accessed 23 July 2012).

Bookchin, M. (1971) *Post-Scarcity Anarchism*. Berkeley, CA: Ramparts Press.

Booth, K. and Smith, S. (eds) (1995) *International Relations Theory Today*. Cambridge: Polity Press.

Booth, K. and Wheeler, N.J. (2008) *The Security Dilemma: Fear, Cooperation and Trust in World Politics*. Basingstoke: Palgrave Macmillan.

Bowen, J.D. (2011) 'Theory in Action: Liberalism', 11 May, http://www.youtube.com/watch?v=tZbDMUaqwE8 (accessed 10 July 2012).

Brown, C. (2001) *Understanding International Relations*, 2nd edn. Basingstoke: Palgrave.

Bull, H. (2002) *The Anarchical Society: A Study of Order in World Politics*, 3rd edn Basingstoke: Palgrave.

Burchill, S. (2009) 'Liberalism', in S. Burchill et al. *Theories of International Relations*, 4th edn. Basingstoke: Palgrave, pp. 57–85.

Burchill, S. and Linklater, A. (2009) 'Introduction', in S. Burchill et al. *Theories of International Relations*, 4th edn. Basingstoke: Palgrave, pp. 1–30.

Buzan, B. (no date) 'English School of International Relations', University of Leeds, www.leeds.ac.uk/polis/englishschool/

Buzan, B. (2004) *From International to World Society? English School Theory and the Social Structure of Globalisation*. Cambridge: Cambridge University Press.

Cabrera, M.A. (2005) *Postsocial History: An Introduction*, trans. M. McMahon. Lanham, MD: Lexington Books.

Cafruny, A.A. (2006) 'Historical Materialism: Imperialist Rivalry and the Global Capitalist Order', in J. Sterling-Folker (ed.) *Making Sense of*

International Relations Theory. Boulder, CO: Lynne Rienner Publishers, pp. 209–24.

Cameron, D. (2006) 'A New Approach to Foreign Affairs – Liberal Conservatism', Speech to the British American Project, 11 September, http://www.conservatives.com/News/Speeches/2006/09/Cameron_A_new_approach_to_foreign_affairs__liberal_conservatism.aspx (accessed 8 December 2011).

Campbell, D. (1998) *Writing Security: United States Foreign Policy and the Politics of Identity*. Manchester: Manchester University Press.

Campbell, D. (2007) 'Poststructuralism', in T. Dunne, M. Kurki and S. Smith (eds) *International Relations Theory: Discipline and Diversity*. Oxford: Oxford University Press, pp. 203–28.

Carlsnaes, W., Risse, T. and Simmons, B.A. (eds) (2006) *Handbook of International Relations*. London: Sage.

Carr, E.H. (2001a) *The Twenty Years' Crisis 1919–1939*. Basingstoke: Palgrave.

Carr, E.H. (2001b) *What is History?* Basingstoke: Palgrave.

Carter, N. and Huby, M. (2005) 'Ecological Citizenship and Ethical Investment', *Environmental Politics*, 14(2): 255–72.

Cheng, A. and Lu, T.K. (2012) 'Synthetic Biology: An Emerging Engineering Discipline', *Annual Review of Biomedical Engineering*, 14.

Chomsky, N. (2007) 'Year 501: World Orders Old and New, Part 1', Z Magazine, September, http://www.zcommunications.org/year-501-world-orders-old-and-new-part-i-by-noam-chomsky (accessed 22 November 2012).

Council of the European Union (2006) 'Review of the EU Sustainable Development Strategy: Renewed Strategy', 9 June, http://register.consilium.europa.eu/pdf/en/06/st10/st10117.en06.pdf (accessed 27 July 2012).

Cox, R.W. (1996a) 'Gramsci, Hegemony and International Relations: An Essay in Method', in R. Cox and T.J. Sinclair (eds) *Approaches to World Order*. Cambridge: Cambridge University Press, pp. 124–43.

Cox, R.W. (1996b) 'Social Forces, States and World Orders: Beyond International Relations Theory', in R. Cox and T.J. Sinclair (eds) *Approaches to World Order*. Cambridge: Cambridge University Press, pp. 85–123.

Cox, R.W. and Sinclair, T.J. (1996c) *Approaches to World Order*. Cambridge: Cambridge University Press.

Crane, G. (1998) *Thucydides and the Ancient Simplicity: The Limits of Political Realism*. Berkeley: University of California Press, http://publishing.cdlib.org/ucpressebooks/view?docId=ft767nb497&brand=ucpress (accessed 26 July 2012).

Crawford, N.C. (2009) 'Jürgen Habermas', in J. Edkins and N. Vaughan-Williams (eds) *Critical Theorists and International Relations*. London: Routledge, pp. 197–8.

Daddow, O. (2007) 'Playing Games with History: Tony Blair's European Policy in the Press', *British Journal of Politics and International Relations*, 9(4): 582–98.

Daddow, O. (2009) '"Tony's War?" Blair, Kosovo and the Interventionist Impulse in British Foreign Policy', *International Affairs*, 85(3): 547–60.

Daddow, O. (2011) *New Labour and the European Union: Blair and Brown's Logic of History*. Manchester: Manchester University Press.

Daddow, O. (2012) 'The UK Media and "Europe": From Permissive Consensus to Destructive Dissent', *International Affairs*, 88(6): 1219–36.

Dalby, S. (2009) 'What Happens If We Don't Think in Human Terms?', in J. Edkins and M. Zehfuss (eds) *Global Politics: A New Introduction*. London and New York: Routledge, pp. 45–69.

Der Derian, J. (1995) 'A Reinterpretation of Realism: Genealogy, Semiology, Dromology', in J. Der Derian (ed.) *International Theory: Critical Investigations*. Basingstoke: Macmillan, pp. 363–96.

Der Derian, J. (2009) 'Critical Encounters in International Relations', *International Social Science Journal*, 59(191): 69–73.

Devetak, R. (1995) 'Incomplete States: Theories and Practices of Statecraft', in J. Macmillan and A. Linklater (eds) *Boundaries in Question: New Directions in International Relations*. London: Pinter, pp. 19–39.

Devetak, R. (2009a) 'Critical Theory', in S. Burchill et al. *Theories of International Relations*, 2nd edn. Basingstoke: Palgrave, pp. 144–78.

Devetak, R. (2009b) 'Post-structuralism', in S. Burchill et al. *Theories of International Relations*, 4th edn. Basingstoke: Palgrave, pp. 183–211.

Dictionary.com (2007a) http://dictionary.reference.com/search?q=an- (accessed 14 July 2012).

Dictionary.com (2007b) http://dictionary.reference.com/browse/archon (accessed 14 July 2012).

Dobson, A. (2003) *Citizenship and the Environment*. Oxford: Oxford University Press.

Dobson, A. (2006a) 'Ecological Citizenship: A Defence', *Environmental Politics*, 15(3): 445–51.

Dobson, A. (2006b) 'Thick Cosmopolitanism', *Political Studies*, 54(1): 165–84.

Dobson, A. (2007) 'Environmental Citizenship: Towards Sustainable Development', *Sustainable Development*, 15(5): 276–85.

Donnelly, J. (1996) 'Twentieth-Century Realism', in T. Nardin and D.R. Mapel (eds) *Traditions of International Ethics*. Cambridge: Cambridge University Press, pp. 85–111.

Doyle, M. (1983) 'Kant, Liberal Legacies, and Foreign Affairs', *Philosophy and Public Affairs*, 12(3) and 12(4), 205–35 and 323–53 respectively.

Doyle, M. (1986) 'Liberalism and World Politics', *American Political Science Review*, 80(4): 1151–69.

Drezner, D. (2011) *Theories of International Politics and Zombies*. Princeton, NJ: Princeton University Press.

Duffield, J. (2007) 'What are International Institutions?', *International Studies Review*, 9(1): 1–22.

Dunne, T. (2005) 'The New Agenda', in A.J. Bellamy (ed.) *International Society and its Critics*. Oxford: Oxford University Press, 65–79.

Dunne, T. (2007) 'The English School', in T. Dunne, M. Kurki and S. Smith (eds) *International Relations Theory: Discipline and Diversity*. Oxford: Oxford University Press, pp. 128–47.

Dunne, T. (2008) 'Liberalism', in J. Baylis, S. Smith and P. Owens (eds) *The Globalization of World Politics: An Introduction to International Relations*, 4th edn. Oxford: Oxford University Press, pp. 108–22.

Dunne, T., Kurki, M. and Smith, S. (eds) (2007) *International Relations Theory: Discipline and Diversity*. Oxford: Oxford University Press.

Dunne, T. and Schmidt, B.C. (2008) 'Realism', in J. Baylis, S. Smith and P. Owens (eds) *The Globalization of World Politics: An Introduction to International Relations*, 4th edn. Oxford: Oxford University Press, pp. 90–106.

Eagleton, T. (1998) 'Postcolonialism and "Postcolonialism"', *Interventions: International Journal of Postcolonial Studies*, 1(1): 24–6.

Eckersley, R. (2007) 'Green Theory', in T. Dunne, M. Kurki and S. Smith (eds) *International Relations Theory: Discipline and Diversity*. Oxford: Oxford University Press, pp. 247–65.

Economist (2010) 'Facebook population: status update', 22 July, http://www.economist.com/node/16660401 (accessed 26 July 2012).

Edkins, J. and Zehfuss, M. (eds) (2008) *Global Politics: A New Introduction*. London and New York: Routledge.

Elshtain, J.B. (1995) 'Feminist Themes and International Relations', in J. Der Derian (ed.) *International Theory: Critical Investigations*. Basingstoke: Macmillan, pp. 340–60.

Encyclopedia of World Biography (2005–6) 'On Hans J. Morgenthau', http://www.bookrags.com/biography/hans-j-morgenthau/ (accessed 31 June 2012).

English Daily (undated) 'Movie Lines', http://www.englishdaily626.com/movie_lines.php?476 (accessed 16 July 2012).

Enloe, C. (2001) *Bananas, Beaches and Bases: Making Feminist Sense of International Politics*. Berkeley, CA: University of California Press.

Epstein, C. (2008) *The Power of Words in International Relations: Birth of an Anti-Whaling Discourse*. Cambridge, MA and London: MIT Press.

Europa (undated) 'The History of the European Union', http://europa.eu/about-eu/eu-history/index_en.htm (accessed 16 July 2012).

Evans, G. (2004) 'The Responsibility to Protect: Rethinking Humanitarian Intervention', 1 April, http://www.gevans.org/speeches/speech103.html (accessed 20 July 2012).

Finnemore, M. and Sikkink, K. (1998) 'International Norm Dynamics and Political Change', *International Organization*, 52(4): 887–917.

Finnemore, M. and Sikkink, K. (2001) 'The Constructivist Research Program in International Relations and Comparative Politics', *Annual Review of Political Science*, 4(1): 391–416.

Forde, S. (1996) 'Classical Realism', in T. Nardin and D.R. Mapel (eds) *Traditions of International Ethics*. Cambridge: Cambridge University Press, pp. 62–84.

Friedman, G. (2008) 'Identifying the Place of Democratic Norms in Democratic Peace', *International Studies Review*, 10(3), 548–70.

Foucault, M. (1991) 'Truth and Power', in P. Rabinow (ed.) *The Foucault Reader: An Introduction to Foucault's Thought*. London: Penguin, pp. 51–75.

Fowler, R. (1992) *Language in the News: Discourse and Ideology in the Press*. London: Routledge.

Freyberg-Inan, A. (2006) 'World System Theory: A Bird's Eye View of the World's Capitalist Order', in J. Sterling-Folker (ed.) *Making Sense of International Relations Theory*. Boulder, CO: Lynne Rienner Publishers, pp. 225–41.

Fuller, T. (2006) '"Sweatshop Snoops" Take on China Factories', *International Herald Tribune*, 16 September, available at: http://www.nytimes.com/2006/09/15/world/asia/15iht-inspect.2827852.html?pagewanted=all&_r=0

Geis, A. (2011) 'Of Bright Sides and Dark Sides: Democratic Peace Beyond Triumphalism', International Relations, 25(2): 164–70.

Giddens, A. (1974) 'Introduction', in A. Giddens (ed.) *Positivism and Sociology*. London: Heinemann, pp. 1–22.

Gilpin, R.G. (1984) 'The Richness of the Tradition of Political Realism', *International Organization*, 38(2): 287–304.

Glaser, C.L. (1994/95) 'Realists as Optimists: Cooperation as Self-Help', *International Security*, 19(3): 50–90.

Goodwin, G.L. and Linklater, A. (1975) 'Introduction', in G.L. Goodwin and A. Linklater (eds) *New Dimensions of World Politics*. London: Croom Helm.

Gowa, J. (2011) 'The Democratic Peace After the End of the Cold War', *Economics and Politics*, 23(2): 153–71.

Green Party (2010) 'Green Party Manifesto 2010', http://greenparty.org.uk/policies/policies-2010/2010manifesto-contents.html (accessed 26 July 2012).

Griffiths, M. (2011) *Rethinking International Relations Theory*. Basingstoke: Palgrave Macmillan.

Groom, A.J.R. and Light, M. (eds) (1994) *Contemporary International Relations: A Guide to Theory*. London: Pinter.

Groom, A.J.R. and Taylor, P. (1975) *Functionalism: Theory and Practice in International Relations*. London: University of London Press.

Grovogui, S.N. (2007) 'Postcolonialism', in T. Dunne, M. Kurki and S. Smith (eds) *International Relations Theory: Discipline and Diversity*. Oxford: Oxford University Press, pp. 229–46.

Guilhot, N. (2011) 'One Discipline, Many Histories', in N. Guilhot (ed.) *The Invention of International Relations Theory: Realism, the Rockefeller Foundation, and the 1954 Conference on Theory*. New York: Columbia University Press, pp. 1–32.

Guzzini, S. and Leander, A. (2006) 'Wendt's Constructivism: A Relentless Quest for Synthesis', in S. Guzzini and A. Leander (eds) *Constructivism and International Relations: Alexander Wendt and his Critics*. London: Routledge pp. 73–92.

Haas, E.B. (1958) *The Uniting of Europe: Political, Social and Economic Forces*, 1950–1957. Stanford, CA: Stanford University Press.

Haas, E.B. (1964) *Beyond the Nation-State: Functionalism and International Organization*. Stanford, CA: Stanford University Press.

Hague, W. (2009) 'The Future of British Foreign Policy', Speech to the International Institute for Strategic Studies, 21 July, http://www.conservatives.com/News/Speeches/2009/07/William_Hague_The_Future_of_British_Foreign_Policy.aspx (accessed 17 January 2012).

Harrison, L. (2001) *Political Research: An Introduction*. London: Routledge.

Haynes, J., Hough, P., Malik, S. and Pettiford, L. (2011) *World Politics*. Harlow: Pearson Education.

Hellsten, S. and Mallin, C. (2006) 'Are "Ethical" or "Socially Responsible" Investments Socially Responsible?', *Journal of Business Ethics*, 66(4): 393–406.

Hobbes, T. (2007) *Leviathan*. University of Adelaide e-book, available at: http://etext.library.adelaide.edu.au/h/hobbes/thomas/h68l/ (accessed 30 June 2012).

Hobden, S. and Jones, R.W. (2008) 'Marxist Theories of International Relations', in T. Dunne, M. Kurki and S. Smith (eds) *International Relations Theory*: Discipline and Diversity. Oxford: Oxford University Press, pp. 142–59.

Hobson, C. (2011a) 'The Sorcerer's Apprentice', *International Relations*, 25(2): 171–7.

Hobson, C. (2011b) 'Towards a Critical Theory of Democratic Peace', *Review of International Studies*, 37(4): 1903–22.

Hoffman, S. (1985) 'Raymond Aron and the Theory of International Relations', *International Studies Quarterly*, 29(1): 13–27.

Hoffman, S. (1995) 'An American Social Science: International Relations', in J. Der Derian (ed.) *International Theory: Critical Investigations*. Basingstoke: Macmillan, pp. 212–41.

Holden, G. (2002) 'Who Contextualizes the Contextualizers? Disciplinary History and the Discourse about IR Discourse', *Review of International Studies*, 28(2): 253–70.

Hollis, M. and Smith, S. (1991) *Explaining and Understanding International Relations*. Oxford: Clarendon Press.

Holsti, K.J. (1985) *The Dividing Discipline: Hegemony and Diversity in International Theory*. London: Unwin Hyman Ltd.

Hooghe, L. and Marks, G. (2008) 'A Postfunctionalist Theory of European Integration: From Permissive Consent to Constraining Dissensus', *British Journal of Political Science*, 39(1): 1–23.

Hooper, C. (2006) 'Masculinities, IR and the "Gender Variable"', in R. Little and M. Smith (eds) *Perspectives on World Politics*. Abingdon: Routledge, pp. 376–85.

Hovden, E. (1999) 'As If Nature Doesn't Matter: Ecology, Regime Theory and International Relations', *Environmental Politics*, 8(2): 50–74.

Huggan, G. and Tiffin, H. (2007) 'Green Postcolonialism', *Interventions: International Journal of Postcolonial Studies*, 9(1): 1–11.

Human Rights Watch (2012) 'Women's Rights', www.hrw.org/category/topic/women (accessed 22 November 2012).

Hutchings, K. (1999) *International Political Theory*. London: Sage.

International Labour Organization (1996–2012) Information Leaflet. www.ilo.org/global/about-the-ilo/press-and-media-centre/news/WCMS_181961/lang--en/index.htm (accessed 23 July 2012).

Ish-Shalom, P. (2011) 'Don't Look Back in Anger', *International Relations*, 25(2): 178–84.

Jackson, R. and Sørensen, G. (2007) *Introduction to International Relations: Theories and Approaches*. Oxford: Oxford University Press.

James, A. (1993) 'System or Society?', *Review of International Studies*, 19(3): 269–88.

Jarvis, D.S.L. (2001) 'Identity Politics, Postmodern Feminisms, and International Theory: Questioning the "New" Diversity in International Relations', in R.M.A. Crawford and D.S.L. Jarvis, *International Relations: Still an American Social Science?: Towards Diversity in International Thought*. Albany, NY: State University of New York Press, pp. 101–29.

Jervis, R. (1994) 'Hans Morgenthau, Realism, and the Study of International Politics – Sixtieth Anniversary, 1934–1994: The Legacy of Our Past', *Social Research*, https://asrudiancenter.wordpress.com/2008/06/23/hans-morgenthau-realism-and-the-study-of-international-politics-sixtieth-anniversary-1934-1994-the-legacy-of-our-past/ (accessed 30 June 2012).

Joker Scene from the Dark Knight (2008), http://www.youtube.com/watch?v=GGwHUr0b4yE (accessed 16 July 2012).

Jørgensen, K.E. (2010) *International Relations Theory: A New Introduction*. Basingstoke: Palgrave Macmillan.

Joynt, C.B. and Corbett, P.E. (1978) *Theory and Reality in World Politics*. Basingstoke: Macmillan.

Kadir, D. (1995) 'Postmodernism/Postcolonialism: What Are We After?', *World Literature Today*, 69(1): 17–21.

Keohane, R.O. (1982) 'The Demand for International Regimes', *International Organization*, 36(2): 325–55.

Keohane, R.O. (ed.) (1986) *Neorealism and its Critics*. New York: Columbia University Press.

Keohane, R.O. (1986) 'Realism, Neorealism and the Study of World Politics', in R.O. Keohane (ed.) *Neorealism and its Critics*. New York: Columbia University Press, pp. 1–26.

Keohane, R. (1995) 'International Institutions: Two Approaches', in J. Der Derian (ed.) *International Theory: Critical Investigations*. Basingstoke: Macmillan, pp. 279–307.

Keohane, R.O. and Nye, J.S. (1977) *Power and Interdependence: World Politics in Transition*. Boston: Little Brown and Co.

Ki-moon, B. (2008) 'Statement to Regional Groups of Member States', January, http://www.un.org/apps/news/infocus/sgspeeches/search_full.asp?statID=170 (accessed 5 July 2012).

Krasner, S.D. (ed.) (1983) *International Regimes*. Ithaca, NY: Cornell University Press.

Kratochwil, F. (1982) 'On the Notion of "Interest" in International Relations', *International Organization*, 36(1): 1–30.

Kratochwil, F. (1989) *Rules, Norms and Decisions*. Cambridge: Cambridge University Press.

Kratochwil, F. (2000) 'Wendt's "Social Theory of International Politics" and the Constructivist Challenge', *Millennium: Journal of International Studies*, 29(1): 73–101.

Kratochwil, F. and Ruggie, J.G. (1986) 'International Organization: A State of the Art on an Art of the State', *International Organization*, 40(4): 753–75.

Kreisler, H. (2003) 'Conversation with Kenneth Waltz', available at: http://globetrotter.berkeley.edu/people3/Waltz/waltz-con0.html (accessed 2 July 2012).

Kuhn, T.S. (1996) *The Structure of Scientific Revolutions*, 3rd edn. Chicago and London: The University of Chicago Press.

Kumar, M.P. (2011) 'Postcolonialism: Interdisciplinary or Interdiscursive?', *Third World Quarterly*, 32(4): 653–72.

Lamy, S.L. (2008) 'Contemporary Mainstream Approaches: Neo-realism and Neo-liberalism', in J. Baylis, S. Smith and P. Owens (eds) *The Globalization of World Politics: An Introduction to International Relations*, 4th edn. Oxford: Oxford University Press, pp. 124–41.

Langlois, A.J. (2007) 'Worldviews and International Political Theory', in M. Griffiths (ed.) *International Relations Theory for the Twenty-First Century*. London: Routledge, pp. 146–56.

Lebow, R.N. (2007) 'Classical Realism', in T. Dunne, M. Kurki and S. Smith (eds) *International Relations Theory: Discipline and Diversity*. Oxford: Oxford University Press, pp. 52–70.

Lehane, D. (2003) *Shutter Island*. London: Bantam Press.

Linklater, A. (1990) *Beyond Realism and Marxism*. London: Macmillan.

Linklater, A. (1995) 'Neo-Realism: Theory and Practice', in K. Booth and S. Smith (eds) *International Relations Theory Today*. Cambridge: Polity Press, pp. 241–61.

Linklater, A. (1998) *The Transformation of Political Community*. Cambridge: Polity Press.

Linklater, A. (2009a) 'Marx and Marxism', in S. Burchill et al. *Theories of International Relations*, 4th edn. Basingstoke: Palgrave, pp. 111–35.

Linklater, A. (2010) 'Global Civilizing Processes and the Ambiguities of Human Connectedness', *European Journal of International Relations*, 16(2): 155–78.

Little, R. (1995) 'International Relations and the Triumph of Capitalism', in K. Booth and S. Smith (eds) *International Relations Theory Today*. Cambridge: Polity Press, pp. 62–87.

Little, R. (2005) 'The English School and World History', in A.J. Bellamy (ed.) *International Society and its Critics*. Oxford: Oxford University Press, pp. 45–63.

Little, R. and Smith, M. (eds) (2006) *Perspectives on World Politics*. Abingdon: Routledge.

Lupovici, A. (2009) 'Constructivist Methods: a Plea and Manifesto for Pluralism', *Review of International Studies*, 35(2): 195–218.

Lynch, M. (2006) 'Critical Theory: Dialogue, Legitimacy, and Justifications for War', in J. Sterling-Folker (ed.) *Making Sense of International Relations Theory*. Boulder, CO: Lynne Rienner Publishers, pp. 182–97.

Macmillan, J. (2003) 'Beyond the Separate Democratic Peace', *Journal of Peace Research*, 40(2): 233–43.

Macmillan, J. and Linklater, A. (eds) (1995) *Boundaries in Question: New Directions in International Relations*. London: Pinter.

Mansbach, R.W. and Rafferty, K.L. (2008) *Introduction to Global Politics*. Abingdon: Routledge.

Martin, L.L. (2007) 'Neoliberalism', in T. Dunne, M. Kurki and S. Smith (eds) *International Relations Theory: Discipline and Diversity*. Oxford: Oxford University Press, pp. 110–26.

Marx, K. (2008) *Capital: A New Abridgement*. Oxford: Oxford University Press.

Marx, K. and Engels, F. (1998) *The Communist Manifesto*. Oxford: Oxford University Press.

Martinsson, J. and Lundqvist, L.J. (2010) 'Ecological Citizenship: Coming Out "Clean" Without Turning "Green"?', *Environmental Politics*, 19(4): 518–37.

McLuhan, M. and Powers, B.R. (1989) *The Global Village: Transformations in World Life and Media in the 21st Century*. New York: Oxford University Press.

Mearsheimer, J.J. (2001) *The Tragedy of Great Power Politics*. London: W.W. Norton and Company.

Mingst, K.A. and Snyder, J.L. (2011) *Essential Readings in World Politics: An Introduction*, 4th edn. London: W.W. Norton and Company.

Mishra, V. and Hodge, B. (2005) 'What was Postcolonialism?', *New Literary History*, 36(3): 375–402.

Mitchell, R.B. (2006) 'International Environment', in W. Carlsnaes, T. Risse and B.A. Simmons (eds) *Handbook of International Relations*. London: Sage, pp. 500–16.

Mitrany, D. (1933) *The Progress of International Government*. New Haven, CT: Yale University Press.

Mohanty, C.T. (1988) 'Under Western Eyes: Feminist Scholarship and Critical Discourse', *Feminist Review*, 30(3): 61–88.

Moravcsik, A. (1998) *The Choice for Europe: Social Purpose and State Power from Messina to Maastricht*. Ithaca, NY: Cornell University Press.

Morgenthau, H.J. (1985) *Politics Among Nations: The Struggle for Power and Peace*, 6th edn. New York: Knopf.

Morris, J. (2005) 'Normative Innovation and the Great Powers', in A.J. Bellamy (ed.) *International Society and its Critics*. Oxford: Oxford University Press, pp. 265–81.

Morris, J. (2011) 'How Great is Britain? Power, Responsibility and Britain's Future Global Role', *British Journal of Politics and International Relations*, 13(3): 326–47.

Navon, E. (2001) 'The "Third Debate" Revisited', *Review of International Studies*, 27(4): 611–25.

Neal, A.W. (2009) 'Michel Foucault', in J. Edkins and N. Vaughan-Williams (eds) *Critical Theorists and International Relations*. London: Routledge, pp. 161–70.

Norris, C. (1993) *Deconstruction: Theory and Practice*. London: Routledge.

Nye, J.S. and Welch, D.A. (2011) *Understanding Global Conflict and Cooperation: An Introduction to Theory and History*. London: Pearson.

Onuf, N. (1998) 'Constructivism: A User's Manual', in V. Kubálková, N. Onuf and P. Kowert (eds) *International Relations in a Constructed World*. Armonk, NY: M.E. Sharpe, pp. 58–78.

Onuf, N.G. (1989) *A World of Our Making: Rules and Rule in Social Theory and International Relations*. Columbia: University of South Carolina Press.

Onuf, N. (2002) 'Institutions, Intentions and International Relations', *Review of International Studies*, 28(2): 211–28.

Onuf, N. (2009) 'Structure? What Structure?', *International Relations*, 23(2): 183–99.

Owen, J.M. (2011) 'Liberal Tradition not Social Science', *International Relations*, 25(2): 158–63.

Palacios, J.J. (2004) 'Corporate Citizenship and Social Responsibility in a Globalized World', *Citizenship Studies*, 8(4): 383–402.

Panke, D. and Risse, T. (2007) 'Liberalism', in T. Dunne, M. Kurki and S. Smith (eds) *International Relations Theory: Discipline and Diversity*. Oxford: Oxford University Press, pp. 89–108.

Paterson, M. (1995) 'Radicalizing Regimes? Ecology and the Critique of IR Theory', in J. Macmillan and A. Linklater (eds) *Boundaries in Question: New Directions in International Relations*. London: Pinter, pp. 212–27.

Paterson, M. (2009) 'Green Politics', in S. Burchill et al. *Theories of International Relations*, 2nd edn. Basingstoke: Palgrave, pp. 260–83.

Peoples, C. (2009) 'Theodore Adorno', in J. Edkins and N. Vaughan-Williams (eds) *Critical Theorists and International Relations*. London: Routledge, pp. 7–18.

Peterson, V.S. (1992) 'Introduction', in V.S. Peterson (ed.) *Gendered States: Feminist (Re)Visions of International Relations Theory*. Boulder, CO: Lynne Rienner Publishers, pp. 1–29.

Phythian, M. (2011) 'From Asset to Liability: Blair, Brown and the "Special Relationship"', O. Daddow and J. Gaskarth (eds) *British Foreign Policy: The New Labour Years*. Basingstoke: Palgrave Macmillan, pp. 188–204.

Prichard, A. (2007) 'Justice, Order and Anarchy: The International Political Theory of Pierre-Joseph Proudhon, 1809–1865', *Millennium: Journal of International Studies*, 35(3): 623–45.

Prichard, A. (2011) 'What Can the Absence of Anarchism Tell us About the History and Purpose of International Relations?', *Review of International Studies*, 37(4): 1647–69.

Ralph, J. (2011) 'A Difficult Relationship: Britain's "Doctrine of International Community" and America's "War on Terror"', in O. Daddow and J. Gaskarth (eds) *British Foreign Policy: The New Labour Years*. Basingstoke: Palgrave Macmillan, pp. 23–38.

Ramakrishnan, A.K. (1999) 'The Gaze of Orientalism: Reflections on Linking Postcolonialism and International Relations', *International Studies*, 36(2): 129–63.

Redman, P. (2006) *Good Essay Writing*, 3rd edn. London: Sage.

Reus-Smit, C. (2002) 'Imagining Society: Constructivism and the English School', *British Journal of Politics and International Relations*, 4(3): 487–509.

Reus-Smit, C. (2005) 'The Constructivist Challenge After September 11', in A.J. Bellamy (ed.) *International Society and its Critics*. Oxford: Oxford University Press, pp. 81–94.

Reus-Smit, C. (2012) 'International Relations, Irrelevant? Don't Blame Theory', Milennium: *Journal of International Studies*, 40(3): 525–40.

Rosato, S. (2003) 'The Flawed Logic of Democratic Peace Theory', *American Political Science Review*, 97(4): 585–602.

Rosenau, J.N. (1976) 'International Studies in a Transnational World', *Millennium*, 5(1): 1–20.

Rosenau, J.N. (2002) 'Unfulfilled Potential: Sociology and International Relations', *International Review of Sociology*, 12(3): 545–9.

Rosenau, J.N. (2003) 'The Theoretical Imperative: Unavoidable Explication', *Asian Journal of Political Science*, 11(2): 7–20.

Rosenau, J.N. (2004) 'Many Globalizations, One International Relations', *Globalizations*, 1(1): 7–14.

Ruane, K. (2000) *The Rise and Fall of the European Defence Community: Anglo-American Relations and the Crisis of European Defence, 1950–55*. Basingstoke: Macmillan.

Ruggie, J.G. (1998a) *Constructing the World Polity: Essays on International Institutionalization*. London: Routledge.

Ruggie, J.G. (1998b) 'What Makes the World Hang Together? Neo-Utilitarianism and the Social Constructivist Challenge', *International Organization*, 52(4): 855–85.

Rupert, M. (2007) 'Marxism and Critical Theory', in T. Dunne, M. Kurki and S. Smith (eds) *International Relations Theory: Discipline and Diversity*. Oxford: Oxford University Press, pp. 148–65.

Rupert, M. (2009) 'Antonio Gramsci', in J. Edkins and N. Vaughan-Williams (eds) *Critical Theorists and International Relations*. London: Routledge, pp. 176–86.

Russett, B. (1995) 'Correspondence on The Democratic Peace: "And Yet It Moves"', *International Security*, 19(4): 164–75.

Said, E. (1994) *Culture and Imperialism*. London: Vintage Books.

Said, E. (2003) *Orientalism*. London: Penguin.

Salter, M.B. (2010) 'Edward Said and Post-colonial International Relations, in C. Moore and C. Farrands (eds) *International Relations and Philosophy: Interpretive Dialogues*. London: Routledge, pp. 129–43.

Schenk, R. (1997–2006) 'A Case of Unemployment', http://ingrimayne.com/econ/EconomicCatastrophe/GreatDepression.html (accessed 18 July 2012).

Schmidt, B.C. (2006) 'On the History and Historiography of International Relations', in W. Carlsnaes, T. Risse and B.A. Simmons (eds) *Handbook of International Relations*. London: Sage, pp. 3–22.

Scholte, J.A. (2008) 'Defining Globalisation', *The World Economy*, 31(11): 1471–1502.

Schweller, R. (2011) 'Theory in Action: Realism', 4 May, http://www.youtube.com/watch?v=UnKEFSVAiNQ&feature=relmfu (accessed 10 July 2012).

Scott, G.M. and Garrison, S.M. (2006) *The Political Science Student Writer's Manual*, 5th edn. Upper Saddle River, NJ: Prentice Hall.

Scriven, M. (1994) 'A Possible Distinction between Traditional Scientific Disciplines and the Study of Human Behaviour', in M. Martin and L.C. McIntyre (eds) *Readings in the Philosophy of Social Science*. Cambridge, MA: The MIT Press, pp. 71–7.

Shinko, R.E. (2006) 'Postmodernism: A Genealogy of Humanitarian Intervention', in J. Sterling-Folker (ed.) *Making Sense of International Relations Theory*. Boulder, CO: Lynne Rienner Publishers, pp. 168–81.

Sinclair, T.J. (1996) 'Beyond International Relations Theory: Robert W. Cox and Approaches to World Order', in R.W. Cox and T.J. Sinclair, *Approaches to World Order*. Cambridge: Cambridge University Press, pp. 3–18.

Smallman, S. and Brown, K. (2011) *Introduction to International and Global Studies*. Chapel Hill: University of North Carolina Press.

Smith, M.J. (2005) 'Obligation and Ecological Citizenship', *Environments*, 33(3): 9–23.

Smith, S. (1995) 'The Self-Images of a Discipline: A Genealogy of International Relations Theory', in K. Booth and S. Smith (eds) *International Relations Theory Today*. Cambridge: Polity Press, pp. 1–37.

Smith, S. (1997) 'Power and Truth: A Reply to William Wallace', *Review of International Studies*, 23(4): 507–16.

Smith, S. (2004) 'Singing Our World into Existence: International Relations Theory and September 11', *International Studies Quarterly*, 48(3): 499–515.

Smith, S. (2007) 'Introduction: Diversity and Disciplinarity in IR Theory', in T. Dunne, M. Kurki and S. Smith (eds) *International Relations Theory: Discipline and Diversity*. Oxford: Oxford University Press, pp. 1–12.

Smith, S., Booth, K. and Zalewski, M. (eds) (1996) *International Theory: Positivism and Beyond*. Cambridge: Cambridge University Press.

Smith, S. and Owens, P. (2008) 'Alternative Approaches to International Theory', in J. Baylis, S. Smith and P. Owens (eds) *The Globalization of World Politics: An Introduction to International Relations*, 4th edn. Oxford: Oxford University Press, pp. 174–91.

Smith, T. (2011) 'Democratic Peace Theory: From Promising Theory to Dangerous Practice', *International Relations*, 25(2): 151–7.

Spiro, D. (1995) 'Correspondence on The Democratic Peace: The Liberal Peace – "And Yet It Squirms"', *International Security*, 19(4): 177–80.

Sterling-Folker, J. (2006a) 'Liberal Approaches', in J. Sterling-Folker (ed.) *Making Sense of International Relations Theory*. Boulder, CO: Lynne Rienner, pp. 55–62.

Sterling-Folker, J. (ed.) (2006b) *Making Sense of International Relations Theory*. Boulder, CO: Lynne Rienner.

Sterling-Folker, J. (2006c) 'Historical Materialism and World System Theory Approaches', in J. Sterling-Folker (ed.) *Making Sense of International Relations Theory*. Boulder, CO: Lynne Rienner, pp. 199–208.

Sterling-Folker, J. (2006d) 'Postmodern and Critical Theory Approaches', in J. Sterling-Folker (ed.) *Making Sense of International Relations Theory*. Boulder, CO: Lynne Rienner, pp. 157–67.

Sterling-Folker, J. (2006e) 'Realism', in J. Sterling-Folker (ed.) *Making Sense of International Relations Theory*. Boulder, CO: Lynne Rienner, pp. 13–17.

Sterling-Folker, J. (2006f) 'Making Sense of International Relations Theory', in J. Sterling-Folker (ed.) *Making Sense of International Relations Theory*. Boulder, CO: Lynne Rienner, pp. 1–12.

Suganami, H. (2005) 'The English School and International Theory', in A.J. Bellamy (ed.) *International Society and its Critics*. Oxford: Oxford University Press, pp. 29–44.

Sutch, P. and Elias, J. (2007) *International Relations: The Basics*. London: Routledge.

Thucydides (2004) *History of the Peloponnesian War*, trans. R. Crawley. Mineola, NY: Dover.

Tickner, A.J. (1988) 'Hans Morgenthau's principles of political realism: a feminist reformulation', *Millenium: Journal of International Studies*, 17(3): 429–34.

Tickner, J.A. and Sjoberg, L. (2007) 'Feminism', in T. Dunne, M. Kurki and S. Smith (eds) *International Relations Theory: Discipline and Diversity*. Oxford: Oxford University Press, pp. 185–202.

Ullmann-Margalit, E. (1977) *The Emergence of Norms*. Oxford: Clarendon Press.

UN (1997) 'A Summary of United Nations Agreements on Human Rights', http://www.hrweb.org/legal/undocs.html#Geneva (accessed 25 July 2012).

UN (1997–2010) 'Directory of UN Resources on Gender and Women's Issues', http://www.un.org/womenwatch/directory/statistics_and_indicators_60.htm (accessed 25 July 2012).

UN (1998) 'Kyoto Protocol to the United Nations Framework Convention on Climate Change', http://unfccc.int/resource/docs/convkp/kpeng.pdf (accessed 27 July 2012).

UN (2005) 'History of the United Nations', http://www.un.org/en/aboutun/history/index.shtml (accessed 16 July 2012).

UN (2006) Organization Chart, http://www.un.org/en/aboutun/structure/index.shtml (accessed 16 July 2012).

UN (2009) Division for Sustainable Development, http://sustainabledevelopment.un.org (accessed 22 November 2012).

UN (2011) 'Growth in United Nations membership, 1945–present', http://www.un.org/en/members/growth.shtml (accessed 16 July 2012).

Varadarajan, L. (2009) 'Edward Said', in J. Edkins and N. Vaughan-Williams (eds) *Critical Theorists and International Relations*. London: Routledge, pp. 292–304.

Wæver, O. (2007) 'Still a Discipline After All These Debates?', in T. Dunne, M. Kurki and S. Smith (eds) *International Relations Theory: Discipline and Diversity*. Oxford: Oxford University Press, pp. 288–308.

Wainwright, M. and Carvel, J. (2006) 'Blair Heralds End of "Nanny State" Advice', *Guardian*, 26 July, http://www.guardian.co.uk/society/2006/jul/26/health.politics2?INTCMP=SRCH (accessed 18 July 2012).

Walker, R.B.J. (1993) *Inside/Outside: International Relations as Political Theory*. Cambridge: Cambridge University Press.

Walker, R.B.J. (1995) 'History and Structure in the Theory of International Relations', in J. Der Derian (ed.) *International Theory: Critical Investigations*. Basingstoke: Macmillan, pp. 308–39.

Wallace, W. (1996) 'Truth and Power, Monks and Technocrats: Theory and Practice in International Relations', *Review of International Studies*, 22(3): 301–21.

Wallerstein, I. (1974) *The Modern World System. Vol. 1: Capitalist Agriculture and the Origins of the European World-Economy in the Sixteenth Century*. New York and London: Academic Press.

Wallerstein, I. (1980) *The Modern World-System. Vol. II: Mercantilism and the Consolidation of the European World-Economy, 1600–1750*. New York and London: Academic Press.

Wallerstein, I. (1989) *The Modern World System. Vol. III: The Second Era of Great Expansion of the Capitalist World-Economy, 1730s–1840s*. New York and London: Academic Press.

Walliman, N. (2006) *Social Research Methods*. London: Sage.

Walt, S.M. (2006) 'International Relations: One World, Many Theories', in R. Little and M. Smith (eds) *Perspectives on World Politics*. Abingdon: Routledge, pp. 386–94.

Waltz, K.N. (1959) *Man, the State and War*. New York: Cambridge University Press.

Waltz, K.N. (1990) 'Realist Thought and Neorealist Theory', *Journal of International Affairs*, 44(1): 21–37.

Waltz, K.N. (1997) 'Evaluating Theories', *American Political Science Review*, 91(4): 913–7.

Waltz, K.N. (2010) *Theory of International Politics*. Long Grove, IL: Waveland Press.

Watson, A. (1990) 'Systems of States', *Review of International Studies*, 16(2): 99–109.

Watson, A. (2001) *The Evolution of International Society*. London; Routledge.

Watson, A.M.S. (2006) 'Children and International Relations: A New Site of Knowledge?', *Review of International Studies*, 32(2): 237–50.

Weber, C. (2010) *International Relations Theory: A Critical Introduction*, 3rd edn. London: Routledge.

Welch, D.A. (2003) 'Why IR Theorists Should Stop Reading Thucydides', *Review of International Studies*, 29(3): 301–19.

Wendt, A. (1992) 'Anarchy is What States Make of It: The Social Construction of Power Politics', *International Organization*, 46(2): 391–425.

Wendt, A. (1999) *Social Theory of International Politics*. Cambridge: Cambridge University Press.

Wendt, A. (2000) 'On the Via Media: A Response to the Critics', *Review of International Studies*, 26(1): 165–80.

Wexler, L. (2003) 'The International Deployment of Shame, Second-best Responses, and Norm Entrepreneurship: The Campaign to Ban Landmines and the Landmine Ban Treaty', *American Journal of International and Comparative Law*, 20(3): 561–606.

Wheeler, N.J. and Dunne, T. (1996) 'Hedley Bull's Pluralism of the Intellect and Solidarism of the Will', *International Affairs*, 72(1): 91–107.

Wight, M. (1987) 'An Anatomy of International Thought', *Review of International Studies*, 13(3): 221–7.

Wight, M. (1995) 'Why Is There No International Theory?', in J. Der Derian (ed.) *International Theory: Critical Investigations*. Basingstoke: Macmillan, pp. 15–35.

Williams, J. (2005) 'Pluralism, Solidarism and the Emergence of World Society in English School Theory', *International Relations*, 19(1): 19–38.

Wilson, W. (1918) 'President Woodrow Wilson's Fourteen Points', http://avalon.law.yale.edu/20th_century/wilson14.asp (accessed 16 July 2012).

Windschuttle, K. (1996) *The Killing of History: How Literary Critics and Social Theorists are Murdering Our Past*. San Francisco: Encounter Books.

Woods, N. (1999) 'Order, Globalization, and Inequality in World Politics', in A. Hurrell and N. Woods (eds) *Order, Globalization, and Inequality in World Politics*. Oxford: Oxford University Press, pp. 8–35.

Yale Law School (2007) 'The Covenant of the League of Nations', http://avalon.law.yale.edu/20th_century/leagcov.asp (accessed 20 July 2012).

Zalewski, M. and Enloe, C. (1995) 'Questions about Identity in International Relations', in K. Booth and S. Smith (eds) *International Relations Theory Today*. Cambridge: Polity Press, pp. 279–305.

Zehfuss, M. (2006) 'Constructivism and Identity: A Dangerous Liaison', in S. Guzzini and A. Leander (eds) *Constructivism and International Relations: Alexander Wendt and his Critics*. London: Routledge, pp. 93–117.

Zehfuss, M. (2009) 'Jacques Derrida', in J. Edkins and N. Vaughan-Williams (eds) *Critical Theorists and International Relations*. London: Routledge, pp. 137–49.

INDEX